Laurence Nowell, William Lambarde and the Laws of the Anglo-Saxons

COSTERUS NEW SERIES 108

Series Editors:
C.C. Barfoot, Hans Bertens, Theo D'haen and Erik Kooper

Laurence Nowell, William Lambarde, and the Laws of the Anglo-Saxons

Raymond J. S. Grant

Amsterdam-Atlanta, GA 1996

ISBN 90-420-0076-7

Cover design: Hendrik van Delft

Printed in The Netherlands

And now I will unclasp a secret book
And to your quick-conceiving discontents
I'll read you matter deep and dangerous.

(*I Henry IV*, 1. iii, 188-90)

For Pieterke

Preface and Acknowledgements

It is many years now since the late Professor Dorothy Whitelock suggested to me that I should work on the texts of II Athelstan, V Athelstan, Iudex, and the laws of Alfred and Ine as contained in Laurence Nowell's transcript of the burnt manuscript BL Cotton Otho B. xi and in William Lambarde's *Archaionomia*. This would, she said, complement the work I had begun in my very first article, on *The Seasons for Fasting* (1972), continued in the one on the Nowell transcript found in BL Additional 43703 in *Anglo-Saxon England* (1974), and needed to consider in my work on the B text of the Old English Bede (1989). Flatteringly, in her work on Henry Spelman and David Wilkins (1981) she assumed the results she expected from my researches to supplement her own observations on the texts involved. Sadly, Professor Whitelock is longer around to chide her recalcitrant *protégé*, but I hope I have not betrayed her confidence in me as much as I used to try her patience. She is sorely missed.

Since Professor Whitelock's time and my earlier work on Laurence Nowell the picture has become a little more complicated than of yore. There are now *two* Laurence Nowells and at least *three* Nowell transcripts of Cotton Otho B. xi — *four* or more, if indeed the work formerly ascribed to William Somner is really that of (the *right*) Nowell. Alongside these complications, a mere detail that pales into insignificance in comparison is the observation that William Lambarde's name is nowadays usually spelled with a final *-e* except by Kenneth Sisam. Likewise, Abraham Wheloc's surname is limited to one *-e-* and is denied a final *-k*.

Essentially what I have done is to print the texts of the Anglo-Saxon laws found originally in BL Cotton Otho B. xi and transcribed in BL Additional 43703 by Laurence Nowell (Nw1 and Nw2) in 1562 alongside those printed by William Lambarde in his *Archaionomia* of 1568. While the great Felix Liebermann printed readings from his Ot and Ld texts (1903-16), his versions are not always continuous and his readers can bog down in his footnotes and other apparatus; it is unfortunate that Liebermann's edition is so ponderous and complicated to use, especially for those uncomfortable with academic German. Besides, he was unaware of the existence of most of the Nowell transcripts, though he had access to the work hitherto taken to be that of William Somner.

It is my hope that it will prove useful to have the Nowell and Lambarde texts side by side in clear editions for comparison, with a minimum of footnoting and commentary. It is to be regretted that Lambarde did not print the unusual text known as *Iudex*. This text is otherwise known only through Liebermann's edition, which draws on G (Nero A. 1, fol. 48) and on the *Quadripartitus*. Rather than leave several pages blank where Lambarde does not print this text, I have reproduced *Iudex* as Liebermann prints it from G.

I acknowledge with deep gratitude the kind assistance extended me in my present modest endeavour by the following colleagues, to whom I owe a great debt of thanks: Mr. W.H. Kelliher, Curator of Manuscripts at the British Library, for the gracious permission of the British Library Board to print the texts from BL Additional 43703; Professor Raymond Page of Corpus Christi College, Cambridge for his encouragement and advice; Dr. Richard Dammery of Melbourne for his generous willingness to share the results of his own more extensive researches and deeper insights; and Mr. Fred van der Zee of Editions Rodopi, Amsterdam and Atlanta, for his continuing patience with my work. For errors, omissions, computer problems and sheer ignorance I must perforce accept total responsibility.

R.G.

Table of Contents

Introduction

i. The Laws of the Anglo-Saxons

The Anglo-Saxon legal system most probably operated on the basis of custom as preserved by popular and oral tradition more than it depended on any written code, and there is no evidence for the laws' having existed in an official form. The corpus of the surviving manuscripts of the laws of the Anglo-Saxons is consequently not a large one, comprising some fifteen manuscripts in all,[1] and the nature of their contents requires careful consideration and evaluation.

The Anglo-Saxon codes of law come from ecclesiastical scriptoria whose endeavour was directed towards preservation rather than legislature, so we are not dealing with official law books in our present-day sense of the legal system. Further, the laws are associated with the names of the monarchs who promulgated them and whose law-giving was a declaration of sovereignty, the assertion of the rule of the law-maker over those he governed. Wallace-Hadrill emphasizes the ideological function of law-giving as the enhancement of kingship:

> ... Alfred resumed a practice that had been lost in England because he knew that, up to the time of Charles the Bald, the Carolingians had found a use for it. Most of the best surviving manuscripts of continental Germanic law belong to the ninth century, and it was not for nothing that Charles the Bald had bothered himself with the Theodosian Code. To assemble the *Volksrechte* and reissue them as their own had seemed an enhancement of kingship to the Carolingians; it was a legislative function with political overtones.[2]

The individual manuscripts' contents are not necessarily restricted to law; Cambridge, Corpus Christi College 173 had the laws added on quire 3 after annal 923 of the Anglo-Saxon Chronicle before annals 924-95 were added on quire 4, for instance, and those in British Library, Cotton Otho B. xi were bedfellows for the Chronicle and the Old English Bede *inter alia.*[3] The surviving laws are therefore associated with both historical and ecclesiastical concerns while constituting the closest we can come to a collection of Anglo-Saxon legal texts equivalent to our modern code of laws. Dorothy Whitelock comments as follows in her useful overview of the Anglo-Saxon laws:

> It is not the official law-books, if such there were, kept by the kings at some headquarters, that have come down to us. It is to the activity of ecclesiastical scribes that we owe our extant laws... It is only the copies kept by religious institutions that had any chance of survival to our times... But it should be

> noted that we do not owe all our extant codes simply to a tendency to preserve and re-copy, out of respect for the past, sets of laws that were no longer in force; some codes have come down to us in compilations made for a practical use. The clergy were not only the preservers and transcribers of the laws; they were also often the drafters of it, and therefore required copies of earlier statutes for their guidance. This is particularly clear in the early eleventh century, when the actual form taken by several of Ethelred's codes and by those of Cnut is due to Wulfstan, archbishop of York and bishop of Worcester, and it is therefore of interest to find in several manuscripts, which on other grounds we can connect with him, collections of earlier statutes, some of which he has used for his own compilations.[4]

Collections of laws survive associated with the names of such kings as Æthelberht, Hlothhere, Eadric, Wihtred, Ine, Alfred, Edward, Athelstan, Edmund, Edgar, Æthelred, and Cnut, but not all of these have come down to us in pre-Conquest manuscripts. In certain cases we have to rely almost entirely on transcriptions and early editions made during the Elizabethan age by such scholars as Joscelyn, Somner, Nowell and Lambarde.

There have been many complete or partial editions of the Anglo-Saxon laws from the sixteenth century to the present day, and these have provided information for both direct commentary and more general histories of English law. The most significant of these editions and studies merit mention in discussion of Anglo-Saxon law in general as well as in specific treatment of the laws of Ine, Alfred and Athelstan.

The pioneering printed editions were those of the Elizabethan jurist, scholar and antiquary William Lambarde (1536-1601). He first called the Anglo-Saxon laws from the darkness into the light, as he put it, in his *Archaionomia*, published in London by John Day in 1568 and reissued in a revised edition prepared by Abraham Wheloc in 1644.[5] Lambarde's *A Perambulation of Kent* of 1576 contained extracts from the Textus Roffensis and ran to a second edition in 1596.[6]

Henry Spelman's *Concilia* was the next important contribution. The first volume appeared in London in 1639, and dealt with matters from the introduction of Christianity to the Norman Conquest, while the second volume of 1664, edited by William Dugdale, continued the study from the Norman Conquest to the reign of Henry VIII.[7] Spelman's work formed the basis of the vast four-volume *Concilia* produced in London in 1737 by David Wilkins to follow his earlier *Leges Anglo-Saxonicae ecclesiasticae et civiles* of 1721.[8] Built on the foundation of the work of Spelman and Wilkins are such significant contributions as John Baron's *Report on the Anglo-Saxon Documents in Wilkins's Concilia* from Oxford in 1859, Arthur Haddan and William Stubbs's three-volume *Councils and Ecclesiastical Documents Relating to Great Britain and Ireland, Edited after Spelman and Wilkins* produced in Oxford 1869-78, and Dorothy Whitelock's *Councils and Synods* from Oxford in 1981.[9]

Thomas Hearne's edition of the Textus Roffensis from Oxford in 1720[10] was followed in the next century by Reinhold Schmid's *Die Gesetze der Angelsächsische* produced in Leipzig in 1832 with a second and revised edition coming out in 1858.[11] Subsequent editions of the Anglo-Saxon laws habitually follow Schmid on the vexed question of the division of the Old English texts into individual paragraphs. 1840 saw the publication in London of Benjamin Thorpe's *Ancient Laws and Institutes of England*, in two volumes,[12] dealing in turn with the secular and ecclesiastical laws enacted by the Anglo-Saxon Kings from Æthelberht to Cnut. Albert Cook published extracts from the laws in New York in 1880,[13] and in his Leipzig dissertation of 1890 Milton Turk concentrated on the legal code of Alfred the Great.[14]

Felix Liebermann offered an edition of the Quadripartitus (a collection of Anglo-Saxon laws in Latin made about 1114) in Halle in 1892 and wrote comments on the Textus Roffensis in 1898, then the present century was ushered in in Halle in grand style in 1903-1916 by his monumental edition *Die Gesetze der Angelsachsen.*[15] This extremely thorough, scholarly and accurate edition is indispensable to all subsequent students of the Anglo-Saxon laws. Liebermann's compact and condensed style of writing and his formal and learnèd German can make some of his introduction and commentary rather opaque, and individual statements of his have been challenged by scholars such as Kenneth Sisam and Dorothy Whitelock,[16] but none can deny the high value of this seminal work. Dammery would deny Liebermann's work the accolade "definitive," because of three major problems: the discussion of the textual transmission of the laws and the unnecessary postulation of "ghost" manuscripts; the division of the texts into chapters following unsatisfactory earlier divisions by Schmid, based in turn on those of Wilkins and Thorpe; and the numbering and classification of the law codes, taken from Schmid's description of the manuscripts as derived from Wanley's *Catalogus Historico-Criticus* of 1705.[17] It would be far from gracious to Liebermann's memory to chide him as a critic once chided a prolix colleague of mine, saying, "she should be kicked to death with her own footnotes," so Dammery quotes the kinder yet still wry remarks made by Maitland in his review of Liebermann's first volume:

> If Englishmen cannot or will not do these things, they can at least rejoice that others can and will... It looks like the full score of an opera, and some time must be spent before we can master the manifold typographical devices which have been invented to save time and space. At first the editor seems to have a rooted objection to printing six consecutive words without a change of type; and the natural man sighs for the simplicity of a pianoforte arrangement.[18]

Made more for the natural man, shorter and easier to use than Liebermann's, but ultimately untrustworthy are the edition of the laws of the earliest English kings (Æthelberht I to Æthelstan) brought out in Cambridge in 1922 by Frederick Attenborough[19] and that of the laws of the kings of England from Edmund to Henry I by Agnes Robertson in 1925, also from Cambridge.[20] In 1958 Karl Eckhardt's *Leges Anglo-Saxonicum 601-925* appeared in Göttingen,[21] and in 1990 Richard Dammery's fine Cambridge thesis on the law code of King Alfred the Great brings discussion of the laws of Alfred and Ine right up to date by incorporating readings from the Nowell transcripts in an exhaustive treatment of his important topic.[22]

For discussion of the Anglo-Saxon laws in general and supplementary to the editions and commentaries already mentioned, recourse should be had to such works as the following: Franz Mone, "Zur Geschichte und Kritik der angelsächsische Gesetze," 1830;[23] John Stearns, *The Germs and Developments of the Laws of England, Embracing the Anglo-Saxon Laws Extant*, 1889;[24] H.M. Chadwick, *Studies on Anglo-Saxon Institutions*, 1905;[25] W.S. Holdsworth, *A History of English Law*, 1923;[26] F. Pollock and F.W. Maitland, *The History of English Law*, 1923;[27] T.F.T. Plucknett, *A Concise History of the Common Law*, 1948;[28] and D. Whitelock, *English Historical Documents c. 500-1042*, 1979 and *History, Law and Literature in 10th-11th Century England*, 1981.[29] A thorough treatment of the topic by Patrick Wormald is keenly anticipated.[30]

ii. The Law Codes II and V Athelstan, Iudex, Alfred and Ine

The concern of the present discussion is with certain texts and later transcripts of the codes known in established practice as II Athelstan, V Athelstan, Iudex, and Alfred and Ine. These codes will be treated in the order in which they are found in the Nowell transcript contained in British Library Additional 43703 rather than in strict chronological order. It should be borne in mind that Liebermann and his contemporaries were unaware that all four texts exist in transcripts made by Laurence Nowell.

Six series of laws, plus an ordinance on charities, survive from the reign of Athelstan (925?-939?). II Athelstan deals with the administration of justice and was promulgated at a council held Æt Greatanlæge (Grately, near Andover, Hants.) 925-*c.* 935, most likely early in the king's reign *c.* 929, while V Athelstan dealing with similar matters was promulgated at a council held at Exeter *c.* 927-937, at least a year or two before the end of the king's reign.[31]

II Athelstan is to be found in Liebermann's H (Textus Roffensis, fols. 32^{v}-37, from Rochester Cathedral, early twelfth century—the only complete version), B (Cambridge, Corpus Christi College 383, pp. 10-12, early twelfth century, at St. Paul's, London—the text is incomplete), Ot (British Library, Cotton Otho B. xi, fols. 48 and 51, early eleventh century—the text is fragmentary following the Cotton Fire, but was previously transcribed by Nowell in British Library, Additional 43703, fols. 233^{r}-236^{r}, 265^{r}), and So (the seventeenth-century paper transcription which is now Canterbury Cathedral Library, B 2, n. 8); the Quadripartitus carries a Latin version. Liebermann, 1. 150-67, prints all versions; Attenborough, pp. 126-43, prints H and variants; Lambarde's edition is on fols. 58^{v}-67^{v} of *Archaionomia*, that of Wilkins on pp. 56-61 of *Leges*. Selections are to be found in Spelman, 1. 398-401, followed by Wilkins, *Concilia* 1. 206-07, and in Whitelock, *Councils and Synods*, 1. 49-53.

II Athelstan begins without preamble, but Whitelock draws attention to the addition at the end of the version in the Quadripartitus of a passage which could take the place of a preface:

> Totum hoc institutum (et confirmatum) est in magna synodo apud Greateleyam, cui archiepiscopus Wulfhelmus interfuit et omnes optimates et sapientes quos Æþelstanus rex congregare potuit.[32]

Lambarde, fol. 68^{v}, prints a version of this in grammatically unsound Old English which is a back-translation from the Latin, and this translation is followed by Spelman and Wilkins, *Concilia*:

Ealle ðis pær gesetted on ðam miclan synoþ
æt Greatanleage; on þam pær se ærcebisceop
Wulfhelme mid eallum þæm æþelum man-
num 7 piotan, ðe Æþelstan cyning
gegadrian.

V Athelstan is to be found in H, fols. 37-38, printed by Liebermann, 1. 166-68; Attenborough, pp. 152-55; Lambarde's *Archaionomia*, fols. 68^{v}-70^{v}; and Wilkins, *Leges*, pp. 62-63. A brief extract is to be found in Whitelock, *Councils and Synods*, 1. 54. The text is also to be found in Additional 43703, fols. 265^{r}-266^{r} (Nowell's transcript of Ot.), and the Quadripartitus carries a Latin version.

V Athelstan has the following introduction:

> Æþelstan cẏnȝ cẏð, ꝥ ic hæbbe ȝeachsod, ꝥ ure friþ is pẏrs ȝehealden, þoñ me lẏst, oþþe hit æt Greatanlæȝe cpeden pære; 7 mine peotan seȝȝaþ, ꝥ ic hit to lonȝe forboren hæbbe.
>
> Nu hæbbe ic funden mid þæm piotū, þe æt Æxsancestre mid me peron to middūpintra, ꝥ þa ealle sẏn ȝearope mid hine seolfū 7 mid pife 7 mid erfe 7 mid eallū þinȝū to fearenne þider þider ic þoñ — butan hio ofer þis ȝespican pillen — on þa ȝerad þe heo næfre æft on earda ne cumen.
>
> *[Additional 43703, fol. 265^{r}]*

The text known as Iudex is dated *c*. 980-*c*. 1050 by Liebermann, and is to be found in G (British Library, Cotton Nero A. 1, fol. 48, mid eleventh century), Additional 43703, fols. 266^{r}-267^{v}, So, and the Quadripartitus. Iudex is printed by Liebermann, 1. 474-76; Spelman, 1. 532; and Wilkins, *Leges*, p. 242, and *Concilia*, 1. 295.

The laws of Alfred and Ine are closely associated, for in all the manuscripts the laws of Ine of Wessex (who reigned, Bede tells us, 688-725) are appended to those of Alfred the Great (who reigned 871-*c*. 900). The close association is thanks to Alfred himself, since he directly acknowledges his debt to the earlier lawmakers Offa of Mercia, Athelberht of Kent, and particularly Ine of Wessex:

> Ic þa Ælfred cẏninȝ þæs toȝædere ȝeȝaderode, 7 apritan het, moniȝ þara þe ure foreȝenȝan heoldon, (þa þe me licodon; 7) þa þe me ne licodon ic apearp, mid minra pitena ȝeþeahte, 7 on oþre pisan bebead to healdanne. Forþā ic ne dorst ȝ̄þristlæcan þæra minra apuht feala on ȝ̄prit settan, forþā me pæs uncuþ hpæt þæs þā lician polde þe æfter us pæren; ac þa þe ic ȝ̄mette apðer, oþþe on Ines dæȝe, mines mæȝes, oþþe on Offan Mẏrcna cyninȝes,

oþþe on Æþelbirhtes, þe ærest fulpiht underfenȝ on Anȝelcýnne, þa þe me rýhtost þuhton, ic þa heron ȝȝaderode, 7 þa oþre forlet.

Ic þa Ælfred, Ƿesseaxna cýninȝ, eallū minū pitū þæs ȝeeopde, 7 hie þa cpædon ꝥ hī ꝥ licode eallū to healdanne.

[Additional 43703, fol. 241ᵛ-242ʳ]

Attenborough dates the code of Ine "in all probability" between 688 and 694, and for that of Alfred suggests Liebermann's "892-893" is perhaps a little late, sometime in the 880s seeming likelier;[33] neither code admits of close dating. The laws of Alfred and Ine survive in E Cambridge, Corpus Christi College 173, fols. 33-52ᵛ, mid tenth century, at Winchester—the laws now follow the A version of the Chronicle known as the Parker Chronicle); B, pp. 13-42; H, fols. 9-31ᵛ; fragments of Ot, fols. 49, 50, 52 and 53; Additional 43703, fols. 236ᵛ-255ʳ; G, fols. 45-48, 51-57ᵛ, incomplete; and the first part of Ine's code is also in Bu (a fragment in British Library Burney 277, fol. 42, late eleventh century. There is a Latin version in the Quadripartitus. Again, the work of Nowell was unknown to Liebermann and his contemporaries. Liebermann prints all versions save Nowell's, 1. 44-78, while E forms the basis of the versions in Attenborough, pp. 62-87; Lambarde's *Archaionomia*, fols. 18ᵛ-43ᵛ, 0ᵛ-17ᵛ; Wilkins, *Leges*, pp. 28-46; and selections in Spelman, 1. 354-71, and Wilkins, *Concilia*, 1. 186-94. Richard Dammery's edition is unfortunately not available except in the form of his Cambridge dissertation.

Whitelock comments on the Old English texts succinctly as follows:

> All texts stem from a version rather badly divided into paragraphs: different topics may be dealt with in the same paragraph, or the division may come in the middle of a topic. The list of chapter headings was drawn up to fit a text thus divided, with the result that some important matters are not mentioned in it.
>
> Ot agrees so closely with E that Liebermann thought it was a direct copy, but Nowell's transcript of Ot avoids some of the errors in E, from which Ot's exemplar must have been free. G is closer to E than to B and H, which share a common exemplar, which was not G, for this has readings peculiar to it; the exemplar of B and H was not E or a copy of E, for it has some readings omitted in E. Thus, though E is the oldest text, the other manuscripts occasionally preserve better readings; but significant variants are few.[34]

In undertaking the act which Wallace-Hadrill would characterize as the enhancement of kingship, Alfred has both a practical and a didactic purpose—it is practical in that he is the first Anglo-Saxon monarch to attempt the codification of earlier law, and it is didactic in that he seeks to place the law in its spiritual context, offering the earliest surviving translations of parts of the Bible into the Old English vernacular. Alfred therefore offers a lengthy preamble which is basically a history of law-giving. It contains a translation of the Decalogue, passages from Exodus (21, 1 to 23, 13) and Acts (15, 23-29), and a discussion of the growth of church law before Alfred acknowledges his debt to Ine. The archetype of the surviving manuscripts viewed the end of the Biblical quotations as the finish of the introduction, numbered the following paragraph "i," and gave the capitula-list at this point. In B the rubrics are normally placed before each law, but in the other manuscripts they are gathered into the capitula-list just before Alfred's history of Christian law-making, his crediting of Ine, Offa and Æthelberht, and his own code.

Some of the language of Ine's code has been updated to that of the time of Alfred, and Whitelock sounds a warning note concerning how far Alfred may have tampered with Ine's code:

> Ine's code constitutes a more important instance of the survival of an early code because it was used as a basis for later legislation; it survives because it was copied as a sort of appendix to Alfred's laws, of which it was one of the main sources, as the king tells us himself. We are left in uncertainty whether, as there copied, it represents Ine's code exactly and completely, or whether it has already been partially edited for the king's immediate purpose. He tells us that he rejected many of the observances of his forefathers which he did not like, and for all we know some of these may have been omitted from the copy of Ine's code appended to his own. But, though one must always bear in mind this possibility of modification in the course of transmission of texts which survive only in versions of much later date, it must not be assumed that there was a widespread practice of modernisation, for the presence of much archaic diction and syntax proves that in general the text was rendered much as it stood.[35]

The Transcribers and Editors

iii. Laurence Nowell

Present-day Anglo-Saxon studies owe their beginnings to the work of a group of dedicated antiquarians in the latter half of the sixteenth century preeminent among whom was Matthew Parker(1504-75). A fellow of Corpus Christi College, Cambridge, Parker became Master of Corpus in 1544, Dean of Lincoln in 1552, then Archbishop of Canterbury in 1559 upon the accession of Elizabeth I. Parker was the close friend of Sir William Cecil and Sir Nicholas Bacon, and he gathered around himself a circle of like-minded scholars whose interest lay in England's Anglo-Saxon past.[36] Parker's primary purpose was to undo the worst effects of Henry VIII's dissolution of the monasteries, and C. E. Wright does well to remind scholars that the impetus behind Parker's efforts was *not* in the first instance antiquarian but had, rather, a utilitarian, ecclesiastical purpose and a political motivation:

> The period of the Archbishop's greatest activity in the building-up of his collections, in the prosecution of historical and Anglo-Saxon studies, and in the publication of various works under his patronage or guidance is roughly the decade immediately preceding his death (say, 1565-75). There can be no doubt at all that the antiquarian studies which were the motive force in this were not (as they would be to-day) disinterested; the rescue of the MSS. dispersed by the dissolution of the monastic houses was undoubtedly pressed forward by Parker with a view to securing material not otherwise accessible and was perceived by him to be essential to the purpose of supplying the evidence needed to underpin the ecclesiastical settlement envisaged by Elizabeth and her advisers such as Cecil and Sir Nicholas Bacon. The utilitarian character of antiquarian studies in the sixteenth and seventeenth centuries must never be lost sight of and it is remarkable to observe how the shift of emphasis in the character of these reflects exactly the corresponding change of emphasis in political affairs. The first and most important subject requiring attention in the early years of Elizabeth's reign was the ecclesiastical settlement, the firm establishment of the 'Ecclesia Anglicana,' and on Parker as Primate rested the responsibility for securing the necessary material to supply the official propaganda for those constitutional and doctrinal principles on which the 'Ecclesia Anglicana' was to be established—the royal supremacy, the rejection of transubstantiation, the right of the people to read the Scriptures in the vernacular, the theory that the Church as then established represented a return to the purity of the Primitive Church (for as such the Saxon Church appeared to their eyes). The Archbishop had therefore to obtain as far as possible material from before the

> period of the fully developed papal claims, that is, as much as possible pre-thirteenth century. Hence the interest in the works in Anglo-Saxon (the Homilies of Ælfric, Alfred's translation of the *Cura Pastoralis*, the Anglo-Saxon versions of the Gospels and the Psalter) and in the pre-Conquest writers like Bede, Gildas and Asser in Latin, and in the great historians of the period immediately following the Conquest—William of Malmesbury, Henry of Huntingdon and Matthew Paris. The library that Parker collected was therefore emphatically a working library, an arsenal, on which he and his assistants were to draw for the materials they needed.[37]

Parker's library was, happily, not as widely dispersed as were those of the monasteries, and most of the items surviving from his collection are to be found today in four depositories—the Parker Library at Corpus, the Cambridge University Library, the Library of Trinity College in Cambridge, and the British Library. Details of Parker's collection and its disposition can be found in the discussions of Wright, James, Ker and Page[38] and in the manuscript catalogues of I(ames), Nasmith, James and Ker.[39]

Wright notes, further, that the focus of interest shifted from the ecclesiastical to the political front later in the sixteenth century:

> As the century went on the emphasis shifted to constitutional problems in political controversy and this is reflected in the activities of the Elizabethan Society of Antiquaries, the starting-point of which may be attributed to 1586 on the basis of a statement in the Preface to Spelman's *Discourse on Law Terms*: 'About 42 years since, divers gentlemen in London, studious in antiquities, framed themselves into a College or Society of Antiquaries.'[40]

Whatever the original motives of Matthew Parker and his circle, the effect of their work is far-reaching in the modern sense of the word "antiquarian," for from their efforts arose manuscript transcriptions, place-name studies, maps, dictionaries and printed editions of great interest to modern-day scholars of Anglo-Saxon. Laurence Nowell developed a "hand" quite distinct from his normal handwriting of Latin for copying Anglo-Saxon, and John Day developed for his 1566 printing of Ælfric's *The Testimonie of Antiquitie* an Anglo-Saxon font which was subsequently used for William Lambarde's *Archaionomia* two years later. Anglo-Saxon studies thus had their true birth in the reign of the first Elizabeth, thanks to Archbishop Parker and his friends.

Wright not only lists the names of many of these friends and contributes brief biographical notes about them but, most usefully, also offers samples of their handwriting—George Acworth, John Bale, William Bowyer, John Dee, John Joscelyn, William Lambarde, Laurence Nowell, John Parker, and Robert Talbot.[41] These facsimiles were also published as extra pulls, and their usefulness is enormous; for instance, one can determine at a glance that, indeed, Nowell glossed a first edition (1552) of Richard Huloet's *Abcedarium Anglico Latinum*[42] and annotated his own transcript of the Anglo-Saxon laws in BL Additional 43703. From the pioneering work of these men (and others such as Sir Thomas Cotton, Sir Robert Cotton, William Camden, William Dugdale, Franciscus Junius, William L'isle, Holinshed, John Leland, and Sir Simonds D'Ewes) arose our modern discipline of Anglo-Saxon studies.[43] And two principal players on the roster are the immediate concern of the present study, namely, Laurence Nowell and William Lambarde.

Laurence Nowell's importance as a pioneer in Anglo-Saxon studies is second only to that of John Joscelyn, yet the details of his biography are open to question. Until comparatively recent researches raised serious doubts, it was assumed that Laurence Nowell the antiquary was to be identified with Laurence Nowell the Dean of Lichfield. The standard account of Nowell's life is given in *The Dictionary of National Biography* and in Robin Flower's seminal article on the work and manuscripts associated with Nowell's name. Nowell was born in Lancashire, a younger son of John Nowell of Read Hall, Whalley by his second wife, Elizabeth, *née* Kay, and brother of Alexander Nowell, Dean of St. Paul's, and of Robert Nowell, attorney-general of the Court of Wards. In 1546 he was appointed master of the grammar school at Sutton Coldfield, Warwickshire; he was accused of neglect of his duty, but an order from the privy council stayed the proceedings against him in February, 1550. A Protestant of strong views, Nowell fled on the accession of Queen Mary, first to the home of Sir John Perrot at Carew Castle in Wales and then to Germany, where his brother Alexander was in exile. On the death of Mary and the accession of Elizabeth he returned to England, where he was appointed Dean of Lichfield in March 1560.

In 1562 Nowell made transcripts of Anglo-Saxon manuscripts in the house of his patron Sir William Cecil, principal secretary to the Queen and later the first Baron Burghley.[44] Letters survive from November and December of 1562 in which Thomas Windebank writes from Frankfurt, Heidelberg and Strasbourg to recommend Nowell for the post of guardian-tutor to Cecil's son Thomas. For the next few years Nowell lived in Cecil's house in the Strand, and came to enjoy a productive relationship with his pupil and friend William Lambarde, the legal scholar and future Keeper of the Records of the Tower of London. In 1563 Nowell was appointed tutor to Richard de Vere, 17th Earl of Oxford and at that time ward of Sir William Cecil, and was installed prebendary of Chichester; he held the rectory of Haughton and Drayton Basset, in Staffordshire, and in 1566 received a prebend also in York. In 1570 he answered the accusation brought against him by Peter Morwent of having uttered scandal about Queen Elizabeth and the Earl of Leicester, and in 1575 bought a house and estate at Sheldon and land at Coleshill, both in Warwickshire. He died in or about October, 1576 leaving two sons and three daughters, and is thought to lie buried at Weston, Derbyshire.[45]

Such is the biography of Laurence Nowell which scholars assumed to be correct until 1977; see, for example, the summary given by Albert Marckwardt in his discussion of Nowell's *Vocabularium Saxonicum*.[46] But in 1974 Retha Warnicke drew attention to a Court of Requests case of 1571 which serves to demonstrate clearly that there were *two* Laurence Nowells, the Dean of Lichfield and the antiquarian.[47] The two men were cousins, and their lives followed very similar patterns in many respects. Their being confused, then, is understandable, and their false identification has been traced back through Flower and the *DNB* entry to Anthony à Wood and William Dugdale.[48] For a while after Warnicke's article appeared the confusion persisted; in 1977 Pamela Black dealt with the same Court of Requests case in detail but interpreted her results along the traditional line that Nowell the antiquary was also the Dean of Lichfield, only later accepting Warnicke's arguments to the contrary.[49] To the discussions of Warnicke and Black have now been added those of Thomas Hahn and Carl Berkhout,[50] and the ramifications of there being two Laurence Nowells have now been worked out in some detail, though some questions still remain unanswered.

In summary, Berkhout offers the following biographical information about Laurence Nowell the antiquary. He was born between 1510 and 1520, and was a cousin of Laurence Nowell the Dean of Lichfield, having the same maternal grandparents in Roger Nowell of Read Hall and his wife Grace, daughter of Sir Richard Towneley, all of Whalley parish in northern Lancashire. The antiquary's father was their son Alexander (possibly their youngest) and his mother Grace Caterall; he had three brothers and possibly as many as three sisters. He grew up in Whalley and later in Eccles, and may have been educated at Whalley Abbey.

It cannot be shown definitely which Laurence Nowell was the schoolmaster at Sutton Coldfield 1546-50 nor which was ordained a deacon on November 9, 1550.[51] But it is clearly the antiquary who was tutor to the young Earl of Oxford, who transcribed manuscripts in Cecil's house in London, and who was the friend and mentor of William Lambarde. And it was Laurence Nowell the antiquary who left his transcripts and other possessions with Lambarde before undertaking an extended study leave on the Continent in 1568, a trip from which he seems never to have returned. Although Lambarde protested the assumption of his death in the Request of 1571, it remains likely that Nowell died abroad in 1571 or 1572.

Armed with the 20/20 vision afforded by hindsight, one can now revisit the biographical information about Nowell offered by the *DNB* entry, Flower and Marckwardt and share it between the Dean and the antiquary. The *DNB* entry was always uncomfortable about the university education apparently on record in Oxford and Cambridge:

> ... entered Brasenose College, Oxford, in 1536, and, desiring to study logic at Cambridge, migrated to that university, where he graduated B.A. in 1544. He is said at one period to have been a member of Christ Church; but this is extremely doubtful.[52]

Flower and Marckwardt are also unhappy about this sequence of colleges, for why would a member of Brasenose become a member of Christ Church? Such things do happen in Oxbridge colleges, of course, as witness the poet Gray's migration in Cambridge from Peterhouse across the road to Pembroke after a fake fire alarm had him descend a rope into a barrel of freezing water. Flower has Nowell graduate from Cambridge in 1542 and incorporated B.A. at Oxford, proceeding M.A. there in 1544.[53] Marckwardt simply says, "He appears to have returned to Oxford, this time enrolling in Christ Church, where he remained until 1554, but in the meantime he had taken holy orders."[54] Black concludes that it is probably safe to "assume that the antiquary Nowell is the man who attended Christ Church, Oxford, proceeding M.A. in 1552, and who can be traced in the buttery books from 1550 to 24th December 1554,"[55] and Hahn concurs: "The scholar probably attended Christ Church, Oxford, while the Dean (and his brother and son) attended Brasenose College."[56] This solution is likelier than that of Warnicke, who by a slip of her pen moves Christ Church to Cambridge: "Surely this Laurence Nowell was not the Dean of Lichfield who attended Brasenose College at Oxford and Christ's [*sic*] Church at Cambridge."[57]

It is still controverted which Nowell was the schoolmaster at Sutton Coldfield, the popular view that it was the antiquary being challenged by Berkhout's objection that the Privy Council would be likelier to intervene on behalf of the more influential future Dean of Lichfield. Likewise, there is no hard evidence for or against the possibility that Nowell the antiquary was also ordained; but if he was, did one or more of the livings attributed to the Dean of Lichfield in his undoubted pluralism belong to Nowell the antiquary? It was no doubt the antiquary who was appointed tutor to Richard de Vere, who could spend time in Cecil's house poring over manuscripts and transcripts, and who enjoyed a long and fruitful working relationship with William Lambarde—the Dean would simply have been too busy.

An interesting self-portrait appears in a corner of a map of Britain (undated) which Nowell drew for his patron Cecil. When Flower saw it, the map was in the possession of Lord Landsdowne, but Berkhout reports that the so-called Nowell-Burghley pocket atlas was sold at an auction in December of 1982 to the British Library, where it is now MS Additional 62540.[58] Flower describes the portrait as follows:

> In the two bottom corners of the map a little scene is set out with a delicate art that proves Nowell to have been an exquisite draughtsman in that English school which derived its craft from the writing master's art of engrossing initials in manuscripts with human and animal designs. To the left Nowell

> represents himself seated on a pedestal in an attitude of deep depression, holding an empty purse downwards with its mouth gaping to the ground. A ferocious dog faces him menacingly, barking... Facing him in the right corner sits Cecil, with arms grimly folded, uneasily poised upon an hour-glass, in which we may imagine the sands are running out, inscribed with Greek words bidding his suppliant hope on and endure.[59]

Flower draws parallels with the popular song about dogs barking as beggars come to town and with the obvious lines from the lips of the destitute Lear, pointing out that on the pedestal Nowell has inscribed the words from Hesiod's *Works and Days* which deal with Hope alone lingering in Pandora's opened box. The empty purse links Nowell with the literary tradition of the artist as wayfarer which extends from François Villon, through William Dunbar's bearing "ane teme purs" and Robert Burns's describing himself as "half-mad, half-fed, half-sarkit", to the pedlar-poet James Macfarlan and the tramp-poet Roger Quinn. The older view that the portrait depicts Nowell the Dean of Lichfield, having returned from the Continent in 1572 to find that Lambarde has executed his will, ruefully over-dramatizing his poverty to Cecil[60] must now yield to the likelier view that the portrait depicts Nowell the ever-underfinanced poor scholar and antiquary in supplicant pose before his rich patron. The Dean of Lichfield, with all those livings and benefices to his name, would never have been so poorly off as this.

It follows that if the Dean of Lichfield would have been too busy with his various ecclesiastical responsibilities to tutor the Earl of Oxford, to be a ward of William Cecil, and to spend time with Lambarde transcribing Anglo-Saxon manuscripts, he would also have been too busy to take a few years' sabbatical leave on the Continent—which is what Laurence Nowell the antiquary did, starting in 1567. Both men had been abroad, most probably in exile, during the reign of Mary, the Dean in Wales and then with his brother Alexander in Germany, the antiquary in Paris, but in 1567 the antiquary undertook an extended tour of the Continent, presumably for purposes of research. Before he left, he entrusted his possessions, books and transcripts to William Lambarde for safe-keeping and presumably for disposition should the antiquary fall victim to the hazards of sixteenth-century travel. Lambarde noted in the family diary the date of the antiquary's departure on March 25 of 1567, and received occasional letters from his friend as he visited Paris, Venice, Padua, Vienna, Basle and Leipzig. Black describes the trip as follows:

> From Lambarde's evidence it would appear that Nowell, far from lacking 'the humour' to continue his work, had set out for the Continent in about 1568 to broaden his knowledge and, on the basis of the transcript of William of Jumièges, to augment his collection of historical material. The civil disturbances in France during 1568, in which year the Huguenots attempted to march on Paris, disturbed Nowell's peaceful researches at the University of Paris and prompted him to journey on across Europe to Venice and Padua,

> and from thence north again to Vienna, Basle and finally, as far as we know, Leipzig.[61]

The last letter to Lambarde came from Leipzig in 1569, then nothing more was heard from the antiquary, who was consequently considered missing and feared to be dead. Lambarde employed private detectives to ascertain the antiquary's fate, without success, and remained reluctant to declare his friend and mentor dead and to execute his will.

Details of the bill of complaint brought against Lambarde before the Court of Requests on November 14, 1571 by Thomas, Charles, and John Nowell and others and of Lambarde's reply are given by Warnicke and Black.[62] The petitioners wished Nowell declared "missing presumed dead" and demanded that Lambarde execute the will by paying them their bequests under its terms. In reply Lambarde expressed his reluctance to accept that his friend had died and pleaded that no grant of administration be made. Black quotes his objection that such a grant would make him appear to be:

> ... author of the reporte of the deathe of his so deare a frende, the rather ... that he hath not yet bene so long missed, but that there remayneth hoope that in tyme he maye be revealed.[63]

The judgment made in the case is not recorded, but it seems most likely that Lambarde paid the monetary bequests but held on to Nowell's books, maps, manuscripts and transcripts. Carl Berkhout wryly expresses his gratitude to Lambarde for retaining these materials in his own family library instead of giving them to Sir Robert Cotton for the collection at Ashburnam House.[64]

The action before the Court of Requests proves the contention that there were *two* Laurence Nowells, for it has been demonstrated by Warnicke and Hahn that the Dean of Lichfield was active in England during the period 1567-71 and beyond, especially with the letter to Archbishop Parker dated June 1567 and the Morwent accusation of 1570.[65] The Dean's own will was dated October 17, 1576 and he is presumed to have died later in that same year.

Several consequences follow acceptance of there being two Laurence Nowells. First, the bibliographical items listed in the *DNB* entry have to be apportioned between the two men. Second, there is the uncertainty already mentioned as to which of them was the schoolmaster at Sutton Coldfield. Third, if Laurence Nowell the antiquary was also ordained, he may have claim to some of the Dean of Lichfield's ecclesiastical preferments, as Black points out; Le Neve's listing of the prebendaries of Chichester lists the prebend of Ferring as being in the hands of "Laurence Nowell M.A. 1563-1571" and bears the notation "D(ead) by 22 April, 1571."[66] And fourth, one wonders which Laurence Nowell (if either) was depicted in the portrait mentioned in the *DNB* entry: "A portrait of Nowell, with the inscription 'Nowell, 1601,' but without painter's name, was bequeathed to Dulwich College by Edward Alleyn, and is now in the Dulwich Gallery." Berkhout suggests that this supposed portrait is a red herring in the path of Nowell scholarship:

> The *DNB* says that there is a portrait of (whichever) Laurence Nowell in the Dulwich Picture Gallery, but there is no record or trace of such a portrait; I suspect that the *DNB* author somehow mistook the Gallery's portrait of Dean Alexander Nowell, no. 419 in the Gallery's 1926 *Catalogue*. This portrait, not currently on exhibit, was restored several decades ago and now has no visible inscription.[67]

Logically, there remains the awful possibility that scholars still do not have the right Laurence Nowell and that there may have been a *third* one. This spectre is raised by Berkhout, who has discovered that a Laurence Nowell, representing Knaresborough in Yorkshire, served in the parliament of 1559, in session January 25-May 8. The antiquary spent most of the 1550s in Italy, but could have been back home in the first part of 1559 and have served as an MP. To this speculation one can only assign the grand old Scottish verdict of "not proven."[68]

I fear that the foregoing brief account of recent research into the true identity of Laurence Nowell the antiquary does scant justice to the excellent investigative work of such colleagues as Warnicke, Black, Hahn and Berkhout, but it is to be hoped that it may serve to sketch the biographical background against which to view the work carried out by Nowell on certain of the Anglo-Saxon laws. Of course, the question of Nowell's identity does not affect the main body of Flower's seminal article, which remains the best overall introduction to the work of Laurence Nowell.

Nowell had all the makings of a colleague at a modern-day university save one; he had an excellent Oxbridge education, teaching experience, research ability, knowledge of Anglo-Saxon language and texts, knowledge of the Classical languages, research travel at home and abroad, and so forth, but he did not *publish*. This is probably why he is not always accorded the pride of place he deserves among the pioneers in Anglo-Saxon studies, as Flower suggests in his admirable summing-up on the antiquary:

> I need not compose a eulogy of Laurence Nowell. If the story I have had to tell is true, and I am persuaded that it errs only on the side of incompleteness, his works may be left to speak for him. I hope that my description of him as one of those faithful scholars who, inspired by a devoted patriotism, gave themselves in Tudor times to the discovery of the face of England and the rediscovery of the tradition of England may be accepted as just. He published nothing and his fame has suffered in consequence. He is not so much mentioned in the chapter on the scholars and antiquaries of that age in the

> *Cambridge History of English Literature*. He did his work and handed over the results to another.[69]

Flower provides the fullest account of Nowell's work, which included a *Vocabularium Saxonicum*, a series of maps of the British Isles, and several collections of Anglo-Saxon and Middle English texts and chronicles. The *Beowulf* manuscript and the Exeter Book passed through Nowell's hands, and the antiquary transcribed in whole or in part such varied works as those of Matthew Paris, Florence of Worcester, William of Malmesbury, Higden's *Polychronicon*, King Alfred (the Orosius), William of Jumièges, Symeon of Durham, Alcuin, Giraldus Cambrensis—Flower's list is extensive. Of immediate concern is the complete transcript Nowell made in 1562 in Cecil's house of the Anglo-Saxon manuscript whose burnt remains are now BL Cotton Otho B. xi and whose original contents included a text of the Old English Bede, a text of the Anglo-Saxon Chronicle, the poem *The Seasons for Fasting*, and a collection of Anglo-Saxon laws. To Flower's list other items may be added, such as the other transcripts now known to scholarship of the Anglo-Saxon laws. Alistair Campbell reminds us that the Chronicle text in BL Additional 43703 contains a transcript of *The Battle of Brunanburh* made by Nowell and copied by Lambarde into the manuscript which is now in the Ussher collection, Trinity College, Dublin, E. 5. 19.[70] And Rosier has shown that Nowell annotated a first edition (1552) of Richard Huloet's *Abcedarium Anglico Latinum*.[71]

It is fitting to end this introduction to Laurence Nowell the antiquary by quoting the words of his praise sung by William Camden in 1590:

> ... vir rara doctrina insignis, & qui Saxonicam maiorum nostrorum linguam desuetudine intermortuam, & oblivione sepultam, primus nostra aetate resuscitavit.[72]

iv. William Lambarde

To turn from Nowell to his pupil and friend William Lambarde is to find a man equally estimable, diligent and scholarly whose biography is less open to question and debate than that of Nowell. The features that gaze on us from the 1730 engraving by George Vertue of "William Lambarde of Kent, Eſq." show kindness, understanding, determination to be just to all people, and dedication to a high moral purpose which could lead to hard consequences for those who swerved from the path of rectitude. But above all there can be seen in the portrait a scholarly and emotional devotion to Queen and country which justifies the tag below—"Deo Patriæ Tibi." A reproduction of the engraving serves as frontispiece to Retha Warnicke's biography of Lambarde,[73] and the *DNB* carries a useful account of the eminent lawyer and antiquary.[74]

William Lambarde was born in London on October 18, 1536 in the parish of St. Nicholas Acon. His father was John Lambarde, draper, alderman and sheriff of London, and his mother was John's first wife, Juliana Horne. The eldest child, William had a younger brother Giles and a sister Anna, and at least one stepsister born to his father's second wife, Alice. William's relations with the family became strained when he had to sue his litigious brother Giles in the Court of Chancery in 1566 over their inheritance from their father, John, of Westcombe Manor, Kent. Little is known of Lambarde's childhood years or the source of his wide education, and Warnicke shows that there is grave doubt about his attending either university.[75] On August 15, 1556 he entered Lincoln's Inn, and was called to the bar in 1567. He was chosen an associate of the bench of Lincoln's Inn on February 9, 1579 and was elevated to bencher on June 14, 1597. On August 6, 1579 he was also appointed Justice of the Peace for Kent, his adopted county, and he discharged his duties honourably and thoroughly. He was married three times: to Jane Multon; to Sylvestra Deane, widow of William Dallison; and to Margaret Payne, widow first of John Meryam and then of Richard Reder. Lambarde had three sons and a daughter, all by his second wife, Sylvestra.

Warnicke takes issue with Sir John Neale and Paul Ward, arguing that there is insufficient evidence to show that Lambarde was the William Lambert who, as Member of Parliament for Aldeborough in Yorkshire, helped precipitate the constitutional crisis of 1566.[76] There is no doubt, however, that Lambarde was the founder of an almshouse in East Greenwich which came to be known as the College of the Poor of Queen Elizabeth; the Queen granted the letters patent in 1574, and it was opened on October 1, 1576. His friend Sir William Brooke, Lord Cobham, wished to reestablish a similar charity at Cobham, Kent and it was Lambarde who drew up the rules for its management and acted as one Lord Cobham's trustees on his lordship's death in March of 1597.

Lambarde was appointed a master in chancery by Sir John Puckering, Lord-Keeper of England, on June 22, 1592, and the next Lord-Keeper, Sir Thomas Egerton, made the antiquary keeper of the records at the Rolls Chapel on May 26, 1597. In 1601 Lambarde came to the attention of Queen Elizabeth, who appointed him Keeper of the Records in the Tower of London on January 21 of that year. Elizabeth requested a catalogue of the Tower documents, and on August 4 Lambarde, in a private audience in her privy chamber at East Greenwich, presented the Queen with his "Pandecta Rotulorum." In his description of that meeting, he notes that the Queen called him her "good and Honest" Lambarde. He died shortly after, on August 19, and would no doubt have considered his Queen's words a fitting epitaph. He was buried in the parish church of East Greenwich, which was named after St. Alphege (Ælfheah), the Archbishop of Canterbury who was murdered there by the Vikings in 1011. The actual epitaph on Lambarde's monument is a simple one which reads as follows:

> William Lambarde of Lincoln's Inn, sometime master in Chancery, Keeper of the rolls and records within the Tower, of the Office of Alienations to Queen Elizabeth, founded the College of the Poor of Greenwich and endowed it. Obiit 1601, August 19, at Westcomb in East Greenwich.[77]

Catherine Brown notes that for some reason Lambarde, even in his youth, is always spoken of as "old Lambarde;"[78] no doubt the sobriquet is intended to show both respect and affection. And Dunkel writes eloquently in his summing-up of the antiquary's sterling qualities and his attitude to the law he laboured to determine and uphold:

> Lambarde was a devoutly religious man, of the flesh and blood of which martyrs are made. Living ever in the eyes of his God, he was paradoxically both humble and certain of his convictions. In God's universe, the natural law was order. He therefore could accept without apparent questioning that the sovereign of England was God's anointed deputy; that the English laws were good; and that the spiritual and political isolation of England from Europe would lead to peace, even though he did advocate trade with Europe. He did not question that the "good" might be different from the status quo, except in his desire to improve the administration of the good laws of England in accord with God's orderly universe. So the nature of the "good" was plain as a pikestaff: the good people observed the laws and maintained order, the evil persons committed misdemeanours and felonies and thus disturbed the peace.[79]

The aspect of William Lambarde which is of immediate concern is, of course, that of William Lambarde as the friend and pupil of Laurence Nowell the antiquary. Lambarde was no less active in Anglo-Saxon studies than his fellow antiquary, and indeed seems to have devoted more of his time to antiquarian pursuits than he did to his responsibilities as lawyer and Justice of the Peace. Nowell and Lambarde were pioneers together in Anglo-Saxon studies and also in historical method, for both eschewed the mediaeval reliance on authorities in favour of a return to the authentic records of the past. The close relations between the two men began with their studies of Anglo-Saxon language and letters in the 1560s and their transcription of manuscripts belonging to such as Archbishop Parker or Nicholas Wotton and persisted, as noted earlier, until Lambarde was forced to admit to himself and others that Nowell was not coming back from the travels on which he had embarked in 1567 and to see to the disposition of Nowell's estate. Lambarde retained Nowell's maps, manuscripts and transcripts, and the first fruits of his delving into his friend's collected works may be seen in Lambarde's *'Αρχηαιονομτα*.

Archaionomia, sive De priscis Anglorum legibus libri, sermone anglico, vetustate antiquissimo, aliquot abhinc seculis conscripti, atq: nunc demum, magno iurisperitorum, & amantium antiquitatis omnium commodo, è tenebris in lucem vocati was first published by John Day in London in 1568, and a revised edition appeared in Cambridge in 1644, edited by Abraham Wheloc. This pioneering work offers a working text of certain of the Anglo-Saxon laws, together with a facing translation into Latin, notes on Anglo-Saxon history and customs, and the laws of William I and Edward I. An introductory epistle thanks Nowell for suggesting the undertaking, Matthew Parker for lending the necessary manuscripts, and Sir William Cordell, Master of the Rolls, for his encouragement and assistance. Lambarde goes on to say that his purpose is to present contemporary Englishmen with an edition of the Anglo-Saxon laws which form the basis of contemporary English law; he thus continues the efforts of Parker and his circle to give the English nation its history and to cement the work of the Reformation. The work is dedicated to Queen Elizabeth and to Cordell.

Retha Warnicke considers that the contribution of Nowell to *Archaionomia* is less than is often supposed, and offers the same assessment of the importance of Nowell's collections to the production of Lambarde's next works, the *Alphabetical Description* and the *Perambulation.*[80] *An Alphabetical Description of the Chief Places in England and Wales (Dictionarium Angliæ Topographicum et Historicum...)* was published (with a portrait of Lambarde engraved by Vertue) in London in 1730, long after Lambarde's death, because the antiquary abandoned his scheme for the dictionary-style gazetteer cum Anglo-Saxon history on which he worked from the 1560s until as late as 1577 when William Camden sent Lambarde a manuscript copy of his *Britannia* for review. *A Perambulation of Kent: Conteining the description, Hystorie, and Customes of that Shyre* first saw the light of print in London in 1576 and was reprinted in London in 1596 after further polishing and enlargement by Lambarde with the lengthier title *A Perambulation of Kent: Conteining the description, Hystorie, and Customes of that Shyre. Written in the yeere 1570. First published in the yeere 1576 and now increased and altered after the authors owne last copie*. The work is a very full and thorough treatment of the history, and particularly of the Anglo-Saxon history, of the county of Kent, and contains excerpts from the *Textus Roffensis* and a map of the beacons in the contemporary Elizabethan county. The descriptive method is quite different from the alphabetical arrangement of the *Alphabetical Description*, consisting of perambulations of the two Kentish dioceses of Canterbury and Rochester. Matthew Parker, who did much to encourage and facilitate the appearance of *A Perambulation*, unfortunately died less than a year before its publication.

Lambarde's later publications concentrate more on legal history and on contemporary legal matters. *Eirenarcha, or of the Office of the Justices of the Peace*, a handbook upon justices, first appeared in 1582, was revised in 1588, and was reprinted several times during Lambarde's lifetime and remained popular through the seventeenth century (the 12th edition, for instance, appeared in 1619).

The *DNB* article notes that *The Duties of Constables, Borsholders, Tithing-men, and such other Lowe Ministers of the Peace. Whereunto be also adjoyned the severall Offices of Churchwardens, of Surveyors for amending the Highwayes,* &c. was first published in London in 1583 and reissued with additions six times between 1584 and 1610. The seventeenth century saw later reprints; the 16th edition of 1640 bore the title *The Duties of Constables, Borsholders, Tythingmen, and such other low and lay Ministers of the Peace*, while the 1677 edition bore the slightly different title *The duty and office of high constables of hundreds, petty constables, tythingmen, and such inferior ministers of the peace with the several duties and offices of churchwardens, overseers, and collectors for the poor, of surveyors for amending the high ways, and distributors of the provision for the destruction of noisom fowl and vermin.* This work was often printed along with *Eirenarcha.*

William Lambarde's Notes on the procedures and privileges of the House of Commons (1584) were printed in London by H.M. Stationery Office, *c.* 1977, and Conyers Read has printed his *Ephemeris and Twenty-nine Charges to Juries and Commissions.*[81] But his great legal antiquarian work was undoubtedly *Archeion or, a Discourse upon the High Courts of Justice in England*, although it did not appear until 1635, when it was published *twice*, once by Daniel Frere from the manuscript copy Lambarde gave to Sir Robert Cecil in 1591 and again in a revised, corrected and enlarged edition by Henry Seile and Daniel Frere from an annotated copy of Lambarde's own.[82]

Retha Warnicke, to whose *William Lambarde* the preceding discussion of the antiquary is deeply indebted, sums up on Lambarde as follows:

> He was, after all, a great founder—a pioneer as it were—in many fields. First, because he wrote and published the *Archaionomia*, he was a pioneer in Anglo-Saxon studies—a fame he deserves even if he had assistance in the gathering of the research for the book. In the area of local history he was also an outstanding contributor, writing the first history of the

county of Kent and having the honour of being the first to write a history of any English county. Furthermore, he encouraged others to write topographical histories and had thoughts of expanding his 'Description' into a national history when the appearance of Camden's masterpiece caused the abandonment of that project.

As an author of works which described the institutions of the 16th century, he can hardly be equalled. Not only did he write handbooks for justices of the peace and other local officials, but he also described the English court system in the *Archeion*, a work which has been so highly esteemed by modern legal historians that two of them, Charles McIlwain and Paul Ward, have had another edition of it published. His writings and decisions about Equity and Common Law are of great value for the modern world because they were written on the threshold of an era when the two realms of justice were to undergo a bitter struggle. Although trained in Common Law, he foresaw no inevitable clash between them and could and did praise the system of Equity in the Courts of Chancery and Star Chamber because it was based upon the conscience of the Queen who was the earthly source of all English justice.[83]

If words of Lambarde's own are to be pressed into service to sum up his sterling worth, they should by rights come from Book I of *Eirenarcha*, from the passage in which he defines the good and lawful gentleman who is fit to become a justice of the peace and to subscribe to this oath:

Doe equall right to rich and poor,
  as wit and law extends;
Give none advice in any cause,
  that you before depends:
Your Sessions hold as statutes bid:
  the forfeits that befall;
See entered well, and then estreat
  them to the Chequer all:
Receive no fee, but that is given
  by King, good use, or right:
No precept send to party self,
  but to indifferent wight.[84]

v. William Somner

Brief mention should be made of a third pioneer Anglo-Saxonist at work on the laws and other texts, William Somner (1598-1669). He was a member of the circle which had grown up around Matthew Parker in the sixteenth century and was well acquainted with such as Franciscus Junius, Archbishop Ussher, Sir Simonds D'Ewes and John Selden. He is noted for his publication "Glossarium: in quo obscuriora quæque vocabula, quæ toto hoc opere continentur copiose explicantur" in R. Twysden's *Historiae anglicanæ scriptores X* ... (London, 1652).[85]

But Somner is best remembered for his *Dictionarium Saxonico-Latino-Anglicum. Voces, phrasesque præcipuas Anglo-Saxonicas... Accesserunt Ælfrici Abbatis Grammatica Latino-Saxonica, cum Glossario suo ejusdem generis* (Oxford, 1659).[86] The *Dictionarium* relies heavily on Nowell's *Vocabularium Saxonicum* and on a manuscript copy of it made by Junius.[87] In addition the *Dictionarium* contains a text and glossary of Ælfric's grammar printed from a manuscript belonging to Junius and copied in its turn from a manuscript belonging to the painter Rubens.

Somner's original manuscript and his personal copy of the 1659 printed edition are preserved in Christ Church, Canterbury, where is also to be found a transcript long associated with William Somner. Liebermann attributed MS Canterbury, Christ Church Cathedral Library Literary B 2 to Somner, and referred to it as So. Somner acquired it indirectly from the Lambarde library, and it is now considered to be the work of Laurence Nowell (Dammery's Nw3).

vi. MSS BL Cotton Otho B. xi and BL Additional 43703

The Old English manuscript whose charred and burnt remains are now MS BL Cotton Otho B. xi was written at Winchester during the reign of Æthelred, partly in the middle of the tenth century and partly about the middle of the first half of the eleventh century according to Ker.[88] It belonged in the thirteenth century to the Augustinian priory of Southwick, Hampshire and in its pristine state contained Anglo-Saxon texts of some importance—a Winchester text (fairly closely dated and comparatively early) of the Old English Bede, the West-Saxon Genealogy, a version of the Anglo-Saxon Chronicle taken from the Parker Chronicle before it underwent addition and alteration at Canterbury, a list of popes, archbishops of Canterbury and bishops of various English sees copied from the Parker Chronicle, a collection of laws, a portion of a letter not otherwise extant on the penalties for adultery, the Burghal Hidage, a note on hides and defence not found elsewhere, a poem on the seasons for fasting not otherwise extant, and a collection of medicinal recipes and leechdoms. The manuscript came into the possession of Sir Robert Cotton early in the seventeenth century, certainly before April 23, 1621 when he lent it to William L'isle,[89] and it fell victim to the Cottonian fire of 1731 which largely destroyed it. Descriptions of the burnt manuscript are available from Wanley, Miller, Ker and Grant.[90]

Fortunately, before the fire Otho B. xi was transcribed by Laurence Nowell practically in its entirety. Nowell began with I. 1 of the Bede, omitting all the preliminary matter, and also omitted fols. 23^{v} and 24^{r}, *hiopesclice cuðon — onȝunne hliapettan.*[91] Although the text of the West-Saxon Genealogy in Otho B. xi is a direct copy of the one in the Parker Chronicle, Nowell did not transcribe it either, preferring the longer one in BL Cotton Tiberius A. iii, fol. 178, apparently taken from a stray leaf of the Abingdon Chronicle, BL Cotton Tiberius A. vi; the leaf bearing the West-Saxon Genealogy was later detached from Otho B. xi by L'isle when he borrowed Otho B. xi from Cotton to collate its Chronicle text with the Peterborough Chronicle and, undamaged, is now BL Additional 34652, fol. 2.[92] Nowell also *added* to the Bede text in his exemplar passages of Old English which are not original but which are back-translations from the Latin texts; these additions to the Bede, book I, chapter 15 are on fols. 19^{v}, 20^{rv} and 21^{r} of Additional 43703.[93]

The transcript is important as providing evidence for the contents of Otho B. xi before the disaster of 1731. We have to rely upon Nowell's transcript for the greater part of the Bede, (together with Wheloc's printed text)[94] for the greater part of the Chronicle, and (together with Lambarde's *Archaionomia*) for the greater part of the laws, almost completely for the poem *The Seasons for Fasting*,[95] and entirely for the list of popes,[96] the penalties for adultery, the Burghal Hidage (hitherto known only in fragmentary form), the note on hides and defence, and the herb recipes and leechdoms. The importance of the transcript for the Old English Bede has been demonstrated by Grant, who shows that CN confirms the closer connection of C with texts O and Ca than with texts B or T;[97] Sisam and Grant have demonstrated the importance of the text of *The Seasons for Fasting*;[98] Flower has performed the same service for the Burghal Hidage;[99] and Alistair Campbell comments on the text of the Chronicle, specifically the version of *The Battle of Brunanburh* which constitutes the entry for 937:

> An appendix is devoted to the recovery of the text of the poem in the lost MS. Cotton Otho B. XI. This text is of great interest, for a comparison of it with MS. A [CCCC 173, the Parker Chronicle], of which it is a copy, throws light on the manner in which copyists about A.D. 1000 treated poetical texts. Since nearly all Old English poetry survives only in copies of about that date, this is of great importance.[100]

It is hoped that the present edition will help to emphasize the importance of the legal texts in CN and the *Archaionomia*.

The detached, intact leaf which is now BL Additional 34652, fol. 2 suggests that the original dimensions of Otho B. xi were as follows: each page = 244 mm. x 177 mm., written area = 207 mm. x 144 mm. with 26 lines recto, 21 verso. The surviving fragments of the law code vary as follows: 165 mm. x 100 mm. to 85 mm. x 75 mm. with most likely 27 lines per page. The fragments are in very poor condition, with some portions virtually illegible; sometimes Liebermann prints text which is no longer legible.

Nowell carried out the work of transcription of Otho B. xi in 1562 while resident in the house of Sir William Cecil as tutor to the young Earl of Oxford, according to the note at the foot of fol. 264^{v}: "Haec scripsit Laurentius Nowellus propria manu in aedibus Cecillianis anno đni. 1562. Londini." "Haec ... Cecillianis" has been deleted and rewritten above the original note, which seems to have been identical; it looks as if Nowell is switching from his larger Anglo-Saxon hand to his smaller, more sloping Latin hand for the explicit. This page is reproduced in reduced facsimile by C. E. Wright.[101] The manuscript bears on fol. 2^{r} the inscription, "Laurence Nowell the owner 1562," and was one of eight transcripts by Nowell which were given to the British Museum in 1934. MSS Additional 43703-43710 were donated (along with twenty-eight sixteenth- and seventeenth-century printed books in the original vellum wrappers, twelve of which bore the inscription of ownership of Lambarde and five that of Nowell) by Thomas Evelyn Scott-Ellis, 8th Baron by Lord Howard de Walden.[102] Miscellaneous notes in Nowell's hand are also to be found on fols. 1^{v}, 3^{v}-4, and 268 of Additional 43703. The transcript also bears interlinear annotations in Lambarde's hand made when he glossed CN's law code from a manuscript of the Quadripartitus (e.g., fol. 239^{v}, ll. 5, 8 and fol. 242^{r}, ll. 12, 14.

CN has 277 paper leaves which are paginated in pencil in the top right-hand corner. Each page = 202 mm. x 154 mm., written area = 155 mm. x 100 mm. on average with 25-30 lines of Nowell's Anglo-Saxon hand. Throughout the transcript Nowell uses two different styles of handwriting, his usual hand for Latin and an Anglo-Saxon hand developed for the transcription of Old English texts. The Anglo-Saxon hand looks smaller and rather different when used for the second stratum of CN, the marginal and interlinear corrections and annotations which are distinguished as Nw2.

Nowell greatly revised and altered his transcript, correcting his work, commenting on vocabulary items, collating his texts with those in other manuscripts, adding passages of supposed Old English which were back-translations from Latin sources, or bringing his texts into line with what he considered to be correct Old English. This work must have been carried out not long after the completion of the transcript, since the transcript was made in 1562 and Nowell went abroad early in 1567. It is interesting to note that Nowell's transcript of Otho B. xi was itself transcribed by William Lambarde in 1564 very shortly after its initial completion and before the revisions were made by Nowell. The Chronicle text, an eleventh-century Winchester copy of the Parker Chronicle, was collated with texts B, C and D (MSS BL Cotton Tiberius A. vi, B. i and B. iv) by Nowell between 1564 and 1567, for Lambarde's copy of Additional 43703, now Dublin, Trinity College E. 5. 19 in the Ussher collection, was made before Nowell's marginal variants were added to his transcript. In an appendix to his edition of *The Battle of Brunanburh*, Campbell uses Lambarde's text to establish which readings in Nowell's transcript are original and then compares these original readings of Nowell's with Wheloc's text (printed as an appendix to his edition of the Old English Bede) to decide on the probable readings of Otho.[103]

In order to establish the degree of accuracy of Nowell's transcription, I compared what survives of the Old English Bede text in burnt Otho with Nowell's version in Additional 43703. Bearing in mind that hindsight tends to be 20/20 and that Nowell was carrying out pioneer investigation of Old English rather than coming to Otho B. xi with modern knowledge and experience of Old English and such tools as electric light and ultra-violet lamps, I nevertheless found that certain features of his transcription should not be relied upon. Nowell was accustomed to the Elizabethan spelling system of English, which saw no difference, for instance, between *i* and *y*; contemporary spelling conventions saw *i* and *y* as interchangeable graphs for [ɪ], printers usually preferring to use *y* for [ɪ] next to minims; Nowell quite often alters to *y* by adding a descender, producing a dotted *ẏ*. Nowell was probably unaware of the true phonetic value of *æ*, and in spelling interchanges *æ* with *a*, *e*, and *ea*. The failure to distinguish *e* and *a* is not vital, nor is that of other vowels; *o* and *u* look alike in the Otho hands, so the faults may not all be Nowell's. He has difficulty with *a* and *o*, *a* and *u* and other vowels and diphthongs, final *-e*, and initial *ge-*, and freely interchanges *þ* and *ð*; the adding or dropping of final *-e* is a reflection of Elizabethan spelling practice, of course, and the interchange of *þ* and *ð* is not very significant, but Nowell's behaviour must be noted.

The constant interchange of *þ* and *ð* is acceptable, for this is a realisation that *þ* and *ð* express the same sound and a failure which we all must share to see any reason for observing any distinction. The handwriting in Otho leads one to forgive Nowell's confusion of *r* and *s*, *n* and *r*, *t* and *d*, and so on, and there is little significance in his alternation of single and double consonants, *ꝥ*, *ꝥte* and *þæt*, or *ʒe-* and *ʒ-*. One cannot take exception to an Elizabethan Latin scholar's suspensions and contractions when these vary from the exemplar, and Nowell's cavalier treatment of the accent marks in Otho is insignificant.

In his spelling of inflexional endings Nowell interchanged *-an*, *-en*, and *-on*, thus undermining distinctions between indicative and subjunctive, or infinitive and preterite plural. Medial unaccented vowels, consonants and words are added or dropped; homoeoteleuta and changes of word-order are infrequent. Nowell collated several of his texts with those in other manuscripts (e.g., his version of the Chronicle), and such collation could account for some of the variation from burnt Otho. Nevertheless, as Kenneth Sisam notes, "In such details the transcript seems to show a mixture of mechanically accurate and careless copying, which makes close consideration of its abnormal forms and spellings unprofitable.[104]

Details of the comparison can be found in my original article, along with the following general conclusion:

> On the evidence presented above it is clear that Nowell's transcript of the Bede is of no use to the student of spellings, phonology or inflections and no dialect indications can be drawn from it. C alone must be used for these purposes, fragmentary as it is. I join Sisam in lamenting Nowell's inaccuracy in these fields. Yet we can reflect that very few words are omitted, homoeoteleuta are very rare and changes of word-order are few. The transcript can therefore be used as evidence for the contents and word-order of C ... Far from reliable in detail as Nowell is, we are ever in his debt for substantially preserving texts that otherwise would be lost.[105]

These conclusions have been criticized by Torkar and Lutz in their theses as being too conservative, but to err on the side of caution with Kenneth Sisam is to find oneself in good company.[106] To assess the accuracy of Nowell's work is in no way to detract from its value. For those texts particularly for which Nowell is the sole authority such evaluation is vitally necessary, for we are dealing not with tenth- or eleventh-century texts directly but with tenth- or eleventh-century texts as they have been filtered through sixteenth-century practices, conventions and human fallibility.

When attention is turned to the legal texts that are the main concern of the present study, similar strictures must be borne in mind. The texts as found in the Nowell transcript in Additional 43703 may be used happily by historians, legal experts, and students of syntax, word-order, and lexicon, but they should be approached with caution by students of orthography, phonology, morphology and dialectology.

The Anglo-Saxon laws found originally in BL Cotton Otho B. xi were copied by Ker's scribe no. 2 of the first half of the eleventh century and his scribe no. 3 also of the first half of the eleventh century but probably later than scribe no. 2. The laws originally in Otho fall into two groups, those of Athelstan and those of Alfred and Ine. The following lists give the references to burnt Otho, the Nowell transcript, and vol. I of Liebermann's *Die Gesetze der Angelsachsen*:

The Anglo-Saxon Laws (Athelstan)

Otho B. xi fols. 48, 51 (by scribe no. 3)
Additional 43703 fols. 233-36^{r} and 265-67

There were originally four leaves in Otho B. xi containing these laws. As transcribed in Additional 43703 they are as follows:

(a) fols. 233-36^{r} and 265^{r}— II Athelstan (Liebermann pp. 150-64);
(b) fols. 265^{r}-66^{r} — V Athelstan (Liebermann pp. 166-68);
(c) fols. 266^{r}-67 — Iudex (Liebermann pp. 474-76).

The Anglo-Saxon Laws (Alfred and Ine)

Otho B. xi fols. 49, 50 and 52 + 53 (by scribe no. 2, all bound the wrong way round)
Additional 43703 fols. 236^{v}-55^{r}

Otho B. xi originally contained, on probably nineteen leaves, the laws of Alfred and Ine. Nowell has transcribed them *in toto*, while Liebermann has printed the fragments remaining (pp. 16-20, 72-78 and 118-22). The text is close to that of the Parker Chronicle.

In Additional 43703, fol. 255^{r} the end of Ine's code is followed immediately and without a break by the unique eight-line text on the penalties for adultery to be imposed on both the man and the woman involved (*Ymb æbricas*).[107] This would imply that Otho B. xi marked no boundary between the two texts and that Nowell initially failed to make the distinction either, returning only later to separate the close of Alfred-Ine from the fragment on adultery with a line and the marginal notation *finis legum Ina*.

In the transcribing of the legal texts Nowell is to be found up to his usual tricks as outlined earlier. The transcript as usual has two layers, Nowell's transcript of Otho B. xi (C), referred to as CN and corresponding to Dammery's Nw1, and Nowell's interlinear and marginal additions or corrections/annotations in CN, corresponding to Dammery's Nw2. As usual, Nowell uses two distinct "hands," one for Anglo-Saxon and the other for Latin, with the Anglo-Saxon one smaller and more sloping when interlinear or marginal. Campbell shows Nowell adding a large number of variants in the margins of the Chronicle text, indicating them by the addition of *al.* or *alias*, and the same device is employed in the legal texts, e.g., CN 246ᵛ, l. 7 reads *haliʒ ryht in folc butan leafe álecʒ̄*, with *aliaṣ: haliʒ rift butan rihte alecʒe, i(d est), sāctū velū sine recto deponat* in the left margin Nw2 [*haliʒ ryht* E, H, *haliʒ riht* B, *haliʒ ryht 'ryft al.'* (margin) Nw4, *halıᵹꞃıꝼꞇ* Ld]. Again, CN 253ʳ, l. 10 reads *hida þara ʒ̄þinʒea*, with *ðara ʒ̄þunʒera, alias* with deletion of one letter after the *e* in the right margin Nw2 [*þara ʒeðinʒea* E, *ðara ðinʒa* B, *ðæra ʒeþinʒa* H, *ðæꞃa ðınᵹa* Ld].

Roy Leslie offers examples of Nowell's use of a hooked and undotted variety of *ı* which he often joins to the preceding letter if this ends in a minim—*cymnʒ* for *cyninʒ*, *cymnʒes* for *cyninʒes*, *mœmum* for *mœnium*—and joins Campbell in showing how this peculiarity of Nowell's handwriting misled Lambarde in the making of his transcript of the Chronicle text.[108] The same device is employed in the legal texts, e.g., CN 243ʳ, l. 16 reads *nıon* for *mon*, and CN 252ʳ, l. 6 reads *mon* for *in on* [Ld *mon* shows Lambarde's being misled].

It has already been seen that on fols. 19ᵛ-21ʳ Nowell added to I. 15 of the Bede text in his exemplar passages of Old English which are not original but which are back-translations from the Latin texts; the same sort of back-translations appear in Lambarde's *Archaionomia*. The passages in question have no source in the surviving manuscripts of the Anglo-Saxon laws but are rather back-translations from the Latin Quadripartitus. Kenneth Sisam claimed, and Felix Liebermann denied, that these translations were made by Nowell and consequently printed by Lambarde, which would destroy Liebermann's theory about a lost "ghost" manuscript of the Anglo-Saxon laws, his *lq*.[109] Sisam finds support from Robin Flower,[110] Dorothy Whitelock,[111] and Albert Marckwardt, who demonstrates that in the *Vocabularium* "Nowell was capable upon occasion of composing his own illustrative quotations when nothing convenient happened to be at hand. We find him, for example, citing, 'we behofiað hlafes,' which is dubious at best since *behofian* was an impersonal verb in Old English."[112] And, of course, part of the purpose of my printing the Nowell and Lambarde texts face-to-face is to lay this particular ghost. The passages from the Quadripartitus and Ld, fol. 68ᵛ, are as follows (see pp. 5-6 *supra*):

> Totum hoc institutum (et confirmatum) est in magna synodo apud Greateleyam, cui archiepiscopus Wulfhelmus interfuit et omnes optimates et sapientes quos Æþelstanus rex congregare potuit.

Ealle ðis ƿæs gesetted on ðam miclan sẏnoþ
æt Greatanleage; on þam ƿæs se ærcebisceop
Ƿulfhelme mid eallum þæm æþelum man-
num ⁊ ƿiotan, ðe Æþelstan cẏning
gegadrian.

Whitelock assumes Lambarde was the translator of the spurious passage in Ld, but Sisam ascribes the work to Nowell. I think Nowell was responsible (despite the absence of the passage from CN) because of the two antiquaries he would be the more experienced Anglo-Saxonist and had done this sort of thing before. A commonplace book written by Nowell, now MS Los Angeles, University of California Research Library 170/529 carries a virtually complete transcript of the Quadripartitus. The question whether Nowell or Lambarde did the actual translation does not, of course, affect the argument that the passage of spurious Old English helps disprove the existence of Liebermann's *lq*.

The rubrics of the Alfred-Ine code present scholars with a rather vexed question. All the surviving vernacular texts descend from a version which was divided into paragraphs in a somewhat haphazard manner; a single paragraph may deal with different topics or, conversely, a single topic can sprawl over two or more paragraphs. Four of the six surviving texts carry a list of rubrics between the Biblical Introduction and the law code proper, and this list of rubrics matches the law code poorly, only partly as a result of the unsatisfactory paragraph-division. Some important matters are not mentioned in this rather scrappy list of chapter-headings. Attempts to improve upon the original list can be detected in B, for instance, and in the Latin Quadripartitus. Several of the rubrics have been omitted from B through scribal carelessness, unfortunately.

Surviving portions of Otho B. xi show clearly that Ot was not rubricated. CN 236^{v}-238^{r} has a rubric list which is not found in Ld., and then begins a numbering and rubric system which is almost immediately abandoned. The rubrics to the individual chapters subsequently found in CN are in Nowell's own hand and are interlinear or marginal insertions from Nw2. In the main, they come from the capitula list, but not always; in two or three places where they differ, they agree with Lambarde's headings, but Nowell keeps the rubrics as in the capitula list where Lambarde alters them, partly under the influence of B. Since CN 236^{v}-238^{r} contains this list of chapter-headings which is not found in Ld, in this edition CN's list is collated with the rubrics extracted from the body of Ld's text. The Appendix contains examples which show the rubrics as they are found in all the surviving Old English versions.

Nw2 thus shows how Nowell collated the text of Additional 43703 with those to be found in at least two other sources. While the rubrics constitute the more obvious alterations and corrections to bring CN into line with other versions, instances are by no means restricted to the list of chapter-headings, as the Appendix will show. There are several places where the reviser (Nowell) is definitely comparing another text or texts: sometimes it seems to be G (fols. 236^{v} to the foot of 241^{r}, which is marked by a hand-pointer ☞ in the left margin); sometimes it seems to be H. Many of these variants have been incorporated into Nw3 and Nw4. For example, CN 236^{v}, rubric vii reads *circan*, Nw2 reads *circen'e'* with the first *e* on top of *a*, and G reads *cyricena;* CN 236^{v}, rubric xxvii reads *monnes pif*, Nw2 reads *pifmonnes* in the left margin, and G reads *pifmannes* [*cẏꞃıcena* Ld]. Again, CN 239^{r}, l. 3 reads *læte hie freo*, Nw2 reads *læte hie 'faran' freo*, Nw3 reads *læte hie faran freo*, and G reads *læte hie faran freo*; Ld has *læꞇe hı ꝼaꞃan ꝼꞃeo.* CN 253^{v}, l. 13 reads *sinniȝ* as does E, B reads *synniȝ* (with '*scyldiȝ*' above in a different hand), Nw2 deletes and corrects to '*scyldiȝ*' followed by Nw3, and H reads *scyldiȝ* [*ꞅcẏlꝺıᵹ* Ld].

Most peculiar is CN 253^{r}, l. 3 which reads *se cyninȝ siðcund* where E, H, and B read *ȝesiðcund* and Nw2 reads *'ȝe'siðcund* [*ᵹeꞅıþcunꝺ* Ld]. Since the addition of *se cyninȝ* makes nonsense, I wonder what has happened here. On fol. 233^{v}, does the *Desunt nonnulla* in the margin, then crossed out Nw2, refer to the fact that B has a lacuna beginning about this point?

It is clear enough that Nowell's transcript has sometimes been altered to bring it into line with the other versions after the time of the original transcription. This casts important light on the relation between Ot and E, as Whitelock points out: "Ot agrees so closely with E that Liebermann thought it was a direct copy, but Nowell's transcript of Ot avoids some of the errors in E, from which Ot's exemplar must have been free ... he leaves unchanged some errors in E, presumably because they were in Ot also."[113]

Lambarde copies some of these entries faithfully, e.g., at CN 252^{v}, l. 24, where in CN beside *æfæsne* is written in the margin *æbesne, alias* Nw2 and in Lambarde's edition the text is *æbesne*, and *al. æfesne* is in the margin.

I wonder if one can entirely trust Liebermann's readings of Ot? He is a remarkably accurate man, but some readings may have been difficult. One or two disagreements between Ot and Nowell seem strange, e.g., II Athelstan 14. 1, where Liebermann gives *upp an* for Ot; CN 234^{v}, l. 13 has *uppan* deleted with '*ufan on*' Nw2 [*uꝼan on* Ld]. But I see that Liebermann says his Ot is "ergänzt" from Somner/Nw3, so perhaps *upp an* comes from there [*up on* H].

At II Athelstan 20.2 Ot is said to read *ȝe..dan* where CN 235^{r}, l. 14 has *toridan* [*ꞇo ꞃıꝺan* Ld]; H has only *ridan*. If Ot really did have *ȝeridan*, *toridan* must be an alteration by Nowell, copied by Lambarde.

In II Athelstan l. 2, the older conclusion must have been *ne sparige hine mon ær þam oþer æfter*. Ot, perhaps unfamiliar with the rare *oðer* for "or," spells *oder* and has *æfter* in the margin. Nowell's transcript 233^{r}, l. 5 has *ær þū* (for *ær þam*) but takes *Oder* as beginning the next clause and has no *æfter* [*ne ſpaꞃıᵹe hıne mon æꞃ ðæm. Oþeꞃ* ... Ld]. I think perhaps the whole thing is corrupt, and that Ot, with *æfter* in the margin, was trying to make some sense—perhaps it means "before 12 years of age or after."

Nowell made use of CN for the making of two further transcripts, Nw3 and Nw4. Both incorporate readings from Nw2, so they must have been made after the copying of CN in 1562 and the subsequent addition of Nw2 and have been completed and given to Lambarde before Nowell left for the Continent in 1567. I have seen neither transcript, and gratefully rely for much of my information on the kindness of Richard Dammery.

Canterbury, Christ Church Cathedral Library, MS Literary B 2, n. 8 = Liebermann's So, Dammery's Nw3 contains, on paper leaves of varying dimensions (approximately 297 mm. x 200 mm., written space 230 mm. x 144 mm., 25-28 lines per page), a collection of miscellaneous documents including incomplete copies of II Athelstan, Alfred and Ine, and II and III Edgar. This is a working copy, written by Nowell in his Anglo-Saxon hand. The volume was obtained by William Somner indirectly from the library of William Lambarde, and on the death of Somner was purchased for the Cathedral Library by the Dean and Chapter of Canterbury. Liebermann mistakenly took the work to be that of Somner himself, and accordingly designated the volume So.[114] Assuming Liebermann's representation of the text of his So is accurate, there is no great need to go to Canterbury to obtain readings for Nw3.

London, British Library, Henry Davis Collection, MS M 30 = Dammery's Nw4 has only recently been discovered to be the work of Nowell, and has not been published.[115] Nw4 contains, on 46 vellum leaves 212 mm. x 152 mm., written space 152 mm. x 92 mm., 16 lines per page, extracts from the code of Alfred and translations by Nowell into sixteenth-century English. The text is important on two counts: it carries variants related to those of Nw2 but not corresponding to those of any of the known Anglo-Saxon manuscripts, thus suggesting the existence in the sixteenth century of at least one manuscript of the laws which is now lost and contributing to the discussion of Lambarde's sources for the *Archaionomia*; and second, the translation is the only sustained sixteenth-century one so far known, and the only extant translation into English of any text by Nowell. The Old English text is in Nowell's Anglo-Saxon hand, the translation in his italic one, and both have been executed with great care, leading to Dammery's suggestion that Nw4 was intended for presentation to Cecil, owner of Otho B. xi at the time of that manuscript's transcription by Laurence Nowell. There is no proof Cecil ever received Nw4. Lambarde did not sign the volume, but Thomas Lambarde affixed his *ex libris* in 1634. The book was sold by Sotheby's in 1943, and is currently in the British Library.[116]

It remains now to consider Otho B. xi and the various Nowell transcripts to determine their relationship to one another, to other surviving manuscripts of the Anglo-Saxon laws, and to the *Archaionomia*. After Liebermann's gentle mauling at the hands of Sisam and scholars' subsequent reluctance to postulate the existence of too many "ghost" manuscripts, to say nothing of latter-day suspicion of stemmatics in general, it seems an act of great temerity to suggest that there previously existed manuscripts of the Anglo-Saxon laws which are no longer extant. It must nevertheless be borne in mind that there may well have been such lost manuscripts in either the eleventh or the sixteenth century.

It has been shown above that Otho B. xi is not as direct a copy of E as Liebermann supposed, though the relationship of the two texts is close. Otho presumably drew on an Old English text close to E but not identical with E. Comparison with CN shows that where E is in lacuna at Alfred 1. 2 through homoeoteleuton, CN is continuous, in line with the other manuscripts, which suggests that Otho was not a direct copy of E but of a version which shared certain errors and lacunae with E but also had some superior readings. Alternative possibilities are that Otho was copied from more than one exemplar (rather unlikely) or that Otho indeed copied E, but an E that had been corrected from a more accurate text which no longer exists, which is perhaps the most likely scenario.

The incomplete G was used by Lambarde for the *Archaionomia*, as indicated by Milton Turk:

> The many agreements of Lamb with G probably indicate only the use of G by Lambarde. Only a few are supported by H. The variations are not sufficient to put G out of the class to which the before mentioned Mss. belong. The scribe of G had an original not much different, we should judge, from E. He was somewhat careless, writing rather fast, and introduced often words of his own, still oftener a new word-order.[117]

Agreements in error and scribal innovation between G and H suggest the possibility that G was derived from a manuscript related to H or to H's source. Nowell collated CN with G (*inter alia*) as far as G extends, and it is most likely that Lambarde used CN when preparing the *Archaionomia*.

Following Liebermann and Turk, it is accepted doctrine that the post-conquest B and H preserve similar texts, supposedly derived from a common but no longer extant source, Liebermann's *hb*.[118] On the other hand, their discussions of the very fragmentary Bu are unhelpful; this very fragmentary text contains so many variants from the others that it possibly represents a quite independent tradition.

Of the sixteenth-century transcripts it can safely be said that CN is a copy of unburned Otho B. xi made by Nowell in 1562 in Cecil's house in the Strand. CN contains the second stratum of textual variants known as Nw2 added when Nowell collated CN with other texts. The source for Nw2 was primarily (but not exclusively) G as far as the foot of fol. 241^{r}. Much less certain is where Nowell got the other variants recorded in Nw2, for no single source is apparent; some of the readings agree with H, others with B, suggesting Nw2 drew on a text of the *hb* tradition, while yet others could simply be back-translations from the Quadripartitus. Nowell probably was unfamiliar with H, and Lambarde did not see that manuscript until after the *Archaionomia* was published. Both the paper working copy Nw3 and the vellum presentation copy Nw4 appear to be textually related to CN and Nw2 (or Nw2's source).[119]

And this is all that can be said for now, until thorough studies are done of all Lambarde's sources for the *Archaionomia* and of all the Nowell transcripts—or until *another* Nowell transcript of Otho B. xi or that *third* Laurence Nowell is discovered!

vii. *Lambarde's* *Archaionomia*

The first book printed in Old English, employing types designed and cast for the reproduction of Anglo-Saxon letter forms, was *Ælfric Grammaticus. A Testimonie of Antiquitie, shewing the auncient fayth in the Church of England*, printed by John Day of Aldersgate in 1566 under the patronage of Archbishop Parker. The second substantial printing of Old English using Day's type was William Lambarde's *Archaionomia, sive De priscis Anglorum legibus libri, sermone anglico, vetustate antiquissimo, aliquot abhinc seculis conscripti, atq: nunc demum, magno iurisperitorum, & amantium antiquitatis omnium commodo, è tenebris in lucem vocati*, printed in London in 1568 "Ex officina Joannis Daij."[120]

Sir Henry Spelman (1564-1641), assisted by his son John (1594-1643) and by Jeremiah Stephens (1592-1664), brought out the first printing of church law and of some charters in Latin and Old English under the title *Concilia, decreta, leges, constitutiones, in re ecclesiarum orbis Britannici, Vol. 1* in London in 1639. Vol. 1 ran from the introduction of Christianity to the Norman Conquest and was by Spelman alone; vol. 2, from the Norman Conquest to the reign of Henry VIII, appeared in London in 1664, edited by William Dugdale. A relative of William L'isle (1569?-1637), Spelman founded the Anglo-Saxon lectureship at Cambridge for Abraham Wheloc, and it was Wheloc who continued the publication of Old English civil and church law by producing a second edition of Lambarde's *Archaionomia* in Cambridge in 1644.

Fol. A.i^r of *Archaionomia* bears the following dedication:

Ornatissimo viro, GVLIELMO CORDELLO
Equiti aurato, & Serenissimæ Reginæ
ELIZABETAE ab Archiuis,
Gulielmus Lambardus.
S. D. P.

The dedication is followed by an introductory *Epistola* in which Lambarde expresses his debt of gratitude to Laurence Nowell and to Archbishop Parker. The implication that the work was produced under the aegis of these renowned and influential men assured its success: Sir William Cordell, Master of the Rolls, was soon to become the Governor of Lincoln's Inn; Laurence Nowell the famous antiquary was even then supposedly carrying out research on the Continent; and the imprimatur of the Archbishop of Canterbury would link the pioneering work of Lambarde to that of Parker's circle. Wilbur Dunkel establishes the context for the *Archaionomia*:

In the dedication of this book to Sir William Cordell, Lambarde also gave lavish acknowledgement to Laurence Nowell and Archbishop Parker. To these three men he owed, he wrote, a great debt for assistance. He also stated his reasons for presenting this book, paraphrasing certain well-known classical thinkers about the law. "No nation was ever conquered that had not first suffered disorder from its enemies within." He then explained, also in Latin, that the laws of England were "like a wall built of stone and oak to defend a city." He advocated that severe penalties be given to persons disobeying the law, so that through fear the people would learn to respect the law. He based this thought on the premise that authority was vested in the sovereign, but ultimately the maintenance of order derived from the people themselves.[121]

When Lambarde first came to know Matthew Parker and Laurence Nowell, Parker was living in seclusion during the purges of Queen Mary's reign, poring over ancient documents dealing with legal matters both civil and ecclesiastical as interpreted by the early leaders of the Church in England, and the antiquary, similarly in seclusion, was collecting, transcribing and translating Anglo-Saxon manuscripts. Lambarde showed such scholarly dedication to the decipherment of the Anglo-Saxon tongue and its use in manuscripts that he rapidly progressed from being Nowell's pupil to becoming the antiquary's friend and colleague. When Nowell left for the Continent in March of 1567, it was to Lambarde that he entrusted his possessions, especially his books and manuscripts; if anything were to happen to him overseas (as, apparently, was to be the case), Nowell wished Lambarde to execute his will with regard to his money and possessions and to use the transcripts and manuscripts for the prosecution of the work they had for so long undertaken together of presenting Anglo-Saxon language and letters to a wider audience. Accordingly, Lambarde in his *Epiꞅꞇola*, fols. A.iij^{rv}, credits Nowell with suggesting his present task and with supplying the necessary resource materials:

> Obꞇulıꞇ mıhı ꞅupeꞃıoꞃı anno Lauꞃenꞇıuꞅ Noeluꞅ, ꝺılıgenꞇıßımuꞅ ınueꞅꞇigaꞇoꞃ anꞇıquıꞇaꞇıꞅ, mıhıque mulꞇa & ıucunꝺa conꞅueꞇuꝺıne conıuncꞇuꞅ, ac quı me (quıcunque ın hoc geneꞃe ꞅım) eꝼꝼecıꞇ, pꞃıꞅcaꞅ Anglоꞃum legeꞅ, anꞇıquıꞅꞅıma Saxonum lıngua, eꞇ lıꞇeꞃıꞅ conꞅcꞃıpꞇaꞅ, aꞇque a me (quonıam eı ꞇū eꞃaꞇ ꞇꞃanꞅ maꞃe eunꝺum) uꞇ laꞇınaꞅ ꝼaceꞃem, ac peꞃ uulgaꞃem vehemenꞇeꞃ ꝼlagıꞇauıꞇ. Huıuꞅ ego poꞅꞇulaꞇıonı æquæ & honeꞅꞇæ, cum pꞃopꞃıuꞅ ꞃeꝼꞃagaꞃı ꞃelıgıo ꝼueꞃaꞇ, non ꞇamē pꞃoꞇınuꞅ conceßı, veꞃum vbı ⁊ ıpꞅe ꞅæpıuꞅ auıꝺıßıme lecꞇıꞇaßem, & amıcoꞃū non nulloꞅ (quoꞃum ego ꞇanꞇı ꝼacıo ıuꝺıcıū, uꞇ ꝼacıle eoꞃū cꞃeꝺo ꞅenꞇenꞇıam me ab oībuꞅ Cꞃıꞇıcoꞃū calūnıjꞅ vınꝺıcaꞇuꞃā) ea ꝺe ꞃe conꞅuluıßē, hanc ꞇanꝺē ꞅuꞅcepı pꞃouıncıā, aꞇq̃ uꞇ ıllı obꞅequēꝺo, ꞃeıpub. ınꞅeꞃuıꞃē, uꞇ poꞇuı ꝺıꝼꝼıculꞇaꞇē ꞅupeꞃauı.

The contents of the *Archaionomia* are certain Old English texts of the Anglo-Saxon laws as transcribed and edited by Laurence Nowell on the verso of each folio with on the recto a facing-page translation or paraphrase into Latin by William Lambarde. The texts of immediate interest to the present study are those of II Athelstan, V Athelstan, Alfred and Ine, and Iudex. Also included are notes on Anglo-Saxon history and customs, the laws of William I and Edward I, and the first printed woodcut map of the Anglo-Saxon kingdoms. Two of the texts are not original, but are back-translations by Nowell into Old English from the Latin Quadripartitus.

Dunkel demonstrates the immediate success of the *Archaionomia* by quoting the words of John Foxe, a member of Archbishop Parker's circle. Foxe sent a copy of the work to William Bradbridge, then Dean of Salisbury and later Bishop of Exeter, commending Lambarde on the flyleaf as "*Vir, multis et egregiis dotibus ornatissimus Gulielmus Lambardus, is ipse qui superiores tuas de me literas.*" Dunkel continues:

> A copy of *Archaionomia* in the Folger Shakespeare Library has the signature of William Shakespeare, believed by many scholars to be authentic. This is significant, as Shakespeare was not born until 1564 and thus was only four years old when *Archaionomia* was printed. This book apparently continued in esteem for many years, or why would Shakespeare have acquired it? But no arguments need to be advanced to support the continued use of this book even after the death of Lambarde, since the common lawyers in the seventeenth century avidly searched it for precedents which they evidently highly esteemed. On the other hand, twentieth-century scholars in the fields of Anglo-Saxon, palaeography, and history have pointed out certain inaccuracies in selecting primary texts, misunderstanding of Anglo-Saxon words and syntax, and in general have warned against the use of this book because of these matters unknown to Lambarde and his learned associates. Yet it would seem to an outsider that the historians who have condemned a few items in this book might also have recognized the significance of its reception, use, and influence some three hundred years ago, when it was a veritable landmark on an uncharted road to Old English learning.[122]

Liebermann prints II Athelstan pp. 150-66 (even-numbered pages only). He prints H (Textus Roffensis), B, Ot, Quadripartitus in columns, with other texts including Ld, So in footnotes and then as principal texts when the main manuscripts are in lacuna. He prints Ld as a primary text from p. 154 since B is in lacuna from that point.

Liebermann prints V Athelstan pp. 166-68 (even-numbered pages only). He prints Ld as a principal text alongside H, Quadripartitus. He also prints Iudex pp. 474-76 from G, Quadripartitus; this text is not in Ld, which makes the version in CN doubly important.

In II & V Athelstan, Ld has rubrics which have no counterparts in CN. Sometimes there are counterparts in other OE manuscripts, but many of the rubrics are apparently unique to Ld. The first two are identical to those in B, but then B simply leaves spaces for rubrics and soon goes into lacuna.

As mentioned above, CN 236^{v}-238^{r} has a rubric list which is not found in Ld. In this edition CN's list is collated with the rubrics extracted from the body of Ld's text.

Comparison of CN and Ld shows that there can be little doubt that Lambarde used Otho or a transcript of it made by Laurence Nowell. Whitelock considers that the CN version of V Athelstan is "almost certainly the source of Ld's version,"[123] and continues:

> Lambard's texts are sometimes merely translations of the Latin of *Quadripartitus*, but for Alfred's code he used B and Nowell's transcript of Ot. William Somner's paper manuscript of Anglo-Saxon laws, Canterbury Cathedral Lib. ms. B. 2. n. 8 (cited as So) also seems to have had access either to Ot or to N.[124]

Various manuscripts have been redated since the time of Fehr and Liebermann, and many of the latter's stemmae are vitiated by his faith in a lost MS known to Lambarde. As this agreed so often with Quadripartitus (naturally so, since Lambarde was often merely translating its readings) Liebermann has allowed far too much weight to Quadripartitus. Lambarde used not only B, but the burnt Otho (or rather CN—Nowell's transcript of it—and Nw2), and the mid-eleventh-century part of G. The relationship between Lambarde's text and Somner's papers is now clear: So/Nw3 is derived, like Nw4, from CN and Nw2.

Notes on the Present Editions

viii. The Editing of CN

Pace Bruce Mitchell,[125] I have used sufficient capital letters and modern punctuation to make Nowell's text usable; it is not an original Old English manuscript, after all, but a transcript. Word-division is editorial. The clause numeration follows Schmid and Liebermann; while not necessarily the best arrangement, this is most practical for scholars who wish to put my edition side by side with those of other MSS and transcripts. Contractions are not expanded, nor is the tironian *et* nota, *7*, since any choice between *and* or *ond* involves a dialect decision.

Underlining in the transcript means that the underlined words have been marked for omission or for correction, or else there is a gloss either superscript or in the margin; these matters are recorded in the footnotes. Letters and words interlineated or added in the margins are placed within single inverted commas in the footnotes; where such additions can be detected palaeographically as the work of a later annotator, this has been indicated. Words and phrases incorporated from the margins into the body of the text are placed in brackets, save for rubrics from Nw2.

Problems involving individual letters which have misled readers from Lambarde to the present day have been solved editorially and noted. For instance, problems with *a* and *u*, *-an* and *-um*, with *eo* and *ea*, with *m* and *ni*, and with other letters have been dealt with as follows.

It looks as if the scribes of Otho used an open Anglo-Saxon *a* which Nowell read often as *u*, thus confusing both *a* and *u*, and *-an* and *-um*:

CN 233^{r}, l. 1 *handa ȝefanȝen*—MS looks like *hunda ȝefunȝen*
l. 5 *ær þū*—MS looks like *ær þā*
l. 13 *andaȝā*—MS looks like *andaȝū*

CN 233^{v}, l. 7 *þeofa*—MS looks like *þeofu*
l. 10 *þreofealdū*—MS looks more like *ū* than *ā*
l. 15 *þryfealda*—a clear *a*!
l. 16 *carcerne*—MS looks like *curcerne*

CN 234^{r}, l. 4 *anfealdū*—a clear *ū*

CN 265^{r}, l. 13 *þa aþas*—MS looks like *þu aþas*

CN 237^{r}, l. 20 *preccendan—an* clear, not *um*

CN 250^{r}, l. 3 *præcēdū*—MS looks like *præcēdā*

CN 254^{v}, l. 14 *maȝan*—MS looks a good deal like *maȝum*

Problems with *eo* and *ea* are best illustrated with the form I have standardized to *feoht-*:

CN 247^{r}, l. 4 *feohte*—MS looks like *feahte*
l. 6 *feohtan*—MS looks like *feahtan*
l. 6 *feohte*—MS looks like *feahte*
l. 10 *feohtan*—MS looks like *feahtan*

Problems with *m* and *ni* can be seen in these examples:

CN 240^{v}, l. 4 *nide* above *niede*—both *ni* from *m*

CN 242^{r}, l. 1 *on ines dæȝe*—from *on mesdæȝe*

CN 243^{r}, l. 16 *mon*—from *nion*

CN 252^{r}, l. 6 *in on*—MS looks like *mon*

CN 252^{v}, l. 20 *ȝemete*—MS looks like *ȝemiete*

Problems with other letters have been corrected, e.g., *h* and *n̄* : CN 266^{r}, l. 9 *he bereð*—MS *ne*. And at CN 245^{r} Nowell has started to write the modern word "shilling" before catching his error: CN 245^{r}, l. 20 *sciłł*—from ~~*s h*~~ *sciłł*.

Nowell's contraction *þon̄e* has been altered in the text and instances noted. I have silently standardised *forþam* and *forþon* as single words but have kept following *þe* separate.

Contractions used in the footnotes are usually self-explanatory; e.g., *del.* = "deletion", "deleted", and *del. of one, etc.* = "deletion or erasure of one letter, etc."

Catch words have been given for Additional 43703 but not Ld.

I have made every effort to adjust fonts and spacing to have one page of edition to one page of Additional 43703, but occasionally the system has broken down and I have resorted to having CN 250^{r} and Ld 2^{v}-4^{v} both spill over on to a second page.

ix. The Editing of Ld

Ld is taken directly from the printed text of the *Archaionomia*, and not from Liebermann's edition.

At the start of the *Archaionomia* Lambarde offers a list of errors and omissions which lies outwith his foliation and bears the rubric *Єꞃꞃaꞇa, & ꞃꞃæꞇeꞃmıſſa, ın hunc moꝺum ꞃeſꞇıꞇuıꞇo.* These *errata* and *corrigenda* have been noted as appropriate. Likewise, Lambarde's few marginal corrections in the body of the text are always noted.

For each opening, Ld recto carries the Latin translation, and the corresponding Anglo-Saxon is always on the verso of the preceding folio. This is fair enough as a device to permit facing-page texts, but it does leave one with the anomaly of 0^{v} at the very start.

The division into "laws" follows Ld as far as possible, not the divisions used for CN. It has not been deemed necessary to print Ld's catchwords, even when these can show slight variations, e.g., *hƿæþeꞃ/ hƿæðeꞃ.*

Capital letters and word-division are original to Ld. On the other hand, the minimal punctuation is editorial, and accords as closely as is reasonable with that of the edited version of CN. Errors in Ld have been allowed to stand without comment, e.g., *Ᵹıᵹ, ƿuꝺu* for *ᵹıꝼ, ƿuꝺu.*

Endnotes

1. See Mary P. Richards, "The Manuscript Contexts of the Old English Laws: Tradition and Innovation," in Paul E. Szarmach, ed., *Studies in Earlier Old English Prose: Sixteen Original Contributions* (Albany, 1986), pp. 171-92.

2. J.M. Wallace-Hadrill, *Early Germanic Kingship in England and on the Continent* (Oxford, 1971), pp. 148-499.

3. Neil Ripley Ker, *Catalogue of Manuscripts Containing Anglo-Saxon* (Oxford, 1957, repr. with supplement 1990), pp. 58, 232.

4. Dorothy Whitelock, ed. and trans., *English Historical Documents c. 500-1042*, 2nd ed. (London and New York, 1979), 1. 357, 358.

5. William Lambarde, ed. and trans., *Archaionomia, sive De priscis Anglorum legibus libri, sermone anglico, vetustate antiquissimo, aliquot abhinc seculis conscripti, atq: nunc demum, magno iurisperitorum, & amantium antiquitatis omnium commodo, è tenebris in lucem vocati* (London, 1568); Abraham Wheloc, ed., *Archaionomia, sive de priscis Anglorum legibus libri, sermone Anglico, vetustate antiquissimo, aliquot abhinc seculis conscripti, etc. Accessere in hac nostra ultima editione Leges Henrici Primi nunc primum editæ, ex manuscripto in fisco regis habito: Una cum gloßario* (Cambridge, 1644).

6. William Lambarde, *A Perambulation of Kent: Conteining the description, Hystorie, and Customes of that Shyre. Written in the yeere 1570. First published in the yeere 1576 and now increased and altered after the authors owne last copie* (London, 1576, 2nd ed. London, 1596, repr. Bath, 1970). Pp. 307-12, 357-62, 364-66 contain excerpts from the *Textus Roffensis*, the only surviving manuscript of the Kentish laws, compiled at Rochester, probably at the behest of Bishop Ernulf (1115-24).

7. Henry Spelman, *Concilia, decreta, leges, constitutiones, in re ecclesiarum orbis Britannici*, vol. 1 (London, 1639), vol. 2, ed. William Dugdale (London, 1664).

8. David Wilkins, *Concilia Magnae Britanniae et Hiberniae, a Synodo Verolamiensi A.D. CCCCXLVI. ad Londinensem A.D. MDCCXVII. Accedunt constitutiones et alia ad historiam ecclesiae Anglicanae spectantia: a Davide Wilkins, S.T.P., Archidiacono Suffolciensi, et Canonico Cantuariensi, collecta*, 4 vols. (London, 1737) with dedicatory letter to William Wake, Archbishop of Canterbury 1715-37; *Leges Anglo-Saxonicae ecclesiasticae et civiles... cum codd. Mss. contulit, notas, versionem et glossarium adjecit D.W.* (London, 1721). For further information about Wilkins, see Sidney Lee, ed., *The Dictionary of National Biography* (London, 1909), 21. 260-61 and Eleanor N. Adams, *Old English Scholarship in England from 1566-1800*, Yale diss., Yale Studies in English

55 (New Haven, London and Oxford, 1917), pp. 99-100. The Corpus Christi College, Cambridge Archives B. 3, records of Library and Plate, fols. 16^{v}-17^{r} note that a "Mr. Wilkins" consulted MSS 173, 201, 265, 190 and 191 between May 20 and July 24, 1717.

9. John Baron, *Report on the Anglo-Saxon Documents in Wilkins's Concilia* (Oxford, 1859); Arthur Haddan and William Stubbs, eds., *Councils and Ecclesiastical Documents Relating to Great Britain and Ireland, Edited after Spelman and Wilkins*, 3 vols. (Oxford, 1869-78); Dorothy Whitelock, M. Brett and C.N.L. Brooke, eds., *Councils and Synods, with other documents relating to the English Church*, 2 vols. (Oxford, 1981).

10. Thomas Hearne, ed., *Textus Roffensis* (Oxford, 1720).

11. Reinhold Schmid, ed., *Die Gesetze der Angelsächsische. In der Ursprache mit Übersetzung und Erläuterungen. I. Teil, den Text nebst Übersetzung enthaltend* (Leipzig, 1832, 2nd rev. ed. 1858).

12. Benjamin Thorpe, ed., *Ancient Laws and Institutes of England; comprising Laws enacted under the Anglo-Saxon Kings from Æthelbirht to Cnut, with an English Translation of the Saxon... also, Monumenta Ecclesiastica Anglicana from the Seventh to the Tenth Century*, 2 vols. (London, 1840).

13. Albert S. Cook, ed., *Extracts from the Anglo-Saxon Laws* (New York, 1880).

14. Milton Haight Turk, ed., *The Legal Code of Alfred the Great*, a Leipzig dissertation published in Halle, 1890 and subsequently republished under the same title (Halle and Boston, 1893).

15. Felix Liebermann, ed. and trans., *Die Gesetze der Angelsachsen*, 3 vols. (Halle, 1903-16, repr. Aalen, 1960); *Quadripartitus, ein englisches Rechtsbuch von 1114* (Halle, 1892); "Notes on the *Textus Roffensis,*" *Archaeologia Cantiana* 23 (1898), 101-12.

16. Kenneth Sisam, "The Authenticity of Certain Texts in Lambard's *Archaionomia, 1568,*" from *Modern Language Review* 18 (1923), 98-104 and 20 (1925), 253-69, repr. and expanded in *Studies in the History of Old English Literature* (Oxford, 1953, repr. 1962), pp. 232-58; Dorothy Whitelock, "Wulfstan and the so-called Laws of Edward and Guthrum," *English Historical Review* 56 (1941), repr. in Dorothy Whitelock, ed., *History, Law and Literature in 10th-11th Century England* (London, 1981), 19-21, appendix: "On the supposed lost manuscript used by Lambarde." Liebermann replied to Sisam's first review article in "Ist Lambardes Text der Gesetze Æthelstans neuzeitliche Fälschung?" *Anglia Beiblatt* 35 (1924), 214-18 and to Sisam's second article in "Angelsächsische Gesetztext gefälscht?" *Anglia Beiblatt* 36 (1925), 345-47.

17. Richard Dammery, "Editing the Anglo-Saxon Laws: Felix Liebermann and Beyond," a paper delivered at the Manchester Centre for Anglo-Saxon Studies, University of Manchester, 25-27 May, 1990 contained in his dissertation, pp. 323-44, and in the published proceedings of that conference in *The Editing of Old English* (Cambridge, 1994), pp. 251-61.

18. Dammery, pp. 252, 261, quoting F.W. Maitland, "The Laws of the Anglo-Saxons," *Quarterly Review* 200 (1904), 139-57, at pp. 139, 152.

19. Frederick L. Attenborough, ed. and trans., *The Laws of the Earliest English Kings (Æthelberht I to Æthelstan)* (Cambridge, 1922 reissued New York, 1963). Attenborough collated only "the more important manuscripts," p. vi.

20. Agnes J. Robertson, ed., *The Laws of the Kings of England from Edmund to Henry I* (Cambridge, 1925, repr. New York, 1974). Robertson began her work in Cambridge and for convenience took as much of her text as possible from Corpus Christi College (p. v); this decision was unfortunate, as B (Corpus 383) is the most corrupt version of the law-code.

21. Karl August Eckhardt, ed., *Leges Anglo-Saxonicum 601-925 (Gesetze der Angelsachsen, 601-925)* (Göttingen, 1958).

22. Richard Dammery, ed., *The law code of King Alfred the Great.* Cambridge diss. (Cambridge, 1990). Vol. 1 deals with the manuscripts, the textual transmission, the structure of the law-code, and bibliography; vol. 2 is an edition of the law-code which takes E as the base text. Dr. Dammery's planned facsimile of Lambarde's *Archaionomia* is to appear in the series *Early Studies in Germanic Philology*, published in Leiden and ed. Rolf Bremmer.

23. Franz Joseph Mone, "Zur Geschichte und Kritik der angelsächsische Gesetze," *Quellen und Forschungen zur Geschichte der teutschen Literatur und Sprache* 1 (Aachen 1830), 482-548, 562.

24. John M. Stearns, *The Germs and Developments of the Laws of England, Embracing the Anglo-Saxon Laws Extant... as Translated into English under the Royal Record Commission... with Notes and Comments* (New York, 1889).

25. Henry Munro Chadwick, *Studies on Anglo-Saxon Institutions* (Cambridge, 1905).

26. W.S. Holdsworth, *A History of English Law*, 3rd ed. (London, 1923).

27. F. Pollock and F.W. Maitland, *The History of English Law*, 2nd ed. (Cambridge, 1923).

28. T.F.T. Plucknett, *A Concise History of the Common Law*, 4th ed. (London, 1948).

29. Whitelock, *English Historical Documents* I; *History, Law and Literature in 10th-11th Century England* (London, 1981).

30. Dammery mentions (p. 18) that Patrick Wormald's book carries the provisional title *The Making of English Law: King Alfred to the Norman Conquest.*

31. Attenborough, pp. 112-13; Liebermann, 1. ix ff., 3. 96, 98 ff., 107 f., 110, 112, 114; Whitelock, *Councils and Synods*, 1. 48-49, 54.

32. *Councils and Synods*, 1. 49; Liebermann, 1. 167.

33. Attenborough, pp. 34-35; Liebermann, 3. 32, 34.

34. *Councils and Synods*, 1. 15-16.

35. *English Historical Documents* 1. 358.

36. For a general discussion of Parker's circle and the Society of Antiquaries, see Catherine Drinker Brown, "Historians Courageous", an essay prefatory to Wilbur Dwight Dunkel, *William Lambarde, Elizabethan Jurist, 1536-1601* (New Brunswick, N.J., 1965), pp. xi ff.

37. C.E. Wright, "The Dispersal of the Monastic Libraries and the Beginnings of Anglo-Saxon Studies: Matthew Parker and his Circle—A Preliminary Study," *Transactions of the Cambridge Bibliographical Society* 1 (1949-53), part 3 (1951), 226-27.

38. Wright, 224-25; Montague Rhodes James, *The Sources of Archbishop Parker's Collection of MSS at Corpus Christi College, Cambridge, with a reprint of the Catalogue of Thomas Markaunt's Library* (Cambridge, 1899); Neil Ripley Ker, *Medieval Libraries of Great Britain* (London, 1941; 2nd ed. London, 1964); Raymond I. Page, *Matthew Parker and his Books* (Kalamazoo, Michigan, 1993).

39. T(homas) I(ames), *Ecloga Oxonio-Cantabrigiensis, tributa in Libros duos* (London, 1600), Book 1, pp. 70-98, Libri Manuscripti Cantabrigiæ—Libri Manuscripti in Bibliotheca Collegij Sancti Benedicti, Cantabrigiæ; J. Nasmith, *Catalogus librorum manuscriptorum quos Collegio Corporis Christi et B. Mariæ Virginis in Academia Cantabrigiensi legavit Reverendissimus in Christo Pater Matthæus Parker,*

Archiepiscopus Cantuariensis (Cambridge, 1777); Montague Rhodes James, *A Descriptive Catalogue of the Manuscripts in the Library of Corpus Christi College, Cambridge*. 2 vols. (Cambridge, 1912), 1; Ker, *Catalogue*), and "A supplement to *Catalogue of Manuscripts Containing Anglo-Saxon*," *Anglo-Saxon England* 5 (1976), 121-31.

40. Wright, 226, n. 1. Wright cites L. van Norden, "Sir Henry Spelman on the Chronology of the Elizabethan Society of Antiquaries," *Huntington Library Quarterly* 13 (1950), 131-60 and his own "Sir Edward Dering: a Seventeenth Century Antiquary and his 'Saxon' Charters," *The Early Cultures of North-West Europe* (1950), 371-93.

41. Wright, 229-37.

42. See James L. Rosier, "A new Old English glossary: Nowell upon Huloet," *Studia Neophilologica* 49 (1977), 189-94.

43. See further Adams, *Old English Scholarship.*

44. On Sir William Cecil (later Lord Burleigh or Burghley), his manuscripts and his relations with Nowell and Parker, see Dorothy Whitelock, ed., *The Peterborough Chronicle*, EEMF 4 (1954), 25-26.

45. Details from *DNB* 14, 695-96 and Robin Flower, "Laurence Nowell and the Discovery of England in Tudor Times," *Proceedings of the British Academy* 21 (1935), 50-51.

46. Albert H. Marckwardt, ed., *Laurence Nowell's Vocabularium Saxonicum*, University of Michigan Publications in Language and Literature 25 (Ann Arbor, 1952), pp. 2-3.

47. Retha M. Warnicke, "Note on a Court of Requests Case of 1571," *English Language Notes* 11 (1974), 250-56, and "The Laurence Nowell Manuscripts in the British Library," *British Library Journal* 5, no. 2 (Autumn, 1979), 201-02. The actual complaint of 1571 and Lambarde's response may be seen in the Public Record Office, Requests 2/45/13, ff. 1-2.

48. See Carl T. Berkhout, "The Pedigree of Laurence Nowell the Antiquary," *English Language Notes* 23 (1985), 24. Sir William Dugdale in *The Antiquities of Warwickshire* (London, 1656), p. 670 identifies Nowell the antiquary as the unfortunate Sutton Coldfield schoolmaster, and Anthony à Wood in *Athenae Oxonienses* (first ed. London, 1691-02), 1. 186 identifies the antiquary as both Dean of Lichfield and the teacher. See also Warnicke, 250.

49. Pamela M. Black, "Laurence Nowell's 'disappearance' in Germany and its bearing on the whereabouts of his *Collectanea* 1568-1572," *English Historical Review* 92 (1977), 345-53, and "Some New Light on the Career of Laurence Nowell the Antiquary," *Antiquaries Journal* 62 (1982), 116-23.

50. Thomas Hahn, "The Identity of the Antiquary Laurence Nowell," *English Language Notes* 20, nos. 3-4 (March/June, 1983), 10-18, and Carl J. Berkhout, *English Language Notes* 23 (1985), 15-26.

51. Condensed from Berkhout, 17-25.

52. *DNB* 14, 695.

53. Flower, *Proc. Brit. Acad.*, 50.

54. Marckwardt, p. 2.

55. Black, *Antiquaries Journal*, 117.

56. Hahn, 17.

57. Warnicke, *ELN*, 254.

58. Berkhout, 16, n. 4. Berkhout notes that a "(rather poor) reproduction of the map appears in G. R. Crone, *Early Maps of the British Isles, A.D. 1000-A.D. 1579* (London, 1961), plate 17.

59. Flower, *Proc. Brit. Acad.*, 61-62.

60. Black, *EHR*, 350.

61. Black, *EHR*, 348.

62. Warnicke, *ELN*, 251 and Black, *EHR*, 346-48.

63. Black, *EHR*, 347.

64. Berkhout, 21-22.

65. Warnicke, *ELN*, 251-54 and Hahn, 16.

66. Black, *Antiquaries Journal*, 120-21.

67. Berkhout, 16, n. 4.

68. Berkhout, 25-26 and n. 33.

69. Flower, *Proc. Brit. Acad.*, 70.

70. Alistair Campbell, ed., *The Battle of Brunanburh* (London, 1938), pp. 133-35.

71. Rosier, 189-90.

72. William Camden, *Britannia* (London, 1590), p. 118, as quoted by Berkhout, 15.

73. Retha M. Warnicke, *William Lambarde, Elizabethan Antiquary 1536-1601* (London and Chichester, 1973), frontis.

74. *DNB* 11, 438-39.

75. Warnicke, *William Lambarde*, pp. 13-14.

76. Warnicke, *William Lambarde*, pp. xii-xiii, 17-22. The traditional view is also held by Dunkel, pp. 32-33.

77. Warnicke, *William Lambarde*, p. 137. The monument was moved to St. Nicholas' Church at the family seat in Sevenoaks by his son Sir Multon Lambarde in 1710 when the roof of St. Alphege's collapsed.

78. Dunkel, p. xiii.

79. Dunkel, pp. 7-8.

80. Warnicke, *William Lambarde*, pp. 23-24, 28-30.

81. Conyers C. Read, ed., *William Lambarde and Local Government: His "Ephemeris" and Twenty-nine Charges to Juries and Commissions* (Ithaca, N.Y., 1962) with a preface for the Folger Shakespeare Library by Giles E. Dawson, pp. v-xi.

82. See Charles H. McIlwain and Paul L. Ward, eds., *Archeion or, a Discourse upon the High Courts of Justice in England* (Cambridge, Massachusetts, 1957).

83. Warnicke, *William Lambarde*, p. 140.

84. Quoted in Warnicke, *William Lambarde*, p. 72 and in Dunkel, p. 2.

85. See White Kennett, "Life of Mr. Somner," in *A Treatise of Gavelkind, Both Name and Thing. Shewing the True Etymologie and Derivation of the One, the Nature, Antiquity, and Original of the Other*, 2nd ed. (London, 1726), pp. 1-136, and William Urry, ed., *the Antiquities of Canterbury*, pp. v-xxiv. [Refs. from Dammery's thesis, p. 96.]

86. William Somner, *Dictionarium Saxonico-Latino-Anglicum. Voces, phrasesque præcipuas Anglo-Saxonicas... Accesserunt Ælfrici Abbatis Grammatica Latino-Saxonica, cum Glossario suo ejusdem generis* (Oxford, 1659). Following specimen copies issued in 1690 and 1699, an abridged edition, ed. Thomas Benson, was published in 1701. The 1659 edition was repr. in facsimile in Menston, England, in 1970, ed. R.C. Alston.

87. See Albert H. Marckwardt, "Nowell's *Vocabularium Saxonicum* and Somner's *Dictionarium*," *Philological Quarterly* 26 (1947), 345-51.

88. Ker, *Catalogue*, pp. 230-34, MS 180. Localisation of Otho B. xi to Winchester is on the basis of texts copied from Corpus 173; see Ker, p. 231; Raymond J. S. Grant, "Laurence Nowell's transcript of BM Cotton Otho B. xi," *Anglo-Saxon England* 3 (1974), 111-12, 115; and Michael B. Parkes, "The palaeography of the Parker manuscript of the *Chronicle*, laws and Sedulius, and historiography at Winchester in the late ninth and tenth centuries," *ASE* 5 (1976), 170-71.

89. BL Harley 6018 records Cotton's book loans, and note 161 (148^v) records the loan of Otho B. xi to "Mr Lill"; see *British Museum Quarterly* 14 (1939-40), 81-82.

90. Humphrey Wanley, *Antiquæ Literaturæ Septentrionalis liber alter. seu Humphredi Wanleii Librorum Vett. Codd. Septentrionalium, qui in Angliæ Bibliothecis extant, nec non multorum Vett. Codd. Septentrionalium alibi extantium Catalogus Historico-Criticus, cum totius Thesauri Linguarum Septentrionalium sex Indicibus* (Oxford, 1705, repr. New York, 1970, the second volume of George Hickes's *Linguarum Vett. Septentrionalium Thesaurus Grammatico-Criticus et Archæologicus*) p. 219; Thomas Miller, ed., *The Old English Version of Bede's Ecclesiastical History of the English People*, EETS OS 95, 96, 110 and 111 (London, 1890-91 and 1898, repr. 1959 and 1963), 1. 1, xv-xvi; Ker, *Catalogue*, pp. 230-34, MS 180; Grant, *ASE*, 111-24, and *The B Text of the Old English Bede: A Linguistic Commentary* (Amsterdam and Atlanta, 1989) pp. 3-7.

91. Miller 1. 386.30-390.9.

92. On MS Additional 34652, see *BMQ* 14 (1939-40), 81-82.

93. See Flower, *Proc. Brit. Acad.*, p. 73, n. 16.

94. Abraham Wheloc, ed., *Historiæ Ecclesiasticæ Gentis Anglorum Libri V* (Cambridge, 1643-44). Wheloc prints a few readings from Otho B. xi and a continuous text of C where his main manuscript (MS Cambridge, University Library Kk. 3. 18, known as Ca) is in lacuna in 2. 5-7 (Miller 1. 110.30-118.16).

95. See Robin Flower, "Laurence Nowell and a Recovered Anglo-Saxon Poem," *British Museum Quarterly* 8 (1933-34), 130-32 and Raymond J. S. Grant, "A Note on 'The Seasons for Fasting,'" *Review of English Studies*, n.s. 23, no. 91 (August, 1972), 302-04.

96. See Ker, *Catalogue*, pp. 58 and 232. The list was compiled after 984 and probably before 988. Ker does not point out Nowell's transcript of this item.

97. Grant, *Old English Bede*, pp. 395-410.

98. Sisam, *Studies*, pp. 45-60; Grant, *RES*. See also Flower, *BMQ*, 130-32.

99. Robin Flower, "The Text of the Burghal Hidage," *London Medieval Studies* 1 (1937), 60-64.

100. Campbell, p. v.

101. Wright, 235.

102. On the gift by de Walden, see Flower, *BMQ*, 130-32. On the contents of the transcript, see Flower, *LMS*, 60-64; Ker, *Catalogue*, pp. 230-34; and *The British Museum Catalogue of Additions to the Manuscripts 1931-1935* (London, 1967), pp. 196-97.

103. Campbell, pp. 133-35.

104. Sisam, *Studies*, p. 59, note.

105. Grant, *ASE*, 124; see also 113, n. 2.

106. Roland Torkar, ed. *Eine Altenglische Übersetzung von Alcuins "De Virtutibus et Vitiis," Kap. 20* (München, 1981), pp. 162-67; Angelika Lutz, ed. *Die Version G der Angelsächsischen Chronik* (München, 1981), pp. liii-lviii; and Sisam, *Studies*, p. 58 and n. and p. 60.

107. *Ymb æbricas* is found on fol. 255^r, ll. 12-19 and has been printed by Flower, *LMS*, 62.

108. Roy F. Leslie, "Textual Notes on *The Seasons for Fasting*," *JEGP* 52 (1935) 558 and Campbell, p. 136.

109. See n. 16 *supra*.

110. Flower, *Proc. Brit. Acad.*, n. 16.

111. See n. 16 *supra*, *English Historical Documents* 1. 329, n. 2, and *Councils and Synods* 1. 15.

112. Marckwardt, pp. 9-10 and n. 13.

113. *Councils and Synods*, 1. 15 and n. 5.

114. Dammery, thesis, pp. 96-101.

115. Dammery (thesis, p. 102, n. 107) refers to a paper on Nw4 delivered by Carl T. Berkhout at the Manchester Centre for Anglo-Saxon Studies, University of Manchester, 25-27 May, 1990 and contained in the published proceedings of that conference in *The Editing of Old English* (Cambridge, 1994).

116. Dammery, thesis, pp. 102-11.

117. Turk, p. 21, quoted by Dammery, thesis, p. 139.

118. Liebermann, 3. 31 and Turk, pp. 21-23.

119. Examples are to be found in the Appendix to the present edition and further examples and details in Dammery, thesis, pp. 112-72, to which, as ever, I am much indebted.

120. Day's type was also used for the printing in 1570 of Matthew Parker's edition of Asser's life of King Alfred.

121. Dunkel, pp. 33-34.

122. Dunkel, pp. 35-36.

123. *Councils and Synods*, 1. 53, n. 2.

124. *Councils and Synods*, 1. 15, n. 3.

125. Bruce Mitchell, "The Dangers of Disguise: Old English Texts in Modern Punctuation," *RES* 31 (1980), 385-413, reprinted in his *On Old English* (Oxford, 1988), pp. 172-202.

ATHELSTANI REGIS LEGES

II ATHELSTAN

V ATHELSTAN

IUDEX

THE LAWS OF ALFRED AND INE
LIST OF RUBRICS

THE LAWS OF ALFRED AND INE
BIBLICAL PROLOGUE

THE LAW OF ALFRED

THE LAW OF INE

as transcribed and printed by

LAURENCE NOWELL & WILLIAM LAMBARDE

List of Sigla

Athelstan, Iudex, Alfred & Ine

E = Cambridge, Corpus Christi College, MS 173 [Ker, pp. 57-59, no. 39]

C/Ot = London, British Library, MS Cotton Otho B. xi [Ker, pp. 230-34, no. 180] This is the manuscript I refer to as C in earlier work on the Nowell transcripts, since Otho B. xi contains the C text of the Old English Bede = Liebermann's Ot

G = London, British Library, MS Cotton Nero A.i [Ker, pp. 210-15, nos. 163, 164]

Bu = London, British Library, MS Burney 277, fols. 42^{rv} [Ker, pp. 171-72, no. 136]

H = Maidstone, Kent County Archives Office, MS DRc/R1 [Ker, pp. 443-47, no. 373] formerly Rochester Cathedral Library, MS A.3.5, the *Textus Roffensis*

B = Cambridge, Corpus Christi College, MS 383 [Ker, pp. 110-13, no. 65]

The Nowell Transcripts

CN/Nw2 = London, British Library, MS Additional 43703
This is the transcript I refer to as CN here and in earlier work on the Nowell transcripts, as Additional 43703 contains a transcript of C (Otho B. xi) as transcribed by Nowell = Dammery's Nw1. Additional 43703 also carries Nowell's interlinear and marginal additions or corrections/annotations in CN = Dammery's Nw2

So/Nw3 = Canterbury, Christ Church Cathedral Library, MS Literary B 2, n. 8 = Liebermann's So, Dammery's Nw3

Nw4 = London, British Library, Henry Davis Collection, MS M 30

Lambarde

Ld = *Archaionomia*, printed by John Day, London 1568

Index to the Edited Texts

The following chart shows where the relevant texts are to be found in the Nowell transcript of BL Additional 43703 and in the *Archaionomia*. It will be noted that the two versions do not present the items in the same order, and that this permits the *Archaionomia* to present the text of II Athelstan in continuous form.

CN	*Ld*
Athelstani Regis Leges	***Æthelstanes æ***
233^{r}, p. 60—236^{r}, p. 72— 236^{r}, p. 72—265^{r}, p. 74	58^{v}—67^{v}, pp. 61—75
V Athelstan	***Æthelstanes æ***
265^{r}, p. 74—266^{r}, p. 78	68^{v}—70^{v}, pp. 75—79
Iudex	[not present in Ld]
266^{r}, p. 78—267^{v}, p. 84	text, pp. 79—85, taken from G as edited by Liebermann, 1. 474—76
The Laws of Alfred & Ine ***List of Rubrics***	
236^{v}, p. 86—238^{r}, p. 92	26^{v}—43^{v}, 0^{v}—17^{v}, pp. 87—93
The Laws of Alfred & Ine ***Biblical Prologue***	
238^{v}, p. 94—242^{r}, p. 108	18^{v}—26^{v}, pp. 95—109
The Law of Alfred	
242^{r}, p. 108—249^{r}, p. 136	26^{v}—43^{v}, pp. 109—137
The Law of Ine	
249^{r}, p. 136—255^{r}, p. 160	0^{v}—17^{v}, pp. 137—161

ATHELSTANI REGIS LEGES[1]

II ATHELSTAN[2]

AN ærest ꝥ mon ne spariȝe nanne þeof ðe æt hæbbendre handa ȝefanȝen sie, ofer tƿelf ƿinter 7 ofer viii peninȝas.

7 ȝif hit hƿa do, forȝelde þone þeof be his ƿere — 7 ne sie þǣ þeofe na ðe ȝeþínȝodre — oððe hine be þā ladiȝe.

Gif he hine þon̄ ƿerian ƿille oððe fleon,[3] þon̄ ne spariȝe hine man æþ[4] ær þā.

Oder ȝif mon þeof on carcerne ȝebrinȝe, ꝥ he beo xl nihta on carcerne, 7 hine mon lẏ́se þonne ut mid cxx[5] sciƚƚ; 7 ȝa seo mæȝð hī on borh, ꝥ he æfre ȝesƿice.

7 ȝif he ofer ꝥ stalie, þonne forȝylden hi hine be[6] his ƿere oððe hine eft þærinne ȝebrinȝen.

7 ȝif hine hƿa foran forstande, forȝilde hine be his ƿere, sƿa þā cinȝe sƿa ðam ðe hit toȝebẏ́riȝe; 7 ælc þara þe ðer midstande ȝeselle cxx sciƚƚ to ƿite þā cinȝe.

7 ƿe cƿædon be ðā hlafordleasū mannū, þe mon nan riht[7] ætbeȝitan ne mæȝ, ꝥ mon bude þære mæȝðe, ꝥ heo hine to rẏ́hte[8] ȝehamette 7 hī hlaford funde on folcȝemote.

7 ȝif hie hine ðonne beȝiten nellen oððe ne mæȝen to þā andaȝā, þon̄ beo he sẏ́ððan flẏ́me, 7 hine lecȝe for þeof se ðe hī tocume.

7 se ðe hine ofer ꝥ feormiȝe, forȝelde hine be his ƿere oððe

[1] rubric in MS Nw2 [2] rubric editorial [3] fleon] fleo'n' [4] æþ] del. [5] cc] cc del. before cxx [6] be] be on top of for [7] riht] r'i'ht [8] rhẏ́te] ẏ́ from i

Æthelstanes æ[1]

II ATHELSTAN[2]

Be ðeofum.[3]

1 Ærest ꝥ mon ne sparige nænne ðeof ðe æt hæbbendre hand gefangen sẏ, ofer tƿelf ƿinterne ⁊ ofer eahta peningas. ⁊ gif hƿa hit dô, forgylde ðone ðeof be his ƿere — ⁊ ne sẏ ðæm ðeofe na ðe geþingodre — oþþe hine be ðæm geladige. Gif he hine ðonne ƿerian ƿille oþþe fleon, ðonne ne sparige hine mon ær ðæm. Oþer gif mon ðeof on cƿearterne gebringe, ꝥ he beo feoƿertig nihta ðær inne, ⁊ hine mon alẏse þonne ut mid hund tƿelftigum scill.; ⁊ ga seo mægþe him on borh, ꝥ he æfre gesƿice. And gif he ofer ꝥ stalige, ðonne forgẏldan hi hine be his ƿere oþþe hine eft þær in gebringan. ⁊ gif hƿa hine forstande, forgẏlde hine be his ƿere, sƿa ðæm cẏng sƿa ðæm ðe hit to gebẏrige; ⁊ ælc man ðara ðe þære mid stande gesẏlle cxx scill. to ƿite ðæm cẏng.

Be hlafordleasum mannum.[4]

2 And ƿe cƿædon be ðæm hlafordleasum mannum, ðe nân man nân rihte æt begẏtan ne mæg, ꝥ man bude ðære mægþe, ꝥ hi hine to rihte gehamette ⁊ him hlaforde funden on folcgemote. ⁊ gif hi hine ðonne begẏtan nellon oþþe ne magon to ðæm andagan, ðonne beo he sẏþþan flẏma, ⁊ hine lecge for ðeofe se ðe him to cume. ⁊ se ðe hine ofer ꝥ [Ld 59^{V}] feormige, forgẏlde hine be his ƿere oþþe

In II Athelstan and V Athelstan, Ld has rubrics which have no counterparts in CN. Similarities to those in other OE manuscripts are noted.

[1] rubric in Ld [2] rubric editorial [3] rubric as in B [4] rubric as in B; room left in H for a rubric

oððe hine be ðam[1] ladiʒe.

7 se hlaford þe hryhtes ƿýrne 7 for his ẏfelan men lẏcʒe: 7 mon þoñe cinʒ foresece, forʒylde ꝥ ceapʒẏld 7 ʒesylle þā cẏnʒe cxx sciłł. 7 se ðe þoñ cinʒ sece, ær he hī ryhtes bidde sƿa oft sƿa hī toʒebyriʒe, ʒielde ꝥ ilce ƿite þe se oðer sceolde, ʒif he hī hrihtes forƿẏrnde.

7 se hlaford þe his þeoƿan æt þẏfþū[2] ʒeƿita sie, 7 hit hī on open ƿyrðe, þolie þæs þeoƿan 7 beo his ƿeres scyldiʒ æt frūcẏrre; ʒif he hit oftur do, beo ealles scẏldiʒ ðe he aʒe.

7 eac sƿilce cinʒes hordra oððe ure ʒerefena, sƿelc þara þeofa ʒeƿita ƿære þe staledon, beo be þǣ ilcan.

7 ƿe cƿædon be hlafordsearƿe, ꝥ he ƿære his feores scẏldiʒ, ʒif he his oðsacan ne[3] mehte oððe eft on ðā þreofealdū ordale ful ƿære.

7 ƿe cƿædun be ciricbrẏce: ʒif he ful ƿære on ðā þreofealdū ordale, bete be þā þe seo domboc[4] sæcʒʒe.

7 ƿe cƿædon be þā ƿiccecræftū 7 liblacū 7 morðdædū, ʒif ðær[5] mon acƿeald ƿære, 7 he his oðsacan ne mæʒe, ꝥ he beo his feores scẏldiʒ.[6]

Gif he his þonne oðsacan[7] ƿille 7 on þā þryfealda ordale ful ƿurþe, ꝥ he beo cxx nihta on carcerne; 7 niman þa maʒas hine siððan ut, 7 ʒesellan þā cinʒe cxx sciłł, 7 forʒylden þone ƿer[8] þæs mannes mæʒū 7 ʒanʒen hī on borh, ꝥ he æfre sƿilces ʒesƿice.

7 þa blisʒeras

[1] ðam] ðam above del. of three [2] þẏfþū] þẏfþū followed by del. of one [3] oðsacan ne] oðra emne with ra em del. and sacan written above [4] domboc] m on del. of one [5] ðær] dær [6] in left margin Desunt nonnulla, del. Nw2 [7] oðsacan] oð followed by del. of ðe; originally oððe [8] ƿer] e above del. of one

oþþe hine be ðæm geladie.

3 And se hlaforde ðe rihte wyrne ⁊ for his yfelan men lycge: ⁊ mane[1] ðone cyng forsece, forgylde ꝥ ceapegylde ⁊ gesylle ðæm cynge cxx scill. And se ðe ðone cyng sece, ær he him rihtes bidde swa oft swa him to gebyrige, gylde ꝥ ylce wite ꝥ se oþer sceolde, gif he him rihtes wyrnde. And se hlaforde ðe his ðeowan æt ðyfþe gewita sy, ⁊ hit open wurþe, ðolige ðæs ðeowan ⁊ beo his weres scildig æt frumcyrre; Gif he hit oftor dô, beo ealles scildig ðæs ðe he age. ⁊ eac swylce cynges hordera oþþe ure gerefena, hwylc ðe ðæra ðeofa gewita wære ðe staledon, beo be ðæm ylcan.

Be hlaford syrwum.[2]

4 And we cwædon be hlaford syrwan, ꝥ he wære his feores scyldig, gif he hit ætsacan ne mihte oþþe on ðæm ðryfealdan ordale ful wære.

Be cyric bryce.[3]

5 And we cwædon be cyric bryce: gif he ful wære on ðæm ðryfealdan ordale, bete be þæm seo domboc secge.

Be wiccecræftum.[4]

6 And we cwædon be ðæm wiccecræftū ⁊ be lyblacum [Ld 60V] ⁊ morþdædum, gif ðær mon acwealde wære, ⁊ he hit ætsacan ne mæge, ꝥ he beo his feores scyldig. Gif he hit ðonne ætsacan wille ⁊ on ðæm ðryfealdum ordale ful weorþe, ꝥ he beo cxx nihta on carcarne; ⁊ niman ða magas hine syþþan ut, ⁊ gesyllan ðam cyng cxx scill., ⁊ forgylden ðone wer ðæs mannes magum ⁊ gangen hi on borh, ꝥ he æfre swylces geswice. And ða blisgeras[5]

[1] errata — mane lege manne [2] H, So, room left in B [3] So, room left in B [4] H, So, room left in B [5] margin — al. belisgeras. quod sonat accuratores falsos

-ras 7 þa ðe þeof ƿrecan, beon þæs ilca ƿẏrþe.

7 se ðe þeof ƿreccan ƿille 7 nanne man ne ʒeƿundiʒe, ʒeselle þā cinʒe cxx scilł for þon æhleƿe.

7 ƿe cƿædan be þā anfealdū ordale æt þā mannū þe oft ʒetẏhlode ƿæran: 7 hi fule ƿyrðen 7 hi[1] nẏten, hƿa hi on borh nime, ʒebrinʒe hine mon on carcerne 7 hine mon do[2] ut, sƿa hit her beforan ʒecƿeden is.

7 ƿe cƿædon, ʒif hƿẏlc landleas mon folʒode on oþre scire 7 his mæʒas eft sece, ꝥ he þe hine[3] on þa ʒerad feormiʒe, ꝥ he hine to folcrihte læde, ʒif he þær ʒẏlt ʒeƿẏrce, oððe forebete.

7 se ðe ẏrfe befo, nemne hī mon fīfe[4] men his nehbura 7 beʒite þara fīfa[5] ænne, ꝥ hī sƿerie mid, ꝥ he hit hī on folcrihte toteo; 7 se þe hit hī aʒnian[6] ƿille, nemne hī mon x men, 7 beʒite þara ii[7] 7 selle þone að, ꝥ hit on his æhte ʒeboren ƿære, butan þǣ rimæde; 7 stande þes cyreað ofer xx peninʒa.

7 ꝥ nane man ne hƿẏrfe nanes ẏrfes butan þæs ʒerefan ʒeƿitnesse oððe þæs mæsseƿreostes oððe þæs hordres oððe þæs landhlafordes oþþe oþres unʒeliʒenes mannes. Gif hit hƿa do, ʒilde xxx scilł, 7 fo se landhlaford to þā ʒehƿerfe.

Gif man þoñ onfinde, ꝥ heora æniʒ on ƿore[8] ʒeƿitnesse sie, ꝥ his ʒeƿitnesse næfre eft nauht ne forstande;

[1] hı] ~~hy~~ hı [2] do] followed by del. of one [3] he þe hine] he 'þe' hine [4] fīfe] .v.'fīfe' [5] fīfa] a on del. of ti [6] aʒnian] i on top of one (e?) [7] ii] tƿean in right margin Nw2 [8] ƿore] ƿ on top of one

-ras ⁊ ða ðe ðeof ƿræcan beon, beon ðæs ẏlca ƿẏrþe. ⁊ se ðe ðeof ƿræcan ƿille ⁊ nænne man geƿundige, gesẏlle ðæm cẏng cxx scill. forþon æhlẏpe.

Be anfealdum ordale.[1]

7 And ƿe cƿædon be ðæm anfealdum ordale æt ðæm mannum ðe ðeofþe getẏhtlod ƿæron: ⁊ hi fule ƿẏrden ⁊ hî nẏten, hƿa hi on borh nime, gebringe hine mon on carcerne ⁊ hine man dô ut, sƿa her beforan gecƿeden is.

Be landlearum mannum.[2]

8 And ƿe cƿædon, gif hƿẏlc landlear man folgode on oþer scire ⁊ his mægas eft sece, ꝥ he ðe hine on ða gerade feormige, ꝥ he hine to folcrihte læde, gif he ðær gẏlt geƿẏrce, oððe fore bete.

[Ld 61^{V}] Be ðonne ðe ẏrf befehþe.[3]

9 And se ðe ẏrfe befo, namne hine mon fîf men his nehbura ⁊ begite ðara fifa ænne, ꝥ him sƿerige mid, ꝥ he him on folcrihte to teo; ⁊ se ðe hit him agnian ƿille, nemne him mon x men, ⁊ begẏte ðæra ii ⁊ sẏlle ðone aþ, ꝥ hit on his æhte geboren ƿære, butan ðæm rimaþe; ⁊ stande ðes cẏreaþ ofer xx peninga.

Be ẏrfa gehƿẏrfe.[4]

10 Ðæt nân man ne hƿẏrfe naner ẏrfes butan ðæs gerefan geƿitnẏsse oþþe ðæs mæsse preostes oþþe ðæs horderes oþþe ðæs land hlafordes oþþe oþres ungeligenes mannes. gif hit hƿa dô, gẏlde xxx scill., ⁊ fô se land hlaforde to ðæm gehƿẏrfe. Gif mon ðonne onfinde, ꝥ heora ænig on foregeƿitnẏsse sẏ, ꝥ his geƿitnẏsse næfre eft nawht ne forstande;

[1] So [2] H (from So, Quadr.); So longer rubric than Ld, none in Ot [3] So; different rubric in H supplied by Liebermann [4] H, So different rubrics

-stande; 7 ʒeselle eac xxx scilł to ƿite.

7 ƿe cƿædon: se ðe scyldʒunʒa bæde æt ofsleʒenū þeof, ꝥ he eode þreora sū, tƿeʒen fæderamaʒas 7 þridda on medren, 7 þone að sealde ꝥ hie on heora mæʒ nane þeofþe nẏsten, ꝥ he his feores ƿyrþe nære for þā ʒẏlt; 7 hio ʒan siððan tƿelfa sume 7 ʒescyldʒien hine, sƿa hit ær ʒecƿæden ƿæs; 7 ʒif þæs deadan maʒas þider[1] cumun nellen[2] to ðam andaʒan, ʒelde ælc cxx scilł þe hit ær spræce.

7 ƿe cƿædon, ꝥ mon nanne ceap ne ceapiᵹ buton ƿorte ofer xx peninʒa; ac ceapiᵹ þær binnan on þæs portʒerefan Ᵹƿitnesse oððe oðres unᵹliʒenesse mannes oþþe eft on þæra ʒerefena Ᵹƿitnesse on folcmote.

7 ƿe cƿædon, ꝥ ælc burh sie Ᵹbet feoƿertẏne niht ofer ʒanᵹdaʒas.

Oþær: ꝥ ælc ciepinᵹ[3] sie binnan[4] porte.

Þridde: ꝥ an mẏnet sie ofer eal þæs cinʒes anƿeald; 7 nan man ne mẏnetiʒe[5] butan port.

Gif sie mẏnetere ful ƿurðe, slea man ða hand of, þe he ð[6] ful mid ƿorhte, 7 sette ufan on[7] þa mẏnetsmẏððan. Gif hit þoñ tẏhtle sie, 7 he hine ladian ƿille, þoñ ʒa he to hatū isene 7 ladie þa hand, mid þe man tẏhð, ꝥ ꝥ facen ƿorhte. Gif he þoñ on þǣ ordale ful ƿurþe, do man ꝥ ẏlce sƿa hit her beforan cƿið.

On Cantƿarabyrʒ vii mẏnetras: iiii cinʒes, ii bisceopas 7 i ðæs abbodes;

[1] þider] þeðer, underlined, from þider; in right margin þe ðer Nw2 [2] nellen] second e on top of a [3] ciepinᵹ] ~~cea~~'ie'pinᵹ [4] binnan] binna'n' [5] mẏnetiʒe] mẏne'ti'ʒe, with ti on top of a [6] ð] read ðæt [7] ufan on] ~~uppan~~'ufan on' Nw2

-standе; ⁊ gesẏlle eac xxx scill. to ƿite.

Be ðon ðe scẏldgunge bæde æt ofslegenum.[1]

11 Ƿe cƿædon: be ðon ðe scẏldgunga bæde æt ofslegenum ðeofe, ꝥ he eode ðreora sum, tƿegen fædera magas ⁊ ðridda on medren, ⁊ ðone aþ sealde ꝥ hi on heora mæge nâne ðeofþe nẏsten, ꝥ he his feores ƿẏrþe nære for ðæm gẏlt; ⁊ hio gan sẏþþan tƿelfa sum ⁊ gescẏlden hine, sƿa hit ær gecƿæden ƿæs; ⁊ gif ðær deadan magas ðeder cuman [Ld 62v] nẏllan to ðæm andagan, gẏlde ælc cxx scill. ðe hit ær spræce.

Be ðon ðe mon ne ceapige butan porte.[2]

12 Ƿe cƿædon be ðon, ꝥ mon nænne ceape ne ceapige buton porte ofer xx peninga; ac ceapige þær binnan on ðæs portgerefan geƿitnẏsse oþþe oþres ungeligenes mannes oþþe eft on ðæra gerefena geƿitnẏsse on folcmote.

Be burga gebettunge.[3]

13 Ƿe cƿædon, ꝥ ælc burgh sẏ gebet feoƿertẏne niht ofer gangdagas.
oþær: ẏlc ceapunge sẏ binnan porte.

Be mẏneterum.[4]

14 Ƿe cƿædon, ꝥ ân mẏnet sẏ ofer ealle ðæs cẏnges anƿealde; ⁊ nân man ne mẏnetige butan port. Gif se mẏnetere ful ƿurþe, slea mon ða hand of, ðe ꝥ ful mid ƿorhte, ⁊ sette ufan on ða minetsmiþan. Gif hit ðonne tẏhtle sẏ, ⁊ he hine ladian ƿille, ðonne gâ he to hatum isene ⁊ ladie ða hand, mid ðæm mon tẏhþ, ꝥ he ꝥ facn ƿorhte. Gif he ðonne on ðæm ordale ful ƿurþe, dôman ꝥ ẏlce sƿa hit her beforan cƿẏþ.

On Cantƿaraburig vii mẏneteras: iiii cẏnges, ii biscopes ⁊ ân ðæs abbodes;

[1] So different rubric, room left in H [2] So, room left in H [3] So different rubric, room left in H [4] H, So

abbodes; to Rofeceastre iii: tpeȝen þæs cinȝes 7 i þæs bisceopes; to Lundenbẏrȝ viii; to Ƿinteceastre vi; to Læpe ii; to Hæstinȝaceastre i; oþer to Cẏsseceastre; to Hātune tpeȝen; to Ƿerhā tpeȝen; tpeȝen to Æxeceastre; ii to Sceaftesbẏrȝ; elles to þǣ oþrū burȝū án.

Feorþ: ꝥ nan scẏldpyrhta ne leȝȝe nan scepes fell on sceld; 7 ȝif he hit do, ȝelde xxx sciłł.

Fifte: ꝥ ælc man hebbe æt þære sẏlh tpeȝen pel ȝehorsade men.

Syxte: ȝif hpa[1] æt ðeofe medsceat nime 7 oþers riht afylle,[2] be his peres scẏldiȝ.[3]

Seofoþe: ꝥ nan man ne selle nan hors ofer sæ, butan he[4] hit ȝifan pille.

7 pe cpedon be þeopan men, ȝif he ful pẏrþe æt þǣ ordale, ꝥ mon ȝuld ꝥ ceapȝẏld 7 spunȝe hine þripa oððe ꝥ oþer ȝeld sealde; 7 sie ꝥ pite be healfan pẏrþe æt þǣ ðeopan.

Gif hpa ȝemot forsitte ðripa, ȝelde cinȝes oferhiernesse; 7 hit sie seofon nihtū ȝeboden, ær ꝥ ȝemot sie.

Gif he þoñ rẏht[5] pyrcan nelle ne þa oferhiernesse sellan, ðoñ riden ealle þa ẏldstan men to, ealle[6] ðe to þære bẏrȝ hieren, 7 nimen ealle ꝥ he aȝe 7 setten hine on borh.

Gif þoñe nelle hpa[7] toridan mid his ȝ̄ferū, ȝelde cinȝes oferhiernesse.

7 beode mon on þǣ ȝemote, ꝥ mon friþiȝe eall ꝥ se cinȝ friþian pille; 7 forȝa þifþa be his feore 7 be eallū þā þe

[1] hpa] followed by del. of h [2] afylle] with y del. and æ written over it [3] scẏldiȝ] scẏldinȝ [4] he] h from b [5] rẏht] ~~rẏht~~ rẏht [6] ealle] 'ealle' with ealle repeated in right margin Nw2 [7] nelle hpa] nelle ~~pa~~ hpa

abbodes; [Ld 63v]
to Hrofeceastre iij: tƿegen þæs cynges ⁊ an ðæs biscopes;
to Lundenbyrig viij;
to Ƿinteceastre vj;
to Læƿes ij;
to Hæstingaceastre j;
Oþer to Cysseceastre;
to Hamtun tƿegen;
to Ƿerham ij;
tƿegen to Eaxanceastre;
ij to Sceaftesbyrig;
Elles to ðæm oþrum burgum an.

Be scyldƿyrhtum.[1]

15 Ƿe cƿædon, ꝥ nân scyldƿyrhta ne lecge nân sceapes felle on scyld; ⁊ gif he hit dô, gylde xxx scill.

16 ꝥ ylc man hæbbe æt ðær sylh tƿegen ƿel gehorsade men.

Be ðæm ðe æt þeofe medsceatte nimaþ.

17 Gif hƿa æt ðeofe medsceat nime ⁊ oþres rihte afylle, be he his ƿeres scyldig.

Be horsum.

18 Nân man ne sylle nan hors ofer sæ, butan he hit gyfan ƿille.

Be ðeoƿman ðe ful ƿurþe æt ordale.

19 Ƿe cƿædon be ðeoƿmen, gif he ful ƿyrþe æt þæm ordale, ꝥ mon gylde ꝥ ceapgylde ⁊ sƿynge hine ðriƿa [Ld 64v] oþþe ꝥ oþer gylde sylle; ⁊ sy ꝥ ƿite be healfan ƿyrþe æt ðæm ðeoƿan.

Be ðon ðe gemot forsitte.

20 Gif hƿa gemot forsitte ðriƿa, gylde cyninges oferhyrnysse; ⁊ hit sy seofon nihtum geboden, ær ꝥ gemot sy. Gif he ðonne rihte ƿyrcan nylle ne ða oferhyrnysse syllan, ðonne riden ealle ða yldestan men, ðe to ðær byrig hyren, ⁊ nimen ealle ꝥ he age ⁊ setten hine on borh. Gif ðonne nelle hƿa to ridan mid his geferum, gylde cynges oferhyrnysse. ⁊ beode mā on þæm gemot, ꝥ mon friþige eall ꝥ se cyng friþian ƿille; ⁊ forga ðyfþa be his feore ⁊ be eallum ðæm ðe

[1] So breaks off after scyld-

þā þe he aʒe.

7 se[1] þe be þẏsū ʒesƿican nelle, ðoñ riden þa ieldestan men ealle to, þe to þære bẏrʒ hẏren, 7 nimen eall ꝥ he aʒe — 7 fo se cinʒ to healfū, to healfū þa men ðe on þære rade sion — 7 setten hine on borh.

Gif he nyte, hƿa hine aborʒiʒe, hæften hine.

Gif he nelle ʒeþafian, lætan hine licʒʒan[2] buton he oðƿinde.

Gif hƿa hine þoñ ƿrecan ƿille[3] oðða heora æniʒne falæce, þoñ sie he fah ƿið ðone cinʒ 7 ƿið ealle his friend.[4]

Gif he þoñe oðƿinde, 7 hine hƿa feormiʒe, sie his ƿeres scẏldiʒ, butan he hine ladian durre be þæs flẏman ƿere, ꝥ he hine flemne nyste.

Gif hƿa ðinʒie for ordale, þinʒie on þǣ ceapʒẏlde ꝥ he mæʒe, naƿiht[5] on ðā ƿite, buton se ʒifan ƿille ðe hit toʒebẏriʒe.

7 ne underfo nan man oðres mannes man, butan þæs leafe þe he ær folʒode.

Gif hit[6] hƿa do, aʒife he ðone man 7 bete þæs cinʒes oferhearnesse.

7 nan man ne[7] tæce his ʒetẏhtledan men frā hī, ær he hæbbe rẏht aƿorht.[8]

Gif hƿa ordales ƿeddiʒe, þoñ[9] cume[10] he ðrī nihtū ær to þǣ mæssepreoste ðe hit[11] halʒian scẏle, 7 fede hine seolfne[12] mid hlafe 7 sealte 7 ƿætere 7 ƿẏrtū, ær he toʒan scẏle, 7 ʒestande his mæssan ðara þreoƿa daʒa ælce, 7 ʒoffriʒe to 7 ʒa to husle þẏ dæʒe þe he to þǣ ordale ʒan scyle, 7 sƿeriʒe þone að, ꝥ he sie mid folcryhte unscyldiʒ ðære tẏhtlan,[13] ær he to þǣ ordale ʒa.

7 ʒif hit

[1] se] ꝥ del. before se, presumably in anticipation of þe [2] licʒʒan] li'c'ʒʒan [3] ƿille] ƿ lle with a space left for i [4] friend] e from o [5] naƿiht] naƿ'i'ht with ƿ on u [6] hƿa] one del. before hƿa [7] man ne] man ʒe ne [8] rẏht aƿorht] rẏht ~~aƿort~~ aƿorht [9] þon] tilde above þoñ scratched out and one del. after þoñ [10] cume] 'c'ume [11] hit] hit altered to hī [12] seolfne] se'o'lfne [13] tẏhtlan] tẏht'land'lan

ðæm ðe he age. ⁊ se þe be ðissum gewitan nẏlle, ðonne riden ða ẏldestan men ealle, þe to ðære bẏrig hẏrē, ⁊ nimen ealle ꝥ he age — ⁊ fô se cẏng to healfum, to healfum ða men þe on þære râd sẏn — ⁊ setten hine on borh. Gif he nẏt, ƿha hine aborgige, hæften hine. Gif he nẏlle geþafian, lætan hine licgan butan he oþƿinde. Gif hine ðonne ƿha arrecan ƿille oþþe heora ænigne falæce, ðonne sẏ he fah ƿiþ ðone cẏng ⁊ ƿiþ ealle his freond. Gif he ðonne oþƿinde, ⁊ ƿha hine feormige, sẏ his ƿeres scẏldig, butan he hine ladian durre be ðæs flẏman ƿere, ꝥ he hine flẏmene nẏste.

[Ld 65^{v}] Be ðæm ðe for ordale ðingiaþ.

21 Gif ƿha ðingie for ordale, þingie on þæm ceapgẏlde ꝥ he mæge, naƿiht on ðæm ƿite, butan se gẏfan ƿille ðe hit to gebẏrige.

Be ðon ðe oþres mannes man underfehþ.

22 Ne underfô nan man oþres mannes man, butan ðæs leafe ðe he ær folgode. Gif hit ƿha dô, agẏfe he ðone man ⁊ bete ðæs cẏnges oferhẏrnẏsse. ⁊ nan man ne getæce his getẏhtledan men fram him, ær he hæbbe riht geƿorhte.

Be ðon ðe ordales ƿeddigaþ.

23 Gif ƿha ordales ƿeddige, ðonne cume he ðrim nihtum ær to ðæm mæssepreoste ðe hit halgian scẏle, ⁊ fede hine sẏlfne mid hlafe ⁊ sealte ⁊ ƿætere ⁊ ƿẏrtum, ær he to gân scẏle, ⁊ gestande his mæssan ðæra ðreora dage ẏlce, ⁊ geoffrige to ⁊ ga to husle ðẏ dæge ðe he to ðæm ordale gân scẏle, ⁊ sƿẏrige ðone aþ, ꝥ he se[1] mid folcrihte unscẏldig ðære tẏhtelan, ær ðe he to ðæm ordale gâ. ⁊ gif hit

[1] errata — se mid folcrihte lege sẏ mid folcriht

ȝif hit sie ƿæter, ꝥ he ȝedufe oðer healf elne on ðā raƿe; ȝif hit sie isen, sien þreo nihte, ær mon þa hand ondo.

7 ofȝa ælc man his tẏhtan mid foreaþe,[1] sƿa ƿe ær cƿædon; 7 beo þara ælc fæstende on æȝþre hand þe ðær mid[2] sie, Godes bebode 7 þæs[3] ercebisceoƿes; 7 ne beo þær on nauþre healfe ma manna ðon̄ xii. Gif se ȝetẏhtleda[4] man þon̄ maran ƿeorode sie ðon̄ xii sū, þon̄ sie ꝥ ordale forod, buton hie hī frā ȝan ƿillen.

7 se ðe ẏrfe bẏcȝȝe on ȝ̄ƿitnesse 7 hit eft teman scẏle, þon̄ onfo se his ðe he hit ær ætbohte, sie sƿa þeoƿ sƿa freoh, sƿeðer he sie.[5]

(7 ꝥ nan ceaƿinȝ ne seo Sunnandaȝum; ȝif hit hƿa do, liȝe þæs ceaƿes 7 selle xxx scẏll.)

Gif minra ȝerefena hƿelc þis don nelle oððe læs ymb sie þon̄ ƿe ȝecƿedon habbað, ȝelde min oferhyrnesse; 7 ic finde oþerne þe ƿile.

7 se biscop amaniȝe þa oferhyrnesse æt þǣ ȝerefan, ðe hit on his folȝoðe sie.

Se ðe of þisse ȝ̄rædnesse ȝa, ȝelde æt frūcẏrre v pund, æt oþrū cyrre his ƿer, æt (þriddan)[6] þoliȝe ealles þæs þe he aȝe 7 ure ealra freondsciƿes.

Se þe mænne aþ sƿeriȝe, 7 hit him on oƿen ƿeorþ, ꝥ he næfre æft aþƿẏrþ ne seo, ne binnan nanū ȝehalȝodū lictune[7] ne licȝe, þæh he ȝefære, butan he hæbbe

Vide reliqua ad finē libri

ad signū[8]

☞

[1] foreaþe] þſ del. after foreaþe [2] mid] ~~mid~~ [3] þæs] ƿæs [4] ȝetẏhtleda] ȝoa'tẏ'htleda [5] sie] followed by caret mark, with 7....scyll in right margin Nw2 [6] þriddan] in right margin Nw2 [7] lictune] t on top of c
[8] Nw2

gif hit sẏ wæter, ꝥ he gedufe ðreo healf elne on ðæm rape; Gif hit sẏ iren, sẏn ðreo nihte, ær mon ða hand on dô. ⁊ ofga ẏlc man his tẏhtan mid fore aþ, swa we ær cwædon; ⁊ beo ðæra ẏlc fæstende on ægþere hand ðe ðær sẏ, be godes [Ld 66^{v}] bebode ⁊ ðæs biscopes; ⁊ ne beo ðær on nawþre healfa ma manna ðonne xii. Gif ðonne se getẏhtleda man maran weorod sẏ þonne xii sum, ðonne sẏ ꝥ ordale forode, buton hi him fram gân wille.

Be ðæm ðe ẏrfe bẏcgaþ.

24 Se ðe ẏrfe bẏcge on gewitnẏsse ⁊ hit eft mon teaman scẏle, ðonne onfô se his ðe he hit ær æt bohte, sẏ swa þeowe swa freoh, hweþer he sẏ. And ꝥ nân ceaping ne sẏ sunnan dagum; Gif hit hwa dô, ðolige ðæs ceapgẏld ⁊ sẏlle xxx scill.

Be mansworum.[1]

25 Se ðe mænne aþ swerige, ⁊ hit him on open weorþe, ꝥ he næfre aþ wẏrþe ne sẏ, ne binnan nanum gehalgodum lictune ne licge, ðeah he gefære, butan he hæbbe ðæs biscopes gewitnẏsse, ðe he on his scire sẏ, ꝥ he hit swa gebete hæbbe, swa his scrift him scrife. ⁊ his scrift hit gecẏþe ðær biscop binnan þrittigum nihta, hwæþer he to þær bote wille. Gif he swa ne do, bete swa se biscop hine forgẏfan wille.

26 Gif minra gerefena gehwẏlce ðis dôn nẏlle oþþe læsse ẏmb sẏ þonne we gecwæden habbaþ, gẏlde min oferhẏrnẏsse; ⁊ ic finde oþerne ðe wille. ⁊ se biscope amanige ða oferhẏrnẏsse æt ðæm gerefan, [Ld 67^{v}] ðe on his folgoþe sẏ. Se ðe of ðis gerednẏsse gâ, gẏlde æt frumcẏrre v punde, æt oþrum cẏrre his wer, æt ðriddan ðolige ealle ðæs ðe he age ⁊ ura ealra freondscipes.

[1] Ld 25 and 26 are in reverse order to that in CN, Ot, H, Quadr.

he hæbbe þæs bisc̄ ʒeƿitnisse, þe he on his scire seo, ꝥ he hit sƿa ʒebæt hæbbe, sƿa his scrift hī scrife.

7 his scrift hit ʒecẏþe þæn bisc̄ binnan þrittiʒū nihta, hƿeþer he to þere bote ƿille. Gif he sƿa ne do, bæte sƿa se bisc̄ him forʒiofan ƿille.

V ATHELSTAN[1]

Æþelstan cẏnʒ cẏð, ꝥ ic hæbbe ʒeachsod, ꝥ ure friþ is ƿẏrs ʒehealden, þon̄ me lẏst, oþþe hit æt Greatanlæʒe cƿeden ƿære; 7 mine ƿeotan seʒʒaþ, ꝥ ic hit to lonʒe forboren hæbbe.

Nu hæbbe ic funden mid þæm ƿiotū, þe æt Æxsancestre mid me ƿeron to middūƿintra, ꝥ þa ealle sẏn ʒearoƿe mid hine[2] seolfū 7 mid ƿife 7 mid erfe 7 mid eallū þinʒū to fearenne þider þider ic þon̄ — butan hio ofer þis ʒesƿican ƿillen — on þa ʒerad þe heo næfre æft on earda ne cumen.

7 ʒif heo mon æfre æft on þæm ærda ʒemitte, ꝥ heo sion sƿa scẏldiʒe, sƿa se þe æt hæbbendre honda ʒefonʒen sion.

7 þe hi fiormie oððe hiora monna æniʒne, oððe æniʒ mon him tosende, seo he[3] scẏldiʒ his seolfes 7 ealles þæs þe he aʒe: ꝥ is þon̄ forþæm þe þa[4] aþas 7 þa

[1] rubric editorial [2] mid hine] mid ~~mid~~ hine [3] seo he] seo ~~seo~~ he [4] þa] þu

Ealle ðis wæs gesetted on ðam miclan synoþ
æt Greatanleage; on þam wæs se ærcebisceop
Wulfhelme mid eallum þæm æþelum man-
num ⁊ witan, ðe Æþelstan cyning
gegadrian.[1]

[Ld 68v]

Æthelstanes æ[2]

V ATHELSTAN[3]

Ic Æthelstan cyng cyþ, ꝥ ic hæbbe geacsod, ꝥ ure friþ is wyrs gehealden, ðonne me lyst, oþþe hit æt Greatanlæge gecwæden wære; ⁊ mine witan secgaþ, ꝥ ic hit to long forboren hæbbe. Nu hæbbe ic funden mid ðæm witum, ðe æt Eaxceastre mid me wæron to middū wintre, ꝥ ða ealle syn gearwe mid hire sylfū ⁊ mid yrfe ⁊ mid wife ⁊ mid eallū ðingū to færēne ðider ðider ic ðonne wille — butan hi ofer ðis geswican willan — on ða gerade ðe heo næfre eft on eorda ne cumen. And gif hi mon æfre eft on ðæm eorda gemitte, ꝥ hi syn swa scyldig, swa se ðe æt hebbendra handa gefongen syn. And se ðe hi feormige oþþe heora manna ænigne, oþþe ænigmon him to sende, sy he scildig his sylfes ⁊ ealles ðæs ðe he age: ꝥ is ðonne for ðæm ðe ða aþas ⁊ ða

[1] The Epilogue, Ealle ðis ... gegadrian, is not in CN or any other surviving OE text. This is, in fact, a back-translation by Nowell or Lambarde from Quadr. The OE is poor — synoþ, witan, gegadrian. Liebermann suggests reading mihte ȝeȝadrian on the basis of Quadr. congregare potuit. [2] rubric in Ld [3] rubric editorial

7 þa borȝas sint 7 þa ƿed ealle oferhefene 7 abrocene, þe þæs ȝesealde ƿeron. 7 ƿe nẏtun nanū oþrū þinȝū toȝetreoƿiȝanne, butan hit þis sio.

7 se þe oþres monnes mon underfo, þe for his ẏfle hī frō do, 7 hī ȝestioran ne mæȝe his ẏfles, ȝeld hine þam þe ær folȝade, 7 ȝeselle þæm cẏninȝe cxx sciłł.

Gif se[1] hlaford þoñ ƿille þone mon mid ƿo fordon, berecce hine þoñ, ȝif he mæȝe, on folcȝemote; 7 ȝif he laðleas sio, sæte hƿelcne hlaford on þa ȝeƿitnisse sƿelcne he þoñ ƿille; forþoñ ic an, ꝥ ælc þara þe laþleas beo, folȝie sƿelcū hlaforde sƿelce he þoñ ƿille.

7 sƿelc ȝerefa sƿelce þis forȝemeleasiȝe 7 ẏmb beon nelle, ȝeselle þæm cẏninȝ his oferhernisse, ȝif him mon onȝereccen mid soðe, 7 he hine onȝereccan ne mæȝe.

7 sƿelc ȝerefa sƿelc metsceattas nime 7 oþres riht þorh ꝥ aleȝȝe, ȝelde þæs cyninȝes oferhernisse 7 ƿeȝe æt þa unȝerisnu, sƿa sƿa ƿe ȝecƿeden habbaþ.

7 ȝif sio þeȝn þe hit do, seo ꝥ ilce.

7 nemne mon on ælces ȝerefan monunȝe sƿa fiola monna sƿa mon ƿite,

[1] se] from he

⁊ ða boꞃᵹaſ ſẏn ⁊ ða ƿeꝺ ealle oꝼeꞃ heꝼene ⁊ abꞃocene, ðe ðæꞃ ᵹeſealꝺ ƿæꞃon. Anꝺ ƿe nẏꞇen nanum oþꞃum ðinᵹum ꞇo ᵹeꞇꞃeoƿiᵹanne, buꞇan hiꞇ ðiſ ſẏ.

Be ðon oþꞃeſ monneſ man unꝺeꞃꝼehþ.

1 Anꝺ ſe ðe oþꞃeſ manneſ man unꝺeꞃꝼô, ðe he ꝼoꞃ hiſ ẏꝼle him ꝼꞃom ꝺô, ⁊ him ᵹeſꞇeoꞃan ne mæᵹe hiſ ẏꝼleſ, ᵹilꝺe hine ðæm ðe he æꞃ ꝼolᵹoꝺe, ⁊ ᵹeſẏlle ðæm cẏnᵹ cxx ſcill. Ᵹiꝼ ſe hlaꝼoꞃꝺ ðonne ƿille ðone mon miꝺ ƿoh ꝼoꞃꝺôn, beꞃecce hine ðonne, ᵹiꝼ he mæᵹe, on ꝼolcᵹemoꞇe; ⁊ ᵹiꝼ [Ld 69v] he laþleaſ ſẏ, ſæꞇe hƿẏlcne hlaꝼoꞃꝺe on þa ᵹeƿiꞇnẏſſe ſƿelcne he þône ƿille; ꝼoꞃ þon ic ƿille, ꝥ ẏlc þæꞃa þe laþleaſ beo, ꝼolᵹiᵹe ſƿẏlcum hlaꝼoꞃꝺe ſƿẏlce he ðonne ƿẏlle. Anꝺ ſƿẏlce ᵹeꞃeꝼa ſƿẏlce ðiſ ꝼoꞃᵹẏmeleaſiᵹe ⁊ ẏmb beo nẏlle, ᵹeſẏlle ðæm cẏnᵹ hiſ oꝼeꞃhẏꞃnẏſſe, ᵹiꝼ him mon onᵹeꞃecce miꝺ ſoþe, ⁊ he hine unᵹeꞃeccan ne mæᵹe. Anꝺ ſƿẏlc ᵹeꞃeꝼa ſƿẏlce miꝺſceaꞇꞇaſ nime ⁊ oðꞃeſ ꞃihꞇe ðuꞃh ꝥ alecᵹe, ᵹẏlꝺe ðæꞃ cẏnᵹeſ oꝼeꞃhẏꞃnẏſſe ⁊ ƿeᵹe æꞇ ða unᵹeꞃiſenu, ſƿa ſƿa ƿe ᵹecƿæꝺen habbaþ. Anꝺ ᵹiꝼ hiꞇ ſẏ ðeᵹn ðe hiꞇ ꝺô, ſẏ ꝥ ẏlc. Anꝺ nemne mon on ẏlceſ ᵹeꞃeꝼan monunᵹe ſƿa ꝼeala manna ſƿa mon ƿiꞇe,

ƿite, ꝥ unᵹelæᵹene sion, ꝥ bion to ᵹeƿitnisse ᵹehƿælcre sprece. 7 sion heora aþas unᵹ̄læᵹenra monna be þæs fios ƿeorþe butan cẏre.

7 se þe bespyriᵹe ærfe in on oþres lond: aspyriᵹe hit ut se þe land aᵹe, ᵹif he mæᵹe; ᵹif he ne mæᵹe, stande ꝥ spor for þone foraþ, ᵹif hƿone þærinne teo.

7 mon sinᵹe ælce Friᵹedæᵹe æt ælcū mynstre ealle þa Goddes þioƿas an fiftiᵹ for þone cẏninᵹ 7 for ealle þa þe ƿillen ꝥ he ƿille 7 for þa oþre, sƿa sƿa hio ᵹeearniᵹen.[1]

7 ælc mon þe ƿille mot ᵹebætan ælc stale ƿiþ þone teond butan ælcū ƿite oþ ᵹonᵹdaᵹas; 7 bio siþþan sƿa hit ær ƿæs.

IUDEX[2]

Ælc mon, þe on riht demeþ, he hafaþ ƿæᵹa on honda; 7 on æᵹþær sceale he[3] bereð rihƿinisse 7 mildheortnisse: Ærest for þær rihtƿisnisse he ᵹerecæð þæs ᵹyltes bote 7 þoñ for þær mildheortnisse he ᵹemetᵹaþ þære scyld ƿite.

Sume ᵹyltas beoþ frō þæm ᵹodan deman ðurh riht to bætænne, sume þorh miltheortnisse to forᵹeofenne.

Domas

[1] ᵹeearniᵹen] ᵹeearniᵹen ~~ƿill~~ [2] rubric editorial [3] he] ne

ƿiꞇe, ꝥ unᵹeleᵹene ſẏn, ꝥ beon ꞇo ᵹeƿiꞇneſſe ᵹehƿẏlcꝛe ſƿꝛæce. Anꝺ ſẏn heoꝛa aþaſ unᵹelæᵹenꝛa manna be ðæſ ꝼeoſ ƿẏꝛþe buꞇan cẏꝛe.

Be ðon ðe ẏꝛꝼe beſƿẏꝛiᵹe.

2 Se ðe beſƿiꝛiᵹe ẏꝛꝼe in on oþꝛeſ lanꝺ: aſƿẏꝛiᵹe hiꞇ uꞇ ſe ðe ꝥ lanꝺ aᵹe, ᵹiꝼ he mæᵹe; ᵹiꝼ he ne mæᵹe, ſꞇanꝺe ꝥ ſƿôꝛ ꝼoꝛ þone ꝼoꝛaþ, ᵹiꝼ hƿone ðæꝛ inne ꞇeo.

Anꝺ mon ſinᵹe ẏlce ꝼꝛiᵹꝺæᵹe æꞇ ẏlcum mẏnſꞇꝛe [Ld 70^{v}]ealle ða ᵹoꝺꝺeſ ðeoƿaſ an ꝼiꝼꞇiᵹ ſealmaſ ꝼoꝛ ðone cẏnᵹ ⁊ ꝼoꝛ ealle ða ðe ƿillen ꝥ he ƿille ⁊ ꝼoꝛ ða oþꝛe, ſƿa hi ſƿa ᵹeeaꝛniᵹen. Anꝺ ẏlce man ðe ƿille moꞇ ᵹebeꞇen ẏlce ᵹeſꞇale ƿiþ ðone ꞇeonꝺe buꞇan ẏlcum ƿiꞇe oþ ᵹonᵹ ꝺaᵹaſ; ⁊ beo ſẏþþan ſƿa hiꞇ æꝛ ƿæſ.[1]

IUDEX[2] [Liebermann 474]

Ælc man, þe riht demeð, he hæfð wæga on handa; 7 on ægðere sceale he byrþ rihtwisnesse 7 mildheortnesse: ærest for ðære rihtwisnesse he gereceð ðæs gyltes bote 7 þonne for ðære mildheortnesse he gemetegað þære scylde wíte.

Sume gyltas beoð fram þam godan deman þurh riht to betanne, sume þurh mildheortnesse tó forgyfanne.

Domas

[1] The passage Anꝺ ẏlce man ... ſƿa hiꞇ æꝛ ƿæſ is also present in CN but does not appear in H, Quadr.; Liebermann suggests it was missing from the archetype. [2] rubric editorial. This text does not appear in Ld.; I print from Liebermann's edition of G.

Domas sceolon beon butan[1] ælcra hadarunʒe:[2] ðæt is, ꝥ he ne murne nauþær ne ricū ne heanū, ne (leofum)[3] ne laþū folcriht to ʒereccenne.

Nis nanƿiht unrihtlicre þon is ꝥ mon mætsceatas onfo for domū: for þe þa mætsceattas ablendað þara ƿisra monna heortan 7 heo forcærraþ þeara rihtƿisra monna ƿord.

Drihten seolf cƿæð: "Be þæm ilcan dome, þe ʒe nu oþrū monnū demað, eoƿ bið æft demed."

Forþoñ se dema ondrede he him God, his deman, þẏ læs he æft on domes dæʒe Gode demendū seo ʒeniðrad.

Se þe þa unscylʒan scæþæð, oþþe þa scylʒan scildeþ for medsceattū oððe æniʒes monnes lufan oððe fionʒe, he bið æft ʒeniþrad frō þǣ æcan deman.[4]

Ne sceal næniʒ ealderman him settan dysiʒe deman ne unrihtƿise to ʒionʒrū: se dysiʒa for his unƿisdome ne con ꝥ riht; se unrihtƿisa dema for his ʒitsunʒe cerreþ ꝥ riht, þe he ʒeleornode.

Forneh þa earman men bioð ƿyrs

[1] beon butan] beon ~~beo~~ butan [2] hadarunʒe] hada arunʒe [3] leofum] MS has liefū underlined and leofum in left margin Nw2 [4] deman] e from æ

Domas sceolon beon butan ælcere hadarunge: *þæt* is, *þæt* he ne murne naðer ne rycu*m* ne heanum, ne leofum ne laðum folcriht to recceanne.

Nys nanwiht unrihtlycre ðonne ys *þæt* man medsceattas onfó for domu*m*: for ðan þe ða medsceattas ablendað þæra wisra manna heortan 7 hi forcyrrað ðæra rihtwisra manna word.

Drihten cwæð: 'Be ðam ylcan dome, ðe ge nú mannu*m* demað, eow byð eft gedemed.'

Forðon þonne ondræde he him God, his deman, ðy læs he eft on domes dæge beforan Godes eagum weorðe dumb 7 genýðerad. [Liebermann 475]

Se þe þam unscyldigan sceððeþ, oððe þam scyldegan scyldeþ for metsceattu*m* oðð for æniges mannes lufan oððe feonge, he biþ eft geniðerad fra*m* ða*m* ecan deman.

Ne sceal him nan ealdorman settan dysige deman ne unrihtwise to geongru*m*: se dysega for his unwisdome ne can *þæt* riht; 7 se unrihtwisa for his gitsunge forcyrreþ *þæt* riht, ðe he geleornode.

Forneah ða earman men beoð wyrs

ƿyrs bereafade frō þæm unrihtƿisan deman þoñ frō þæm ƿelrædƿæstan herȝe: ne bið æniȝ heretoȝa sƿa ȝifre on fremdra mon erfe sƿa se unrihtƿisa dema bið on heremonna.

Ða unrihtƿisan deman beoð ƿyrsan þoñ herȝende here: here mon[1] mæȝ ful oft befleon; ac þa deman for hiora onƿalde mon ne mæȝ befleon, þoñ heo him of hiora cæsterƿarena forðrycnisse ȝestreon ȝaderiað.

Oft æc[2] þa ȝodan deman habbaþ yfle ȝinȝran 7 reafiȝende, mid þara scẏlde þa deman beoð besmitene; 7 ȝif heo hī heara reaflaces ne stioraþ, þoñ forƿeorþað þa deman þorh hiora ȝinȝrena synne.

Forþon sƿa sƿa se æþela[3] middanȝeardes laruƿ cƿæð: "No þa ane þe yfel doþ, ac æc þa þe hit þæm dondū ȝeþafiaþ, bioþ ƿyrþe þæs æcan deaþes."

Oft æc þa þƿeorran deman for hiora ȝitsunȝe oððe ðe þone dom ȝeuffriȝaþ oððe hine onƿendaþ 7 ne ȝeendiȝaþ no þa sprece, ær hiara seod bið ȝefullæd; 7 þoñ þon hio demaþ, ne sceaƿiaþ hiora sprece, ac

[1] here: here mon] here: here/mon [2] æc] æc from œt with c repeated in left margin Nw2 [3] æþela] followed by del. of n

wyrs bereafode fra*m* þam unrihtwisan deman þonne fra*m* þa*m* wælgri*mm*estan here: ne bið nan heretoga swa gifre on fræ*m*drea manna yrfe swa se unrihtwisa dema byþ on his hyremanna.

Þa unrihtwisan deman hí beoð wyrsan þonne herigende here: here man mæg foroft befleon; ac þa deman for hira anwealde man ne mæg befleon, ðonne he him of hira ceast*re*warena forðrycnesse gestreon gaderiað.

Oft eac þa godan deman habbað yfele gingran 7 reafgende, mid ðæra scylde þa deman habbað hí besmitene; 7 gyf heo hym hyra reaflaces ne gestyrað, þonne forweorðaþ hí, ða deman, ðurh hyra gyngrena synna.

Forðan se æðela middangeardes lareow cwæð: 'Na ða áne ðe yfel doþ, ac ælc þara þe hit ðam dondum geðafiað, beoð wyrþe ðas ecean deaðes.'

Oft eac ða ðwyran deman for heora gitsungae þone dom geuferiað oððe hyne awendað 7 ne geendiað ná þa spæce, ær heora seod bið afylled; 7 þa*n* þonne hy demað, ne scewiað hy ná þa spæce, ac ac þa medsceatas.

Þa unrihtƿisan deman, æfter þæs ƿitȝan cƿide, sƿa sƿa ƿulfas on æfenne, ne (læfað)[1] noƿiht oð[2] on morȝenne: ꝥ is, ꝥ hio be þisses andƿeardan lifes anes ȝehyþnesse þencaþ 7 noƿiht be þæs toƿardan.

Ƿulfa þiaƿe hio niamað ælcƿiht 7 uneaþa lytles hƿæt[3] hio þæm þearfū læfaþ.

Se hatheorta dema ne mæȝ he behealdan þæs domes riht, for̄þon þe for þæs ierres dimnisse he ne mæȝ ȝeseon þæs rihtes.

On dome mon ne sceal næniȝes monnes med sceaƿiȝan, ac þa spece.

Hit is aƿritenne: "Ne onfoh þu nænine had on dome, ꝥ is, ne ara þu for næniȝum, ꝥ ðu ðæt riht ne deme."

Ða unrihtan deman hio dƿeoliȝiaþ[4] on þære soþfæstnisse cƿiþe, þon̄ hio hialdaþ ða ȝeðinðo þæs monnes; 7 oft hio scæððað þæm rihtƿisū, ðon̄ hio scildað ðæm arleasan.

Sio onfonȝnes mædsceatta on domū is soðfæstnisse leornis.

7 þa þe hī God ondredende[5] riht demaþ,[6] hio onfoð æt Gode ec edlean.

Followed by fol. 267* — r is blank, v has Latin and OE notes. Fol. 268r also has Latin and OE notes, of which the contents seem in part to deal with place-name etymology; the OE includes —

Bold ȝetele .i. botl   vide legē 34

Esne in legibs ælfredi capite Be mæsse dæȝ freolse

ƿesseaxna cyninȝ has been scratched out at the top of the page

[1] læfað] bæfaþ underlined with læfað in left margin Nw2 [2] oð] ascender of ð missing; ot̄ = oð might also be intended [3] hƿæt] hƿiet [4] dƿeoliȝiaþ] dƿeoliȝ'i'aþ [5] ondredende] ondredredende [6] demaþ] þ from ð

ac þa medsceatas. [Liebermann 476]

Þa únrihtwisan deman, æfter witegan cwyde, swa swa wulfas on æfne, ne læfað náwiht oð morgen: þ*æt* ys, þ*æt* hi be þisses anweardan lifes ongehyðnesse ðenceað 7 nawiht be þæs towerdan.

Yfelra gerefena þeaw ýs, þ*æt* hí nymað ælcwiht 7 uneaðe hí þam þearfiendum lytles hwæt læfa[ð].

Se hatheorta dema ne mæg he behealdan ðas domes riht, for ðan þe for ðæs yrres dimnesse he ne mæg geseon ðas rihtes beorhtnesse.

In dóme ne sceal man æniges mannes mæð sceawian, ac þa spæce.

Hyt ys awriten: 'Ne onfoh ðu nænigne had on dome; né ne ara ðú for nanum, þ*æt* þu þ*æt* riht ne deme.'

Þa unrihtwisan deman hí dweliað on ðare soðfæstnesse cwyde, þonne hí behealdaþ þa geðincþo ðas mannes; 7 oft heo scaðað þam unrihtwisu*m*, ðonne hí scyldað þam arleasum.

Seo anfengnes medsceata on domu*m* ys soðfæstnesse forlætnes.

7 þa ðe him God ondrædende riht demeð, hí onfoð æt Gode écc endlean.

THE LAWS OF ALFRED AND INE

LIST OF RUBRICS

1	Be þā þe mon ne scyle oþrū deman, buton sƿa he ƿille ꝥ hī mon deme.
2	Be aþū 7 be ƿeddū.
3	Be circena socnū.
4	Be borhbrẏce.[1]
5[2]	Be hlafordsearƿe.
6	Be circena friþe.
7	Be circene[3] stale.
8	Be þon þe mon on cyninʒes healle feohte.
ix	Be nunnan hæmede.[4]
x	Be bearneacū ƿife ofsleʒenū.
xi	Be tƿelfhẏndes monnes ƿife forleʒenū.
xii	Be ciorliscre[5] fæmnan onfenʒe.
xiii	Be ƿudubærnete.
xiiii	Be dūbra monna dædū.
xv	Be þǣ monnū þe beforan bisceopū feohtað.
xvi	Be nunnena onfenʒe.
xvii	Be þǣ monnū þe hiora ƿæƿen to monslẏhte lænað.
xviii	Be þā þe munecū heora feoh buton leafe befæstað.[6]
xix	Be preosta ʒefeohte.
xx	Be eofetes andetlan.
xxi	Be hundes slyte.
xxii	Be[7] netena misdædū.
xxiii	Be ceorles mennenes nidhæmede.[8]
xxiiii	Be tƿyhẏndū[9] men æt hloðslẏhte.
xxv	Be syxhẏndū men.
xxvi[10]	Be tƿelfhyndū men.
xxvii	Be unʒeƿintredes (ƿifmonnes)[11] nedhæmde.[12]
xxviii	Be sƿa ʒerades monnes sleʒe.
xxix	Be folcleasunʒe ʒeƿyrhtum.
xxx	Be ʒodborʒū.
xxxi	Be ciepemonnum.
xxxii	Be cẏrlisces monnes bẏndellan.
xxxiiii	Be speres ʒemeleasnesse.
xxxiiii	Be boldʒetæle.
xxxv	

[1] borhbrẏce] ẏ on top of e [2] 5] 54 [3] circene] circen'e' with first e on top of a Nw2 [4] hæmede] hæmeðe [5] ciorliscre] ci'ɵ'rl'i'scre with del. of one after first r Nw2 [6] befæstað] f on top of one; f repeated in right margin [7] Be] del. of one after Be [8] nidhæmede] ~~med~~'nid'he'æ'meðe Nw2 [9] tƿyhẏndū] tƿyhẏrdu [10] xxvi] xxvii [11] ƿifmonnes] 'monnes' ƿif with ƿifmonnes in left margin Nw2 [12] nedhæmde] nedhæmðe

THE LAWS OF ALFRED AND INE
LIST OF RUBRICS

	—	[no rubric Ld = CN i]
Ld 26^v	1	Be aþum ⁊ be ƿeꝺꝺum.
Ld 27^v	2	Be cẏꞃıcena ꞅocnum.
Ld 28^v	3	Be boꞃhbꞃẏce.
	4	Be hlaꝼoꞃꝺ ꞅẏꞃƿe.
	5	Be cẏꞃıcena ꝼꞃẏþe.
Ld 29^v	6	Be cẏꞃıcena ꞅꞇale.
	7	Be ðon ðe mon on cẏnınᵹeꞅ healle ᵹeꝼeohꞇe.
Ld 30^v	8	Be ðam ðe nunnan oꝼ mınꞅꞇeꞃ ût alæꝺaþ—[from B]
	9	Be ðon ðe mon oꝼꞅlea beaꞃn eacnenꝺ ƿıꝼ—[from B?]
Ld 31^v	10	Be ꝼoꞃleᵹeꞃum.
	11	[no rubric Ld = CN xii]
	12	Be ƿuꝺu bæꞃneꞇꞇe.
	13	Be ðon ðe mon oþeꞃne oꝼꝼẏlle—[from B?]; not in CN
Ld 32^v	14	Be ꝺumbꞃa manna ꝺæꝺum.
	15	Be ᵹeꝼeohꞇum.
	16	Be ðon ðe mon mẏꞃe oþ cû ꝼoꞃꞅꞇele—[from B?]; not in CN
	17	Be ðon ðe oþꞃu hıꞅ unmaᵹum oþꝼæꞅꞇeþ—[from B?]; not in CN
	18	Be nunnena onꝼenᵹ.
	19	Be ðon ðe heoꞃa ƿæꞃne lænaþ ꞇo manꞅlıhꞇ.
Ld 33^v	20	Be ðam ðe munecum ꝼeoh beꝼæꞅꞇaþ.
	21	Be ƿꞃeoꞅꞇa ᵹeꝼeohꞇe.
	22	Be eoꝼeꞇeꞅ anꝺeꞇlan.
	23	Be hunꝺeꞅ ꞅlıꞇe.
Ld 34^v	24	Be nẏꞇena mıꞅꝺæꝺum.
	25	Be nẏꝺhæmeꝺ. [= CN xxiii]
	26	Be manꞅlıhꞇ mıꝺ hloþe. [= CN xxiiii-xxvii, part 1]
Ld 35^v	27	Be mæᵹleaꞅum monnum. [= CN xxvii, part 2 + xxviii]
	28	Be ꝼolc leaꞅunᵹum ᵹeƿẏꞃhꞇum.
	29	Be ᵹoꝺ boꞃhᵹum.
	30	Be cẏpmannum.
Ld 36^v	31	Be ceoꞃlıꞅceꞅ manneꞅ bınꝺelan.
	32	Be ꞅƿeꞃeꞅ ᵹẏmeleaꞅꞇe.
Ld 37^v	33	Be bolꝺᵹeꞇæle.

xxxv Be þon þe mon befóran ealdormen on Ᵹmote Ᵹfeohte.
xxxvj Be ciorlisces monnes fletᵹefeohte.
xxxvij Be boclondū.
xxxviij Be fæhþe.[1]
xxxix Be mæssedæᵹa freolse.
xl Be heafodƿunde.
xli Be feaxƿunde.
xlij Be earsleᵹe.
xliij Be monnes eaᵹƿunde 7 oðerra missenlicra lioma.[2]
xliiii Be Ines domum.
xlv Be Godes þeoƿena[3] reᵹole.
xlvj Be cildū.
xlvii Be Sunnandæᵹes ƿeorcū.
xlviij Be ciricsceattū.
xlix Be ciricsocnum.
l Be ᵹefeohtū.
li Be stale.
lii Be ryhtes béne.
liii[4] Be reaflace.
liiii[5] Be þǣ ƿreccendan, ær hī man[6] ryhtes[7] bidde.
lv Be þǣ monnū þe heora Ᵹlondan bebyᵹᵹað.
lvi Be ᵹefonᵹenū þeofū.[8]
lvii Be þǣ þe heora Ᵹƿittnessa beforan bisc̄ aleoᵹað.
lviii Be hloðe.
lix Be heriᵹe.
lx Be þeofsleᵹe.
lxi Be forestolenū flæsce.
lxii Be ciorliscū[9] þeofe ᵹefanᵹenū.
lxiii Be cẏninᵹes ᵹeneate.
lxiiii Be feorran cumenū men butan ƿeᵹe Ᵹmetton.
lxv Be sƿa ofsleᵹenes monnes ƿere.
lxvi Be þon þe monnes ᵹeneat staliᵹe.
lxvii Be elþeodiᵹes monnes sleᵹe.
lxviii Be ƿiteþeoƿes monnes sleᵹe.
lxix Be cyƿemonna forefenᵹ uppe on londe.
lxx Be fundenes cildes fostre.
lxxi Be þon þe mon dearnenᵹa bearn ᵹestrẏne.[10]
lxxii Be þeofes onfenᵹe æt þyfþe.[11]
lxxiii

[1] fæhþe] færþe [2] lioma] li'o'ma [3] þeoƿena] þeoƿ'en'a Nw2 [4] liii] liiii [5] liiii] liii [6] man] ~~mar~~ man [7] ryhtes] h from þ [8] ᵹefonᵹenū þeofū] ᵹeforᵹenū þeoƿu [9] ciorliscū] ci'o'rliscū Nw2 [10] ᵹestrẏne] ẏ from i
[11] þyfþe] ~~þeof~~ þyfþe

	34	Be ᵹeꝼeohꞇe beꝼoꞃan ealꝺoꞃmen.
	35	Be cẏꞃlıꞅceꞅ monneꞅ ꝼleꞇꞇe ᵹeꝼeohꞇe.
	36	Be buꞃhbꞃẏce—[from B? cf. Quadr.]
Ld 38^{v}	37	Be boclanꝺe.
	—	Be ᵹeꝼeohꞇe—[in margin, al. fæþe]
Ld 40^{v}-43^{v}	39	Be mæꞅꞅe ꝺæᵹe ꝼꞃeolꞅe.
	40	Be ƿunꝺum. [= CN xl-xliii]
Ld 0^{v}	—	Ineꞅ æ [= CN xliiii]
	1	Be ᵹoꝺeꞅ þeoƿena ꞃeᵹole.
	2	Be cılꝺum.
	3	Be ꞅunnan ꝺæᵹeꞅ ƿeoꞃcum.
Ld 1^{v}	4	Be cẏꞃıcꞅceaꞇꞇe.
	5	Be cẏꞃıc ꞅocnum.
	6	Be ᵹeꝼeohꞇe.
Ld 2^{v}	7	Be ꞅꞇale.
	8	Be ꞃıhꞇeꞅ bene.
	9	Be þam ƿꞃæcenꝺan. [= CN lii(i)]
	10	Be ꞃeaꝼlace. [= CN liiii—order reversed in CN rubric list, but *not* in body of text]
	11	Be leoꝺ bẏᵹene—[from B?]
Ld 3^{v}	12	Be ðam þe heoꞃa ᵹeƿıꞇnẏꞅꞅe ᵹeleoᵹaþ. [= CN lvii]
	13	Be ᵹeꝼanᵹenum þeoꝼum. [= CN lvi—order reversed]
	14	Be hloþum.
	15	Be heꞃᵹe.
	16	Be þeoꝼꞅlæᵹe.
	17	Be ꝼoꞃꞅꞇolenum ꝼlæꞅce.
	18	Be ceoꞃlıꞅcum þeoꝼum ᵹeꝼanᵹenum.
Ld 4^{v}	19	Be cẏnınᵹeꞅ ᵹeneaꞇ.
	20	Be ꝼeoꞃꞃan cumenum men.
	—	[no rubric Ld = CN lxv]
	21	Be ðon ðe monneꞅ ᵹeneaꞇ ꞅꞇalıᵹe.
	22	Be ælþeoꝺıᵹeꞅ manneꞅ ꞅlæᵹe.
Ld 5^{v}	23	Be ƿıꞇe þeoƿum.
	24	Be cẏpmanna on lanꝺe.
	25	Be ꝼunꝺeneꞅ cılꝺeꞅ ꝼoꞅꞇꞃe.
Ld 6^{v}	26	Be ðeoꝼeꞅ onꝼenᵹ. [= CN lxxii]
	27	Be ðam ðe ꝺeaꞃnunᵹa beaꞃn ꞅꞇꞃẏneþ.[= CN lxxi – order reversed]

lxxiii Be þon þe mon sƿeordes onlæne oþres[1] þeoƿe.
lxxiiij Be þon þe cyrlisc mon flymanfeormiȝe.
lxxv Be þon þe mon ƿif[2] bicȝȝ 7 þon̄ sio ȝift tostande.
lxxvi Be Ƿilisces monnes londhæfene.
lxxvii Be cyninȝes horsƿeale.
lxxviii Be monslihte.
lxxviiii Be þeofslihte: ꝥ he mote að ȝecẏþan.
lxxx Be þeofes onfenȝ 7 hine þon̄ forlæte.
lxxxi Be cẏrlisces[3] monnes ontyȝenesse æt þiefþe.
lxxxii Be þon þe ȝrihtȝesīhiƿan[4] bearn hæbben 7 þon̄ se ƿer ȝƿite.
lxxxiii Be unalefedū fære frō his hlaforde.
lxxxiiii Be ceorles ƿeorþiȝ.
lxxxv Be borȝes ondsæce.[5]
lxxxvi Be ceorles ȝærstune.
lxxxvii Be ƿudabærnete.[6]
lxxxvii Be ƿuda onfenȝ buton leafe.
lxxxviii[7] Be burhbryce.
xc Be stæltẏhtlan.
xci Be þon þe mon forstolene ceap befehþ.
xcii Be ƿiteþeoƿū men.
xciii Be unaliefedes mæstines onfenȝe.
xciiii Be ȝsiþcundes monnes ȝeþinȝ.
xcv Be þon þe ȝsiþcund mon fyrd forƿitie.[8]
xcvi Be dyrnū ȝeþinȝe.
xcvii Be forstolenes monnes fore forȝsitte.
xcviii Be ƿerfæhþe tyhtlan.
xcix Be eƿes ƿeorþe.
c[9] Be ȝehƿelces ceapes anȝelde.
ci Be[10] cearlisces monnes stale.
cii Be oxan horne.
ciii Be cuushorne.
ciiii Be hyrȝeiohte.[11]
cv Be ciricsceatte.
cvi Be þon þe mon to ceape fordrefe.
cviii

[1] oþres] oþers [2] ƿif] fif [3] cẏrlisces] cẏlisces [4] ȝrihtȝesīhiƿan] ȝeriht'ȝe'sīhiƿan with ī on top of ā Nw2 [5] ondsæce] ondfæce [6] ƿudabærnete] ƿudabærn'e'te with first e over del. [7] lxxxviii] lxxxv'iii'; Nw2 puts this right, for there is no lxxxix [8] forƿitie] forsytte originally, then ~~sytte~~ was struck out and ƿitie added to give forƿitie Nw2 [9] c] ~~xc~~ c [10] Be] after Be del. of ~~cea'r'l~~ [11] hyrȝeiohte] hyrȝe'i'ohte

Folio	No.	Rubric
	28	Be ðam ðe his ƿæpnu onlæne.
	29	Be ðam ðe flẏman feormige.
	30	Be ðon ðe mon ƿif bicge.
Ld 7^{v}	31	Be cirlisces monnes land hæfene.
	32	Be cẏninges hors ƿealh.
	33	Be manslẏhte.
	34-35	Be ðeofslẏhte.
Ld 8^{v}	36	Be ðon ðe mon þeof forlæte.
	37	Be cẏrlisces monnes betogennẏsse.
	38	Be ðon ðe riht gehiƿan bearn hæbban.
	39	Be unalẏfedum fære fram his hlaforde.
	40	Be ceorles ƿeorþige.
Ld 9^{v}	41	Be borges onsæce.
	42	Be ceorla gemænum land—[from B?]
	43	Be ƿudu bærnete—[errata: ƿudu, lege ƿudu]
Ld 10^{v}	44-45	[no rubric Ld = CN lxxxvii(i)]
	46	Be burhbrẏce.
	47	Be stal tẏhtlan.
Ld 11^{v}	48	Be forstolene ceap befangene.
	49	Be ƿite ðeoƿum mannum—[from B?]
	50	Be unalẏfedes mæstenes onfeng.
	51	Be siþcundes monnes geþinge.
Ld 12^{v}	52	Be ðon ðe gesiþcund mon fẏrd forsitte.
	53	Be dẏrnum geþingþe.
	54	Be forstolenes mannes forfenge.
	55	Be ƿærfæhþe tẏhtlan.
Ld 13^{v}	56	Be eoƿes ƿẏrþe.
	57	[no rubric Ld = CN c]
	58	Be cẏrlisces monnes stale.
	59	Be oxan.
Ld 14^{v}	60	[no rubric Ld = CN ciii]
	61	Be hẏre Geôc.
	62	Be cẏric sceatte.
	63	Be ðon ðe mon to ceape fordræfe.

cvii	Be ȝesiþcundes monnes fære.
cviii	Be þon þe hæfþ tƿenti hida londes.
cix	Be tyn hidū.
cx	Be iii hidū.
cxi	Be ȝẏrde londes.
cxii	Be ȝesiþcundes monnes dræfe of londe.
cxiii	Be sciopes ȝonȝ mid his fliose.[1]
cxiiii	Be tƿyhindū ƿere.
cxv[2]	Be ƿeretẏhtlan.
cxvi[3]	Be ƿerȝeldþeofes[4] forefonȝ.
cxvii[5]	Be anre nihtes þyfþe.
cxviii[6]	Be þon þe þeoƿƿealh frione mon ofslea.
cxix	Be forstolenes[7] ceapes forefonȝe.
cxx	Be þon ȝif mon oþres[8] ȝodsunu slea oþþe his ȝodfæder.

[1] fliose] ~~flese~~ fliose [2] cxv] cxvi [3] cxvi] cxvii [4] ƿerȝeldþeofes] ƿerȝeld þe ofes [5] cxvii] cxviii [6] cxviii] cx~~ix~~'viii' [7] forstolenes] þon stolenes [8] oþres] oþers

	64	Be ᵹeꞅıþcunꝺeꞅ monneꞅ ꝼaꞃe.
Ld 15v	65	Be lanꝺ hæbbenꝺum. [= CN cviii, cix, cx]
	66	[no rubric Ld = CN cxi]
	67	Be ᵹeꞅıþcunꝺeꞅ monneꞅ ꝺꞃæꝼe oꝼ lanꝺe.
	68	Be ꞅceapeꞅ ᵹanᵹe mıꝺ ꝼleoꞅ.
	69	Be ƿeꞃum. [= CN cxiiii, part 1]
	70	Be ꝼoꞅꞇꞃe. [= CN cxiiii, part 2]
Ld 16v	71	Be ƿeꞃꞇẏhꞇlan.
	72	Be ƿeꞃᵹẏlꝺ ðeoꝼeꞅ ꝼoꞃeꝼenᵹ. [= CN cxvi, cxvii]
	73	Be ðon ðe ðeoꝼ ƿealh ꝼꞃıᵹne man oꝼꞅlea.
Ld 17v	74	Be ꝼoꞃꞅꞇoleneꞅ ceapeꞅ ꝼoꞃꝼenᵹ.
	75	Be ᵹoꝺꝼæꝺeꞃeꞅ oþþe ᵹoꝺꞅuneꞅ ꞅlẏhꞇ——[from B?]

The rubric list is not found in Ld. The rubrics found in the text of Ld at the heads of individual items have been gathered here and repeated editorially. Comments such as "from B?" are from Liebermann. Nowell has tried to make some sense of the list of rubrics in CN. However, the numbers and rubrics added in the body of the text (= Nw2) do not necessarily agree with the original list of rubrics.

THE LAWS OF ALFRED AND INE

BIBLICAL PROLOGUE

Drihten pæs sprecende þas pord to Moẏse, 7 þus cpæð: Ic eom Drihten þin God. Ic þe ut ̄ʒlædde of Eʒipta londe, 7 of heora þeopdome.

Ne lufa þu oþþre fremde ʒodas ofer me.

Ne minne noman ne ciʒ ðu on idelnesse, forþon þe þu ne bist unscẏldiʒ piþ me, ʒif þu on idelnesse ciʒst minne noman.

Gemine ꝥ þu ʒehalʒie þone restedæʒ; pyrceað eop vi daʒas, 7 on þā[2] seofaþan restaþ eop; forþā on vi daʒū Crist ̄ʒporhte heofonas 7 eorþan, sæs 7 ealle ̄ʒsceafta þe on hī sint, 7 hine ʒereste on þone seofoþan dæʒe; 7 forþon Drihten hine ̄ʒhalʒode.

Ara þinū fæder 7 þinre meder,[3] þa þe Drihten seald, ꝥ þu sie þy lenʒ libbende on eorþan.

Ne sleah þu.

Ne li ̄ʒ þu dearnenʒa.

Ne stala þu.

Ne se ̄ʒ þu lease ̄ʒpitnesse.

Ne pilna þu þines nehstan ierfes mid unriht.

Ne pyrce þe ʒyldne ʒodas oþþe sylfrene.

Þis sint þa domas þe þu hī settan scealt: Gif hpa ̄ʒbẏcʒʒe[4] Cristenne þeop, vi ʒear þeopiʒ he; þy seofoþan beo he freoh orceapunʒa; mid spilce[5] hræʒle he ineode, mid spilce ʒanʒ he ut. Gif he pif self hæbbe, ʒanʒ hio ut mid hī. Gif se hlaford hī pif sealde, sie hio 7 hire bearn þæs hlafordes.

Gif se þeopa þonne cpeþe: "Nelle ic frō minū hlaforde, ne frō minū pife, ne frō minū bearne, ne frō minū ierfe," brenʒe hine þonne his hlaforde to þære dura tēples 7 þurhþyrliʒe his eare mid æle to tacne ꝥ he

[1] at top of page is a ref. to Exods. 20. The page is also given the number 1 [2] þā] þa [3] meder] me'e'der with o also roughly altered to e [4] ̄ʒbẏcʒʒe] ~~̄ʒbẏ ̄ʒ~~ ̄ʒbẏcʒʒe [5] spilce] spilce corrected from hpelce Nw2

THE LAWS OF ALFRED AND INE
BIBLICAL PROLOGUE

Drihten wæs sprecende ðas word to Moyse, ⁊ ðus cwæþ: Ic eom drihten ðin God. Ic ðe utgelædde of Ægipta lond, ⁊ of heora ðeowdom. Ne lufa þu oþre fremde godas ofer me.

Ne minne noman ne cig þu on idelnesse, forþon ðe ðu ne bist unscildig wiþ me, gif ðu on idelnesse cigst minne noman. Gemine ꝥ ðu gehalgie ðone reste dæg; wyrceaþ eow syx dagas, ⁊ on ða seofoþon restaþ eow, ðu ⁊ ðin sunu, ⁊ ðine dohter, ⁊ ðin ðeowe, ⁊ ðine wylne, ⁊ ðin weorcnyten ⁊ se cuma þe biþ binnan ðinan durum;[1] forþon on syx dagas Crist geworhte heofonas ⁊ eorþan, sæs ⁊ ealle [Ld 19v] gesceafta ðe on him synd, ⁊ hine gerest on ðone seofoþan dæge; ⁊ forþon drighten hine gehalgode. Ara ðinum fæder ⁊ ðinre meder, ða þe drihten sealde, ðe ꝥ ðu sy ðy leng libbend on eorþum. Ne slea ðu. Ne stala ðu. Ne licge ðu dearnunga.[2] Ne sæcge ðu leasgewitnesse wiþ ðinum nehstan.[3] Ne wilna ðu þines nehstan yrfes mid unriht. Ne wyrc ðe gyldene godas oþþe seolfrene. Ðis synd ða domas ðe ðu him settan scealt: Gif hwa gebycge cristenne ðeowe, vi gear ðeowige he; ðy seofoþan beo he freoh orceapunga; Mid swylce hrægle he in eode, mid swilce gang he ut. Gif he wif sylf hæbbe, gang heo ut mid him. Gif se hlaford him wif sealde, sy heo ⁊ hire bearn ðæs hlafordes. Gif se ðeowe ðonne cwæþe: "Nelle ic fram minum hlaforde, ne fram minum wif, ne fram minum bearne, ne fram minum yrf," breng hine ðonne his hlaford to ðære dura ðæs temples ⁊ ðurh þyrlige his eare mid eale to tacne ꝥ he

[1] ðu ⁊ ðin sunu....binnan ðinan durum imported by Ld from Vulgate [2] order reversed from that of other MSS; CN Ne liȝ þu dearnenȝa. Ne stala þu [3] wiþ ðinum nehstan imported by Ld from Vulgate

tacne[2] ꝥ he sie æfre siþþan þeoƿ.

Ðeah hƿa ᵹbicᵹ his dohtor[3] on þeoƿenne, ne sie hio ealles sƿa ðeoƿu sƿa oðru mennenu; naᵹe he hie ut on ælþeodiᵹ folc to bebẏcᵹᵹanne. Ac ᵹif he hire ne recce, se hie bohte, læte hie faran freo[4] on ælþeodiᵹ folc.

Gif he þoñ alefe his suna mid to hæmanne, do hire ᵹifta: lociᵹ ꝥ hio hæbbe hræᵹl; 7 ꝥ ƿeorþ sie hyre mæᵹþhades, ꝥ is se ƿeotuma, aᵹẏfe[5] he hire þone. Gif he hire þara nan ne do, þoñ sie hio frioh.

Se mon se þe his ᵹƿealdes monnan ofslea, ƿelte se deaðe. Se þe hine þoñ nedes ofsloᵹe oþþe unƿillū oþþe unᵹƿealdes, ƿelce hine God sƿa sende on his honda, 7 he hine ne ȳbsẏrede, sie he feores ƿyrþe, 7 folcrihtre bóte, ᵹif he friðstoƿe ᵹsece.

Gif (hƿa)[6] þoñ of ᵹyrnesse 7 ᵹeƿealdes ofslea his þone niehstan þurh searƿa, aluc þu hine frō minū ƿeofode to þā þæt he deaþ ƿelte.

Se þe slea his fæder oþþe his modor, se sceal deaþ ƿeltan.

Se þe frione forstele 7 he hine bebẏᵹᵹe, 7 hit onbestæled[7] sie ꝥ he hine bereccan ne mæᵹ, ƿelt se deaðe.

Se þe ƿyrᵹe his fæder oþþe his[8] modor, ƿelte se deað.

Gif hƿa slea his þone nehstan mid stane, oþþe mid fẏste, 7 he þeah utᵹonᵹan mæᵹe bẏ stafe, beᵹite hī læce, 7 ƿyrce his ƿeorce þa hƿile þe hī silfe ne mæᵹe.

Se þe slea his aᵹen þeoƿne esne oþþe his mennen, 7 he ne sie idæᵹes[9] dead, þeah he libbe tƿa[10] niht oþþe þreo, ne bið he ealle sƿa scẏldiᵹ, forþon þe hit ƿæs his aᵹen fioh. Gif he þonne[11] sie idæᵹes dead, þonne sitte sio scẏld on hī.

Gif hƿa on ceaste[12] eacniende ƿif ᵹeƿerde, bete þone æƿerdlan sƿa hī dome-

[1] page numbered 2 [2] tacne] del. of one before tacne [3] dohtor] ~~dohtor~~ do'h'ctor [4] faran freo] 'faran' freo Nw2 [5] aᵹẏfe] aᵹ'ẏ'fe [6] hƿa] ~~sƿa~~/ with hƿa in right margin Nw2 [7] onbestæled] onbest'æ'led [8] his] s his [9] ıdæᵹes] þ'i'dæᵹes [10] tƿa] ƿ on del. of one [11] Gif he þonne] Gif ~~þon~~ he þonne [12] ceaste] ceast'e' with t on top of one Nw2

tacne ꝥ he sẏ æfre syþþan ðeoƿe. Ðeah hƿa bebẏcge his dohtor to ðeoƿenne, ne sẏ heo ealles sƿa þeoƿu sƿa oþru mennenu; Nage he hi ut on ælþeodig folc to bebẏcganne. Ac gif he hire ne recce, se hi bohte, læte hi faran freo on ælþeodig folc. Gif þōne he alẏfe his sunu mid to hæmænne, dô hire gẏfta: locige ꝥ hio hæbbe hrægle; ⁊ ꝥ ƿeorþ sẏ hẏre mægþhades, ꝥ is se ƿeotoma, agẏfe he hire ðonne. [Ld 20v] Gif he hire ðæra nân ne do, ðonne sẏ heo freoh. Se mon se ðe his geƿealdes monnan ofslea, sƿelte se deaþ. Se ðe ðonne hine nedes ofsloge oþþe unƿillum oþþe ungeƿealdes, sƿẏlce hine god sƿa sende on his honda, ⁊ he hine ẏmb ne sẏrede, sẏ he his feores ƿẏrþe, ⁊ folc rihtre bôt, gif he friþstoƿe gesece. Gif hƿa þonne of gẏrnesse ⁊ geƿealdes ofslea his ðone nehstan ðurh sẏrƿa, aluc ðu hine fram minum ƿeofod to þam ꝥ he deaþ sƿelte. Se þe slea his fæder oþþe his modor, se sceal deaþ sƿeltan. Se ðe frione forstæle ⁊ he hẏne bebẏcge,[1] sƿelt se deaþ. Se ðe ƿẏrge his fæder oþþe his modor, sƿelte se deaþe. Gif hƿa slea his ðone nehstan mid stane, oþþe mid fẏste, ⁊ he ðeah ut gongan mæge be stafe, begẏte him læce, ⁊ ƿẏrce his ƿeorce ða hƿile ðe he sẏlf ne mæge. Se ðe slea his agenne ðeoƿne esne oþþe mennen, ⁊ he ne sẏ þẏ dæges dead, ðeah he libbe tƿa niht oþþe ðreo, ne biþ he ealle sƿa scẏldig, forþon ðe hit ƿæs his agen feoh. Gif he ðonne sẏ idæges dead, ðonne sitte seo scẏld on him. Gif hƿa on ceast eâcniend ƿif geƿerd, bete ðone æfƿẏrdlan sƿa him dome-

[1] omission in Ld; cf. CN ...bebẏȝȝe, 7 hit onbestæled sie ꝥ he hine bereccan ne mæȝ, spelt...

hi demeras[2] ʒereccen.[3] Gif hio dead sie, selle saƿle ƿiþ saƿle.

Gif hƿa oþrū his eaʒ̄ oððó, selle his aʒen fore: toþ fore toþ, honda for honda, fet for fet,[4] berninʒ for berninʒe, ƿund ƿiþ ƿunde,[5] læl ƿiþ læle.[6]

Gif hƿa aslea his þeoƿe oþþe his þeoƿenne[7] ꝥ eaʒ̄ ut, 7 he þoñ hie ʒ̄do aniʒʒ̄,[8] ʒefreoʒ̄ hie for þon. Gif he þon þone toð ofaslea, do ꝥ ilce.

Gif oxa ofhnite[9] ƿer oþþe ƿif ꝥ hie dead syn, sie he mid stanū ofƿeorpod,[10] 7 ne sy his flæsc æten; se hlaford bẏð[11] unscyldẏʒ.[11] Gif se oxa hnetol ƿære tƿā daʒū ær oþþe ðrym, 7 se hlaford hit[12] (nyste, ʒif he hit þonne) ƿiste[13] 7 hine inne[14] betẏnan nolde, 7 he þoñ ƿer oþþe ƿif ofsloʒe, sie mid stanū ofƿorpod, 7 sie se hlaford ofsleʒen oþþe forʒolden sƿa ꝥ ƿitan to rẏhte finden. Sunu oþþe dohtor ʒif he ofstinʒ̄, þæs ilcan domes sie he ƿẏrþe.

Gif he þoñ þeoƿ oþþe þeoƿmennen[15] ofstẏnʒ̄, ʒ̄selle þā hlaforde xxx scill seolfres, 7 se oxa sie mid[16] stanū ofƿorpod.

Gif hƿa adelfe ƿæƭƿẏtt, oþþe betẏnedne ontẏne, 7 hine eft ne betẏne, ʒelde sƿilce neat sƿelc þær on befealle, 7 hæbbe hī þæt deade.

Gif oxa oþres monnes oxan ʒeƿundiʒ̄, 7 he þoñ dead sie, bebycʒʒen þone oxan 7 hæbben hī ꝥ ƿeorð ʒ̄mæne, 7 eac ꝥ flæsc sƿa þæs deadan.[17] Gif se hlaford þoñ ƿiste[18] ꝥ se oxa hnitol ƿære, 7 hine healdan nolde, selle hī oþerne oxan fore 7 hæbbe hī eall ꝥ flæsc.[19]

Gif hƿa forstele oþres oxan 7 hine ofslea oþþe bebicʒe, selle tƿeʒen ƿið 7 feoƿer sceap ƿið anū; Gif he næbbe hƿæt he selle, sie he sylfe boht ƿiþ þā fio.

Gif þeof brece

[1] page numbered 3 [2] demeras] first e from o [3] ʒereccen] ʒerecʒan with ce above cʒ and ʒ̄tæcan above that Nw2 [4] fet for fet] ~~fæt fore fæt~~ fet for fet [5] ƿund ƿiþ ƿunde] ~~ƿiþ~~ ƿund ƿiþ ƿunde [6] above læle, liuore [7] þeoƿenne] þeoƿe'n'ne Nw2 [8] aniʒʒ̄] aniʒʒ̄ has above it luscs̄ (= luscus), almost illegible [9] ofhnite] ofhnite has above it cornu petat [10] ofƿeorpod] ofƿ'e'orpod Nw2 [11] bẏð unscyldẏʒ] bẏð unscyldẏʒ with ẏ on top of i in both words [12] hit] after hit a caret mark with he hit þonne above the line; in left margin nyste, ʒif is added before the interlinear he hit þonne Nw2 [13] ƿiste] ƿis't'e with t on del. of c [14] hine inne] ~~hine~~ hine 'inne' [15] þeoƿmennen] underlined and in left margin þeoƿne, al Nw2 [16] sie mid] 'sie' mid Nw2 [17] deadan] ~~dæ~~deadan [18] ƿiste] ƿiss't'e Nw2 [19] flæsc] f on top of one (s?)

hım ꝺomeꞃaſ ᵹeꞇæcā. Ᵹıꝼ heo ꝺeaꝺ ſẏ, ſẏlle ſaƿle ƿıþ ſaƿle. Ᵹıᵹ hƿa oþꞃū hıſ eaᵹe oþ ꝺô, ſẏlle hıſ aᵹē ꝼoꞃ: ꞇoþ ꝼoꞃ ꞇoþ, hōꝺa ꝼoꞃ hōꝺa, ꝼeꞇ ꝼoꞃ ꝼeꞇ, beꞃnınᵹ ꝼoꞃ beꞃnınᵹ, ƿúꝺ ƿıþ ƿúꝺ, læl ƿıþ læle. Ᵹıꝼ hƿa aſlea hıſ þeoƿe oþþe hıſ ðeoƿenne ꝥ eaᵹe uꞇ, ⁊ he þonne hı ᵹeꝺô anıᵹᵹe[1], ᵹeſꞃeoᵹe [Ld 21V] hı ꝼoꞃþon. Ᵹıꝼ he ðone ꞇoþ oꝼ aſlea, ꝺo ꝥ ẏlce. Ᵹıꝼ oxa oꝼhnıꞇe ƿeꞃe oþþe ƿîꝼ ꝥ he ꝺeaꝺ ſẏnꝺ, ſẏ he mıꝺ ſꞇanum oꝼƿeoꞃƿoꝺ, ⁊ ne ſẏ hıſ ꝼlæſc æꞇen; ⁊ ſe hlaꝼoꞃꝺ bẏþ unſcẏlꝺıᵹ. Ᵹıꝼ ſe oxa hnıꞇol ƿeꞃe ꞇƿam ꝺaᵹum æꞃe oþþe ðꞃẏm, ⁊ ſe hlaꝼoꞃꝺ hıꞇ nẏſꞇ, Ᵹıꝼ he hıꞇ ðonne ƿıſꞇ ⁊ hıne ınne beꞇẏnan nolꝺe, ⁊ he ðonne ƿeꞃe oþþe ƿıꝼe oꝼſloᵹe, ſẏ he mıꝺ ſꞇanum oꝼꞇoꞃꝼoꝺ, ⁊ ſẏ ſe hlaꝼoꞃꝺ oꝼſleᵹen oþþe ꝼoꞃᵹolꝺen ſƿa ꝥ ƿıꞇan ꞇo ꞃıhꞇ ꝼınꝺan. Sunu oþþe ꝺohꞇoꞃ ᵹıꝼ he oꝼſꞇınᵹe, ðæſ ẏlcan ꝺomeſ ſẏ he ƿẏꞃþe. Ᵹıꝼ he ðonne ðeoƿne oþþe ðeoƿemennen oꝼſꞇẏnᵹe, ᵹeſẏlle ðæm hlaꝼoꞃꝺ xxx ſcıll. ſeolꝼꞃeſ, ⁊ ſe oxa ſẏ mıꝺ ſꞇanum oꝼꞇoꞃꝼoꝺ. Ᵹıꝼ hƿa aꝺelꝼe ƿæꞇeꞃƿẏꞇꞇe, oþþe beꞇẏneꝺne unꞇẏne, ⁊ hıne eꝼꞇ ne beꞇẏne, ᵹẏlꝺ ſƿẏlce neaꞇ ſƿẏlce ðeꞃon beꝼealle, ⁊ hæbbe hım ꝥ ꝺeaꝺ. Ᵹıꝼ oxa oþꞃeſ monneſ oxan ᵹeƿunꝺıᵹe, ⁊ he ðonne ꝺeaꝺ ſẏ, bebẏcᵹᵹen ðone oxan ⁊ hæbben hım ꝥ ƿeoꞃþ ᵹemæne, ⁊ eac ꝥ ꝼlæſc ſƿa ðæſ ꝺeaꝺan. Ᵹıꝼ ſe hlaꝼoꞃꝺ þonne ƿıſꞇ ꝥ ſe oxa hnıꞇol ƿæꞃe, ⁊ hıne healꝺan nolꝺe, ſẏlle hım oþeꞃne oxan ꝼoꞃe ⁊ hæbbe hım ealle ꝥ ꝼlæſc. Ᵹıꝼ hƿa ꝼoꞃſꞇæle oþꞃeſ oxan ⁊ hıne oꝼſlea oþþe bebẏcᵹe, ſẏlle ꞇƿeᵹen ƿıþ ⁊ ꝼeþeꞃ ſceaƿa ƿıþ anum; Ᵹîꝼ he næbbe hƿæꞇ he ſẏlle, ſẏ he ſẏlꝼ beboht ƿıþ ðam ꝼeoh. Ᵹıꝼ ðeoꝼ bꞃece

[1] margin — al. aneᵹe

brece mannes hus nihtes, 7 he ƿeorþ þær ofsleʒen, ne sie he na mansleʒes scyldiʒ. Gif he siþþan æft̄ sunnan upʒonʒe þis deð, he biþ mansleʒes scyldiʒ, 7 he þon̄ sẏlfe ƿelte, butan he nieddæda ƿære. Gif mid[2] hī cƿicū sie funden ꝥ he ær stæl, be tƿẏfealdū forʒylde hit.

Gif hƿa ʒeƿerde oþres monnes ƿinʒeard, oþþe his æceras, oþþe his landes aƿuht, ʒebete sƿa hit mon ʒeeahtiʒe.

Gif fẏr sie ontended rẏt to bærnanne,[3] ʒ̄bete þone æfƿerdelsan se þæt[4] fyr ontent.

Gif hƿa (oþ)fæste[5] his friend fioh, ʒif he hit seolf stæle, forʒẏlde be tƿyfealdū. Gyf he nẏte hƿa hit stæle, ʒ̄ladiʒ̄ hine selfne ꝥ he þær nán[6] facn ne ʒ̄fremede. Gif hit þonne cucu[7] feoh ƿære, 7 he secʒ̄, ꝥ hit here name oþþe hit sylf acƿæle, 7 ʒeƿitnesse hæbbe, ne þearf he ꝥ ʒeldan. Gif he þon̄ ʒeƿitnesse næbbe, 7 he hī ne ʒ̄trẏƿe,[8] sƿeriʒe he þonne.

Gif hƿa fǣnan besƿice unbeƿeddode, 7 hire mid slæƿe, forʒylde hie 7 hæbbe hie siþþon hī to ƿife. Gif þære fæmnan fæder hie þon̄ sellan nelle, aʒyfe he ꝥ feoh æft̄ þā ƿeotuman.[9]

Đa fæmnan þe ʒ̄ƿunniað onfon ʒʒaldorcræftiʒan[10] 7 scinlæcan 7 ƿiccan, ne læt þu þa lybban.

7 se þe hæme mid netene,[11] sƿelt se deað.

7 se þe ʒodʒeldū[12] onsecʒ̄ ofer God ænne, sƿelte se deað.

Utancumene 7 elþeodiʒ̄ ne ʒ̄sƿenc þu no, forþon þe ʒ̄ ƿæron ʒiu[13] ælþeodiʒe on Eʒipta londe.

Þa ƿuduƿan[14] 7 þa stioƿcild ne sceaþað ʒe hi,[15] ne hie naƿer deriað. Gif ʒ̄ þonne elles doð, hie cleoƿiað to

[1] page numbered 4 [2] Gif mid] Gif ~~he~~ mid Nw2 [3] bærnanne] bærnan~~ne~~ [4] þæt] ~~ꝥ~~ þæt Nw2 [5] oþfæste] ~~oþþe~~ fæste with ~~of~~ del. over ~~þe~~ and oþ in right margin Nw2 [6] he þær nán] he ~~na~~ þær nán [7] cucu] cucu has cƿicu written above Nw2 [8] ʒ̄trẏƿe] ʒetrẏeƿe—ẏe underlined, complete word underlined, and eo above ẏe; ʒ̄trẏƿe also found in right margin Nw2 [9] ƿeotuman] has dotem above -man [10] ʒʒaldorcræftiʒan] second ʒ broadened to obliterate an e [11] netene] ~~metene~~ with netene above Nw2 [12] ʒodʒeldū] ~~ʒold~~ above ʒod Nw2 [13] ʒiu] u on top of one [14] ƿuduƿan] ~~þu~~ ƿuduƿan Nw2 [15] sceaþað ʒe hi] sceaþ'ðe'að ʒe 'hi' with ~~ði~~ in right margin and að underlined Nw2

brece mannes hûs nihtes, ⁊ wẏrþe ðær ofslægen, ne sẏ he na manslæges scẏldig ðe him sloge. Gif he sẏþþan æfter sunnan upgong ðis deþ, [Ld 22v] he biþ manslegeſ scẏldig, ⁊ he ðonne sẏlfa swẏlte, buton he nẏddæda wære. Gig mid him cwicū sẏ funden ꝥ he ær stale, be twẏfealdum forgẏld hit. Gif hwa gewerd oþres monnes wingeard, oþþe his æceras, oþþe his landes awuht, gebete swa hit mō ge eahtige. Gif fir sẏ ontended wẏþ to bærnanne, gebete ðone æfwẏrdelsan se ꝥ fẏr ontent. Gif hwa oþfæst his freond feoh, gif he hit sẏlf stæle, forgẏld be twẏfealdum. Gif he nẏte hwa hit stæle, geladige hine sẏlfne ꝥ he ðær nân facn ne gefremed. Gif hit ðonne cucu feoh wære, ⁊ he secge, ꝥ hit here name oþþe hit sẏlf acwæle, ⁊ gewitnesse hæbbe, ne ðearf he ꝥ gẏldan. Gif he ðonne gewitnesse næbbe, ⁊ he him ne getrẏwige, swerige he ðonne. Gif hwa fœmnan beswice unbeweddode, ⁊ hire mid slæpe, forgẏld hi ⁊ hæbbe hi sẏþþon him to wife. Gif ðær fœmnon fæder hi ðonne sẏllan nẏlle, agẏfe he ꝥ feoh æfter þam weotoman. Þa fœmnan ðe gewunniað onfôn galdorcræftigan ⁊ scinlæcan ⁊ wiccan, ne læt ðu ða libban. ⁊ se ðe hæme mid nẏtene, swelte se deaþ. And se ðe godgeldum onsæcge ofer god ænne, swelte se deaþ. Vtancumene ⁊ ælþeodige ne geswenc þu na, forþon þe ge wæron ælþeodige on Ægipta londe. Þa wuduwan ⁊ ða steopcilde ne sceaþæþ ge hi, ne hi na hwer deriaþ. Gif ge ðonne elles doþ, hi cleopiaþ to

-ƿiað to me, 7 ic ʒehire hie, 7 ic eoƿ þoñ slea mid minū sƿeorde; 7 ic ʒedo ꝥ eoƿru[1] ƿif beoð ƿẏdeƿan 7 eoƿru bearn beoð steopcild.

Gif þu fioh to borhe ʒ̄selle[2] þinū ʒ̄feran, þe mid þe eardian ƿille, ne nide þu þu hine sƿa sƿa niedlinʒ, 7 (ne ʒ̄hine)[3] þu hine mid þy eacan.

Gif mon næbbe buton anfeald hræʒle hine mid to ƿreone 7 to ƿerianne, 7 he hit to ƿedde selle, ǽr sunnan setlʒonʒ̄ sie hit aʒifen. Gif þu sƿa ne dest, þonne cleoƿað he to me, 7 ic hine ʒ̄hiere, forþon þe ic eom sƿiþe mildheort.

Ne tæl þu þinne Drihten, ne þone hlaford þæs folces ne ƿyrʒ þu.

Þine teoþan sceattas 7 þine frūriƿan ʒonʒendes 7 ƿeaxendes aʒif þu Gode.

Eal ꝥ flæsc[4] ꝥ ƿildeor læfen ne eten ʒe ꝥ, ac sellaþ hit hundū.

Leases mannes ƿord ne rec þu no þæs to ʒehiranne, ne his domas ne ʒ̄þafa þu, ne nane ʒeƿitnesse ne æfter hī ne saʒa þu.

Ne ƿend þu þe no on þæs folces unræd 7 unʒ̄riht ƿille on hiora spræce 7 ʒ̄clips[5] ofer þin riht, 7 on[6] þæs unƿisestan lare ne hī ne ʒeþafa.

Gif þe becume oþres mannes ʒiemeleas fioh on hand, þeah hit sie þin[7] feond, ʒecẏþe hit hī.

Dē þu sƿiþe emne.[8] Ne dem þu oþerne[9] dō þā ƿeolecʒan,[10] oþerne[11] þā earman; ne oðerne[12] þā leofron, 7 oþerne[11] þā laþran ne dē þu.

Onscuna þu a leasunʒa.

Soþfæstne man 7 unscyldiʒne ne cƿele ðu þone næfre.

Ne onfoh þu næfre medsceatū,[13] forþon hie ablendað ful oft ƿisra monna ʒ̄þoht, 7 hiora ƿord onƿendað.

Þā ælþeodiʒan 7 utancumenan ne læt þu no uncuþlice ƿið hine, ne mid nanū unrihtū þu hine ne drece.

Ne sƿerʒen ʒe næfre under hæþene ʒodas, ne on nanū þinʒū ne cleoƿiʒe[14] ʒe to hī.

---

[1] eoƿru] eoƿra with a from u [2] ʒ̄selle] 'ʒ̄'selle [3] ne nide þu þu hine sƿa sƿa niedlinʒ, 7 ne ʒ̄hine] ne niede þu þu hine sƿa sƿa niedlinʒ/ ~~7 ʒhere~~ with nide above niede, nid above nied- (both ni from m), ~~n~~ above r and in left margin ne ʒ̄hine Nw2 [4] flæsc] slæsc; first s is an f without crossbar [5] ʒ̄clips] ʒ̄clips with ep above underlined ip Nw2 [6] 7 on] 7 'on' Nw2 [7] þin] þind [8] Dē þu sƿiþe emne] dē þu sƿiþe emne: dē is underlined and in left margin is ~~deme~~, del. Nw2; the entire phrase is also underlined in the text, and in left margin is Deme þu sƿiþe riht 7 sƿiþe emne Nw2 [9] oþerne] oþ'e'rre with n over second r Nw2 [10] ƿeolecʒan] ~~ƿe~~'ƿeo'lecʒan Nw2 [11] oþerne] oþerre with n over second r Nw2 [12] oðerne] oðerre with n over second r Nw2 [13] munera in right margin Nw2 [14] cleoƿiʒe ʒe] cleo~~ƿinʒu~~ with e over i and u of cleo~~ƿinʒu~~ and ƿiʒe ʒe written below Nw2

-wiaþ to me, ⁊ ic gehire hi, ⁊ ic eowe ðonne slea mid minum sweorde; ⁊ ic gedô, ꝥ eowra [Ld 23ᵛ] wif biþ widuwan ⁊ eora bearn býþ steopcilde. Gif ðu feoh to borh gesýlle ðinum geferan, ðe mid ðe eardian wille, ne nide ðu hine swa nidling, ne gehine þu hine mid ðý eacan; gif mon næbbe butō anfeald hrægle hine mid to wreon ⁊ to werian, ⁊ he hit to wedde sýlle, ær sunnan setl gonge sý hit agýfen. Gif ðu swa ne dest, þōne cleopaþ he to me, ⁊ ic hine gehýre, forþon þe ic eom swiþe mildheort. Ne tæl[1] ðu þinne drihtē, ne þone hlaford þæs folces ne wýrge þu. Þine teoþan sceattas ⁊ þine frūripan gongendes ⁊ weaxendes agýfe ðu gode. Ealle ꝥ flæsc ðe wildeor læfen ne eten ge ꝥ, ac sýllaþ hit hundū. Leases mannes word ne rec þu na þæs to gehýranne, ne his domas ne geþafa þu, ne nân gewitnýsse æfter him ne saga ðu. Ne wend þu þe na on folces unræd ⁊ ungeriht wille on heora spræce ⁊ geclepys ofer þin riht, ⁊ on ðæs unwisestan lare ne him ne geþafa. Gif þe becume oþres mannes gýmeleas feoh on hond, þeah hit sý þin feonde, gecýþe hit him. Deme þu swiþe rihte ⁊ swiþe emne. Ne deme ðu oþerne dom ðæm weolegan, oþerne ðā earman; ne oðerne ðam leofran, ⁊ oþerne ðam laþran ne deme þu. Onscuna ðu â leasunga. Suþfæstne mā ⁊ unscýldigne ne cwæle ðone næfre. Ne onfoþ ðu næfre medsceatas, forþon hi ablendaþ ful oft wisre mōna geþeahte, ⁊ hiora word onwendaþ. Þā ælþeodigan ⁊ utancumenā ne læt ðu na uncuþlic wið hine, ne [Ld 24ᵛ] mid nanū unrihtum þu hine ne drecce. Ne swergen ge næfre under hæþene godas, ne on nanū þingum ne cleopige ge to him.

[1] margin — al. tale

ÞIS SINDAN ða domas ðe se Ælmihteȝa God self sprecende ƿæs to Moẏse, 7 hī bead to healdanne; 7 siþþā se áncenneda Drihtnes sunu, ure God, ꝥ is Halend Crist, on middanȝeard cƿō, he cƿæþ, ꝥ he ne cō no þas bebodu to brecanne[1] ne to forbeodanne, ac mid eallū ȝodū to ecanne; 7 mildheortnesse 7 eaðmodnesse[2] he lærde.

Þa æft̄ his þroƿunȝe, ær þā þe his apostolas tofarenne ƿǽron ȝeond ealle eorþan to læranne, 7 þa ȝiet þa hie ætȝædere ƿæron, moneȝa hæþena þeoda hie to God ȝ̄cerdon. Þa hie ealle ætsōne[3] ƿæron, hie sendan ærendƿrecan[4] to Antiochia 7 to Sẏrie, Cristes æ to læranne.

Þa hie þa onȝiaton ꝥ hī ne speoƿ, þa sendon hie ærendȝ̄ƿrit to hī. Þis is þoñe ꝥ ærendȝ̄ƿrit þa þa apostolas[5] sendon ealle to Antiochia, 7 to Syria, 7 to Cilicia, þa sint nu of hæþenū þeodū to Criste ȝecirde:

"Þa apostolas 7 þa eldran broþor hælo eoƿ ƿiscað; 7 eoƿ cẏþað ꝥ ƿe ȝ̄acscodon ꝥ ure ȝ̄feran sume mid urū ƿordū to eoƿ comon, 7 eoƿ hefiȝran[6] (ƿisan budon)[7] to healdanne þoñ ƿe hī budon, 7 eoƿ to spiþe ȝ̄dƿealdon mid þā maniȝfealdū ȝebodū, 7 eoƿra[8] saƿla ma forhƿerfdon þoñ hie he[9] ȝerihton. Ða ȝesomnodon ƿe us ẏmb ꝥ, 7 us eallū ȝ̄licode þa ꝥ ƿe sendon Paulus 7 Barnabān, þa men ƿilniað hiora saƿla sellan for Drihtnes naman; Mid hī ƿe sendon Iudā 7 Silā, ꝥ eoƿ ꝥ ilce secȝȝen.

Þā Halȝan Gaste ƿæs ȝ̄þuht, 7 us, ꝥ ƿe nane bẏrþene on eoƿ settan noldon ofer ꝥ ðe[10] eoƿ nedþearf ƿæs to healdenne: ꝥ (is)[11] þoñ ꝥ ȝ̄ forberen ꝥ ȝe deofolȝeld ne ƿeorþiȝen,[12] ne blod ne þicȝen ne asmorod, 7 frō diernū ȝ̄liȝerū;[13] 7 ꝥ ȝe ƿillen ꝥ oþre men eoƿ ne don, ne doð ȝe þæt oðrū monnum."

Of þis

☞

[1] brecanne] c from t with c repeated above it [2] eaðmodnesse] eaðmudnesse [3] ætsōne] ō on top of one [4] ærendƿrecan] ƿ has a crossbar on the descender, and in left margin is a d [5] apostolas] aposto~~to~~'las' [6] hefiȝran] del. of one (r?) after f Nw2 [7] ƿisan budan] in right margin Nw2 [8] eoƿra] del. of h before eoƿra [9] hie he] hie 'he' Nw2 [10] ꝥ ðe] ꝥ ~~he eðe~~ Nw2 [11] ꝥ is] ꝥ / with is in left margin Nw2 [12] ƿeorþiȝen] ƿeorþi'ȝ'en Nw2 [13] ȝ̄liȝerū] ȝ̄liȝenū with a hand in lower left margin apparently pointing to -ȝenū

Ðis sẏnd ða domas ðe se ælmihtiga god sẏlf spræcend ƿæs to moẏse ⁊ him bead to healdānne; ⁊ sẏþþan se ancenneda drẏhtenes sunu, ure god, ꝥ is hælend crist, on middan geard come, he cƿæþ, ꝥ he ne come ne þæs bebodu to brecanne ne to forbeodāne, ac mid eallum godū to eacanne; ⁊ mildheortnẏsse ⁊ eaþmodnẏsse he lærde. Þa æfter his þroƿunge, ærþam ðe his apostolas tofarēne ƿærō geond ealle eorþan to lærāne, ⁊ þa gẏt þa hi ætgædere ƿæron, monega hæþena þeode hi to god gecẏrdon. Þa hi ealle æt somne ƿæron, hi sendon ærendrecan to Antiochia ⁊ to Sẏria,[1] Cristes æ to lærāne. Þa hi þa ongẏaton ꝥ him belampe, þa sendon hi ærend geƿrit to him. Þis is þōne ærendgeƿrit þe þa apostolas sendon ealle to Antiochia, ⁊ Sẏria, ⁊ to Cilicia, þa sind nu of hæþenū þeodū to crist gecẏrd:

"Þa apostolas ⁊ þa ẏldran gebroþera hæle eoƿe ƿiscaþ; ⁊ eoƿe cẏþaþ ꝥ ƿe geahsodon ꝥ ure gefera sume mid urū ƿordū to eoƿe comon, ⁊ eoƿe hefigran ƿisan budon to healdanne þonne ƿe him budon, ⁊ eoƿe to sƿiþe gedƿealdon mid þæm mænigfealdum gebodum, ⁊ eoƿre sapla ma forhƿerfdon ðonne hi geƿihton; ða gesomnodon ƿe us ẏmb ꝥ, ⁊ us eallū gelicod þa ꝥ ƿe sendon Paulus ⁊ Bernaba, ða men ƿilmaþ [Ld 25^{v}] heora sapla sẏllan for drẏhtenes naman; Mid him ƿe sendō Iudā ⁊ silā, ꝥ hi eoƿe ꝥ ẏlce secgan. Þā halgā gast ƿæs geþuht, ⁊ us, ꝥ ƿe nane bẏrþē on eoƿe settā noldō ofer ꝥ þe eoƿe ned þearf ƿæs to healdāne: ꝥ þōne ꝥ ge forberē ꝥ ge deofulgẏld ne ƿeorþigē, ne blôd ne þicgē ne asmorod, ⁊ frā dẏrnū geligerū; ⁊ ꝥ ge ƿillē ꝥ oþre men eoƿe ne don, ne doþ ge ꝥ oþrū monnū. On þis-

[1] errata — Post Sẏria interpone hæc verba: ⁊ to Cilicia

Of þissū anū dome mon mæʒ ʒ̄þencean, ꝥ he æʒhƿelcre on ryht ʒ̄demeð; ne þearf he nanra domboca oþerra. Geþence he ꝥ he nanū men ne deme ꝥ he nolde ꝥ he hī demede, Gif he þone dom ofer hine sohte.

Siþþan ꝥ, ʒelāp ꝥ maneʒa þeoda Cristes ʒ̄leafan onfenʒon,[1] þa ƿurdon moneʒa seonoþas ʒeond ealne middanʒeard ʒ̄ʒaderode, 7 eac sƿa ʒeond Anʒelcyn, siþþan hie Cristes ʒeleafan onfenʒon, haliʒra bisceopa 7 eac oþerra ʒeþunʒenra ƿitena; hie þa ʒ̄setton, for þære mildheortnesse þe Crist lærde, æt mæstra hƿelcre misdæde ꝥte þa ƿeoruldhlafordas moston mid heora leafan butan synne æt þǣ forman ʒylte þære feohbote onfon, þe hie þa ʒesettan; buton æt hlafordsearƿe hie nane mildheortnesse ne dorston[2] ʒecƿeðan, forþon þe God Ælmihtiʒ þā nane ne ʒ̄demde þe hine oferhoʒdon, ne Crist, Godes sunu, þā nā ne ʒedemde þe hine to deaþe sealde, 7[3] he bebead[4] þone hlaford lufian sƿa hine.

Hie þa on moneʒū seonoþū moneʒra menniscra misdæda bote ʒesetton,
7 on moneʒa senoðbéc hie ƿritan, hƿær ænne dom, hƿær oþerne.[5]

Ic þa Ælfred cyninʒ þæs toʒædere ʒeʒaderode, 7 aƿritan het, moniʒ þara þe ure foreʒenʒan heoldon,[6] (þa þe me licodon; 7) þa þe me ne licodon[7] ic aƿearp, mid minra ƿitena ʒeþeahte, 7 on oþre ƿisan bebead to healdanne. Forþā ic ne dorst ʒ̄þristlæcan þæra[8] minra aƿuht feala on ʒ̄ƿrit settan, forþā me ƿæs un

[1] onfenʒon] f from s [2] dorston] dor's'ton Nw2 [3] 7] followed by del. of b [4] bebead] 'be'bead Nw2 [5] oþerne] oþerre [6] heoldon] heoldon / with þa þe me licodon 7 in left margin Nw2 [7] ne licodon] 'ne' licodon [8] þæra] þæra ~~þara~~

On þissū anū dome mō mæge geþēnceā, ꝥ he æghƿelcne on riht gedemeþ; ne þearfe he nāra oþerra. Geþence he ꝥ he nanū mē ne deme ꝥ he nolde ꝥ he him demed, gif he ðone dome ofer hine sohte. Sýþþan ꝥ, gelāp ꝥ manega þeoda cristes geleafā onfēgō, þa ƿurdō maniga seonoþas geōd ealne middāgeard gegaderod, ⁊ eac sƿa geond angelcýn, sýþþā hi cristes geleafā onfēgō, haligra biscepa ⁊ eac oþera geþungēra ƿitena; hi þa gesettō, for þær mildheortnýsse þe crist lærde, æt mæstra hƿýlcra misdæde ꝥ þa ƿoruld hlafordas mostō mid heora leafā butā sýnne æt þæm forman gýlt þær feoh bôt onfôn, þe hi þa gesettō; buton æt hlaford searƿe on þæm hi nane mildheortnesse ne dorston ge cƿeþan, forþan þe god ælmihtig þā nane ne gedemed þe hine oferhogdon, Ne crist, godes sunu, þam nane ne gedemde ðe hine to deaþ sealde, ⁊ he bebead ðone hlaford lufian sƿa hine sýlfne. Hi ða on monegum seonoþum monegra menniscra misdæda bote gesettō, ⁊ on monega senoþbêc hi aƿritan hetton, hƿær ænne dom, hƿær oþerne.

[Ld 26v] Ic ða Ælfred cýning þæs togæder gegaderod, ⁊ aƿritan het, monega ðara ðe ure foregengan heoldon, ða þe me licodon; ⁊ ða ðe me ne licodon ic aƿearp, mid minra ƿitena geþeahte, ⁊ on oþre ƿisan bebead to healdāne; forþam ic ne dorste gedýrstlæcan þæra minra aƿuht feala on geƿrita settan, forþan me ƿæs un-

ƿæs uncuþ hƿæt þæs þā lician ƿolde þe æfter us ƿæren; ac þa þe ic ȝmette aƿðer, oþþe on Ines dæȝe,[1] mines mæȝes, oþþe on Offan Mẏrcna cyninȝes, oþþe on Æþelbirhtes, þe ærest fulƿiht underfenȝ on Anȝelcẏnne,[2] þa þe me rẏhtost þuhton, ic þa heron ȝȝaderode, 7 þa oþre forlet.

Ic þa Ælfred, Ƿesseaxna cẏninȝ, eallū minū ƿitū þæs ȝeeoƿde,[3] 7 hie þa cƿædon ꝥ hī ꝥ licode eallū to healdanne.

THE LAW OF ALFRED

ii.

Æt ærestan ƿe lærað ꝥ mæst þearf is: þæt æȝhƿelc mon his að 7 his ƿed ƿerlic healde.

Gif hƿa to hƿæþeru þissa[4] ȝenyd sie on ƿoh,[5] oþþe to hlafordsearƿe oþþe to æniȝū unrẏhtū fultume, ꝥ is þon̄ ryhtre to aleoȝanne þon̄ to ȝlæstanne.[6]

Gif he þon̄ þæs ƿeddiȝ þe hī riht sie to ȝlæstanne, 7 ꝥ aleoȝ, sylle mid eaðmedū his ƿæpn 7 his æhta his freondū to ȝhealdanne, 7 beo feoƿertiȝ nihta on carcerne on cẏninȝes tune; þroƿiȝ þær sƿa bisceop hī scrife, 7 his maȝas hine fedan, ȝif he sylf mete næbbe.

Gif he maȝas næbbe, oþþe þone mete næbbe, fede cẏninȝes ȝerefa hine.

Gif hine mon toȝenedan scẏle, 7 he elles nẏlle,[7] ȝif hine mon ȝbinde, þoliȝ his ƿæpna 7 his ẏrfes.

Gif hine mon ofslea, liȝȝ he orȝilde.

Gif he ut oþfleo ær þā fẏrst, 7 hine mon ȝfo, sie he feoƿertiȝ nihta on[8] carcerne, sƿa he ær sceolde.

Gif he losiȝe, sie he aflȳmed, 7 sie amensumod of eallū Cristes ciricū.

Gif þær þon̄e oþer mennisc borh sie, bete þone borh

[1] Ines dæȝe] corrected from mesdæȝe [2] Anȝelcynne] el crossed out by two strokes; does Nw? intend anȝlecynne? [3] ȝeeoƿde] ȝe~~eode~~eoƿde [4] þissa] þisse'a' with a in left margin also [5] iniuste above on ƿoh [6] implere above ȝlæstanne [7] nylle] y from i [8] nihta on] nihta ~~þā fẏrste 7 hine mon ȝfá sie~~ on

ƿæꞅ uncuþ hƿæꞇ þæꞅ þæm lician ƿolꝺe ðe æꝼꞇeꞃ uꞅ ƿæꞃen; Ac þa þe ic ᵹemeꞇꞇe ahƿæꞃ, oþþe on Ineꞅ ꝺæᵹe, mineꞅ mæᵹeꞅ, oþþe on Oꝼꝼā mẏꞃcna cẏninᵹeꞅ, oþþe on Æþelbẏꞃhꞇeꞅ, þe æꞃeꞅꞇ ꝼulƿihꞇ unꝺeꞃꝼenᵹ on anᵹelcẏnne, ða þe me ꞃihꞇoꞅꞇ þuhꞇon,

ic þa heꞃon ᵹeᵹaꝺeꞃoꝺ, ⁊ þa oþꞃe ꝼoꞃlæꞇe. Ic ða
Ælꝼꞃeꝺ, ƿeꞅꞇeaxna cẏninᵹ, eallū minū ƿiꞇum
þæꞅ ᵹeeoƿꝺe, ⁊ hi þa cƿæþon, ꝥ him ꝥ lico-
ꝺe eallum ꞇo healꝺenne.

THE LAW OF ALFRED

Be aþum ⁊ be ƿeꝺꝺum.

Cap. 1 Æꞇ æꞃeꞅꞇan ƿe læꞃaþ ꝥ mæꞅꞇ þeaꞃꝼ iꞅ: ꝥ æᵹhƿẏlce mon hiꞅ âþ ⁊ hiꞅ ƿeꝺ[1] ƿæꞃlic healꝺe.

Ᵹif hƿa ꞇo hƿæþeꞃum þiꞅꞅum ᵹenẏꝺ ꞅẏ on ƿoh, oþþe ꞇo hlaꝼoꞃꝺe ꞅẏꞃƿe oþþe ꞇo ænigum unꞃihꞇum ꝼulꞇume, ꝥ iꞅ þonne ꞃihꞇꞃe ꞇo aleoᵹanne ðonne ꞇo ᵹelæꞅꞇanne. Ᵹif he ðonne ðæꞅ ƿeꝺꝺiᵹe ðe [Ld 27v] him ꞃihꞇ ꞅẏ ꞇo ᵹelæꞅꞇāne, ⁊ ꝥ aleoᵹe, ꞅẏlle miꝺ eaꝺmoꝺum hiꞅ ƿæpn ⁊ hiꞅ æhꞇa hiꞅ ꝼꞃeonꝺum ꞇo ᵹehealꝺanne, ⁊ beo ꝼeoƿeꞃꞇiᵹ nihꞇa on caꞃceꞃne on cẏninᵹeꞅ ꞇûn; ðꞃoƿiᵹe ðæꞃ ꞅƿa biꞅceop him ꞅcꞃiꝼe, ⁊ hiꞅ mæᵹaꞅ hine ꝼeꝺan, ᵹif he ꞅẏlꝼ meꞇe næbbe. Ᵹif he maᵹaꞅ næbbe, oþþe ðone meꞇe næbbe, ꝼeꝺe cẏninᵹeꞅ ᵹeꞃeꝼa hine. Ᵹif hine mon ꞇo ᵹenẏꝺan ꞅcẏle, ⁊ he elleꞅ nẏlle, ᵹif hine mon ᵹebinꝺe, ðoliᵹe hiꞅ ƿæpna ⁊ hiꞅ ẏꞃꝼeꞅ. Ᵹif hine mon oꝼꞅlea, licᵹe he oꞃᵹẏlꝺ. Ᵹiᵹ he ûꞇ oþꝼleo æꞃ þæm ꝼẏꞃꞅꞇ, ⁊ hine mon ᵹeꝼô, ꞅẏ he ꝼeoꞃꞃꞇiᵹ nihꞇa on cæꞃceꞃne, ꞅƿa he æꞃ ꞅceolꝺe. Ᵹif he loꞅiᵹe, ꞅẏ he aꝼlẏmeꝺ, ⁊ ꞅẏ amanꞅumoꝺ oꝼ eallum cꞃiꞅꞇeꞅ cẏꞃicum. Ᵹif ðæꞃ ðōne oþeꞃ menniꞅc boꞃh ꞅẏ, beꞇe ðone boꞃh-

[1] margin — Sonaꞇ eꞇiā ƿeꝺ ꝼiꝺem ꝺaꞇam

borhbryce spa hī riht pisiȝ̄, 7 þone peddebrice spa hī his scrift scrife.

iii. Be cyrecena socnū.[1]

Gif hpa þara mẏnsťhama hpelcne[2] for hpelcere scẏlde[3] ȝ̄sece hpilne þe cẏninȝes feorm to belimpe, oððe oþerre frione hyred þe arpyrþe sie, aȝe he þreora nihta first hī to ȝ̄beorȝanne, butan he þinȝian pille.

Gif hine[4] mon on þā firste ȝeẏfliȝe mid sleȝe oððe mid bende oþþe[5] þurh punde, bete þǣra[6] æȝhpelc mid rihte þeodscipe, ȝ̄ mid pere ȝ̄ mid pite, 7 þā hipū[7] hundtpelftiȝ[8] sciƚƚ, ciricfriþes to bote, 7 hæbbe his aȝene forfonȝen.[9]

iiii. Be borhbryce.[1]

Gif hpa cẏninȝes borh abrece,[10] ȝ̄bete þone tẏht spa hī riht pisiȝ̄, 7 þæs borȝes brice mid v pundū mærra peninȝa. Arcebisceopes[11] borȝes bryce, oþþe his mundbẏrd, ȝ̄bete mid þrȳ pundū. Oþres bisceopes oþþe ealdormannes borȝes bryce[3] oþþe mundbyrd ȝebete mid tpā pundū.

v. Be hlafordsyrpe.[1]

Gif hpa ẏmb cẏninȝ feorh sierpe, þurh hine oþþe þurh precena[12] feormunȝe oþþe his manna, sie he his feores scẏldiȝ 7 ealles þæs ðe he aȝe.

Gif he hine sielfne triopan pille, do ꝥ be cyninȝes perȝylde.

Spa pe eac settaþ be eallū hadū, ȝ̄ ceorle ȝ̄ eorle: se þe ȳb his hlafordes fiorh sẏrpe, sie he piþ þone his feores scẏldiȝ 7 ealles þæs þe he aȝe; oþþe be his hlafordes pere ȝetriope.

vi. Be cyrccena friþe.[1]

Eac pe settaþ æȝhpelcre cirican þe bisceop ȝ̄halȝode þis fryþ: ȝif hie fahmon[13] ȝ̄ẏrne oþþe[14] ȝ̄ærne,

[1] rubrics inserted into text Nw2 [2] hpelcne] ~~hpelcéne~~ [3] scylde] y from i [4] hine] hine ~~þǣ~~ [5] oþþe] oþþe ~~mid~~ [6] þæra] e of æ del. [7] hipū] ȝ above p Nw2 [8] hundtpelftiȝ] on above f Nw2 [9] hæbbe ... forfonȝen underlined Nw2 [10] abrece] 'a'brece Nw2 [11] Arcebisceopes] arcebisce'o'pes [12] precena] pre~~ce~~cena [13] factiosus above fahmon [14] oþþe] oþþe ~~oþþe~~

borhbrẏce sƿa him riht ƿisige, ⁊ ðone ƿedde brẏce sƿa him his scrift scrife.

Be cẏricena socnum.

2 Gif hƿa ðæra mẏnster hama for hƿẏlcre scẏlde gesece ðe ne cẏninges feorme to belimpe, oþþe oþerne frione hẏred ðe ærƿẏrþ sẏ, age he þreora nihta fẏrst him to gebeorganne, butan he ðingian ƿille. Gif hine mon on ðæm fẏrste geẏflige mid slege oððe mid bende oþþe ðurh ƿunde, gebete ðæra æghƿẏlc mid riht ðeodscipe, ge mid ƿere [Ld 28V] ge mid ƿite, ⁊ ðam hiƿum hund tƿelftig scill., cẏricfriþes to bôt.[1]

Be borhbrẏce.

3 Gif hƿa cẏninges borh brece, gebete þone tẏht sƿa him riht ƿisige, ⁊ ðæs borges brẏce mid v pūdum mæra[2] peninga. Ærcebisceopes borhbrẏce, oþþe his mundbrẏce, gebete mid ðrẏm pundum; oþres bisceopes oþþe ealdormannes borgesbrẏce oþþe mund brẏce gebete mid tƿam pundum.

Be hlaford sẏrƿe.

4 Gif hƿa ẏmb cẏninges feorh sẏrƿe, ðurh hine oþþe þurh ƿreccena feormunge oþþe his manna, sẏ he his feores scẏldig ⁊ ealles ðæs ðe he age. Gîf he hine sẏlfne treoƿian ƿille, dô ꝥ be cẏninges ƿergẏlde. Sƿa ƿe eac settaþ be eallum hadum, ge ceorle ge eorle: se ðe ẏmb his hlafordes feorh sẏrƿe, sẏ he ƿiþ ðone his feores scẏldig ⁊ ealles ðæs ðe he age; oþþe be his hlafordes ƿere getreoƿe.

Be cẏricena friþe.

5 Eac ƿe settaþ æghƿẏlcre cẏrican ðe bisceop gehalgode ðis friþe: gif hi gefahmon geẏrne,

Nw2 rubrics inserted into CN [1] Nw2 inserts 7 hæbbe his aȝene forfonȝen into CN; Ld and Quadr. omit
[2] margin — al. mærcna. Sonat etiā mundbrẏce, læsæ dignitatis crimen.

ʒærne, þ hine seofan nihtū nan mon ut ne teo. Gif hit þoñ hpa dó, þoñ sie he scyldiʒ cẏninʒs mundbyrde[1] 7 þære cirican fryþes; mare ʒif he þær mare ofʒefo—Gif he for hunʒre libban mæʒe, buton he seolf[2] utfeohte.

Gif hipan[3] hiora cirican maran þearf hæbben,[4] healde hine mon on oþrū ærne,[5] 7 þ næbbe þoñ ma dura þoñ sio cirice; ʒepite þær cirican ealdor þ hī mon on þā fyrste mete ne sylle.

Gif he self his pæpno his ʒfan[6] utræccan pille, ʒhealden hie hine þrittiʒ nihta, 7 hie hine his mæʒū ʒbodien.

Eac cirican friþ: ʒif hpylc mon cirican ʒyrne for þara ʒylta hpilcū þara þe ær ʒẏpped nære, 7 hine ðær on Godes noman ʒandette, sie hit healf forʒyfen.

Se þe stalað on Sunnanniht oþþe on Gehhol oþþe on[7] Eastron oððe on þone halʒan (Þunres)dæʒ[8] on ʒanʒdaʒas, þara ʒhpelc pe pillað sie tpẏbote, spa on Lenctenfæsten.

vii. Be cyrecena stale.[9]

Gif hpa on cirican hpæt[10] ʒþeofiʒ, forʒẏlde þ anʒẏlde, 7 þ pite spa to þā anʒylde belȳpan pille, 7 slea mon þa hand of þe he hit mid dide.

Gif he þa hand lesan pille,[11] 7 hī mon þæt ʒeþafian pille, ʒelde spa to his pere belȳpe.

viii. Be þoñe þe mon on cynīʒes healle ʒefeoht.[9, 12]

Gif hpa in cẏninʒes healle ʒefeohte, oþþe his pæpn ʒbrede, 7 hine mon ʒfó, sie þ on cyninʒes dome, spa deað spa lif, spa he hī forʒifan pille.

[1] fractione pacis above mundbyrde [2] after seolf a space for two or three left blank [3] editui above hipan [4] hæbben] a altered to e [5] domo above ærne [6] inimicis above ʒ—fán [7] on] oné [8] on þone halʒan Þunresdæʒ] on þone "dæʒ halʒan Þunres" with Þunresdæʒ in right margin Nw2 [9] rubrics Nw2 [10] hpæt] hpæʒ't' [11] redimere uelit added above lesan pille [12] Be ... ʒefeoht] be borh bryce Nw2 del. with Be ... ʒefeoht in right margin Nw2

geýrne, ꝥ hine seofan nihtum nân man ut ne teo. Gif hit ðonne hƿa dô, ðonne sý he scildig cýninges mundbýrd ⁊ ðære cýricean friþes; mare gif he ðær mare ofgefô—gif he for hungre libban mæge, buton [Ld 29^{V}] he sýlf ut feohte. Gif hiƿan heora cýricean mare ðearf hæbben, heald hine mon on oþrum hûs, ⁊ ꝥ næbbe ðonne ma ðura ðonne seo cýrice; Geƿite ðære cýricean ealdor ꝥ him mon on ðæm fýrst mete ne sýlle. Gif he sýlf his ƿæpnu his gefân utƿæcan ƿille, gehealdan hi hine ðrittig nihta, ⁊ hi hine his mægum gebeoden. Eac cýricean friþe is: gif hƿýlce man cýricean gesece for ðæra gýlta hƿýlcum ðæra ðe ær ge ýppeð nære, ⁊ hine ðær on godes naman geondette, sý hit healf forgýfen.

Be cýricena stale.

6 Gif hƿa on cýricean hƿæt geþeofige, forgýld ꝥ angýlde, ⁊ ꝥ ƿite sƿa to ðæm angýlde belýmpan ƿille, ⁊ slea mon ða hand of ðe he hit mid gedýde. Gif he ða hand lýsan ƿýlle, ⁊ him mon ꝥ geþafian ƿille, gýlde sƿa to his ƿere belimpe. Se ðe stalaþ on sunnan niht oþþe on geol oþþe on eastron oþþe on ðone halgan ðunres dæge ⁊ on gang dagas, ðæra gehƿýlce ƿe ƿillaþ sý tƿýbôt, sƿa on lencten fæsten.[1]

Be ðon ðe mon on cýninges healle gefeohte.

7 Gif hƿa on cýninges healle gefeohte, oððe his ƿæpne gebrede, hine mon gefô, ⁊ sý ꝥ on cýninges dome, [Ld 30^{V}] sƿa deaþ sƿa lif, sƿa he him forgýfan ƿille.

Nw2 rubrics inserted into CN [1] Se ðe stalaþ...lencten fæsten found at end of 5 in other MSS, including CN

ƿille.

Gif he losiʒe, 7 hine món eft ʒ̄fo, forʒylde he hine selfne be[1] his ƿerʒylde, 7 þone ʒilt ʒebete, sƿa ƿer sƿa ƿite, sƿa he ʒeƿyrht aʒe.

ix.[2] Be nunnan hæmede.[3]

Gif hƿa nunnan of mẏnstre ut alæde butan cẏninʒes lefnesse oþþe bisceopes, ʒ̄selle hundtƿelftiʒ sciłł: healf cẏninʒ, healf bisceope 7 þære cirican hlaforde þe[4] þone munuc aʒe.

Gif hio lenʒ lybbe þonne se þe hi utlædde, naʒe hio his yrfes oƿiht.

Gif hio bearn ʒestryne, næbbe ꝥ þæs ierfes þon mare þe sio[5] modor.

Gif hire bearn mon ofslea, ʒylde cẏninʒe þara medrenmæʒa dæl; fæderenmæʒū[6] hiora dæl mon aʒife.

x. Be bearneacnum ƿife ofsleʒenum.[7]

Gif[8] mon ƿif mid bearn ofslea, þonne ꝥ bearn in hire sie, forʒylde þonne ƿifman fullan ʒylde, 7 ꝥ bearn be þæs fædrencnosles ƿere healfan ʒylde.

Á sie ꝥ ƿíte sixti sciłł, oþ ꝥ anʒyld arise to þrittiʒū sciłł; siþþan hit to þā aríse ꝥ anʒylde, siþþan sie ꝥ ƿite hundtƿelftiʒ sciłł.

Geo[9] ƿæs ʒoldþeofe 7 stodðeofe[10] 7 beoþeofe, 7 maniʒ ƿitu, maran þonne oþru; nu sint eal ʒelic butan manþeofe: cxx sciłł.

xi. Be forleʒerum.[7]

Gif mon hæme[11] mid tƿelfhyndes monnes ƿífe, hundtƿelftiʒ sciłł ʒebete þā ƿere; sixhundū men, hundteontiʒ[12] sciłł ʒebete; cyrliscū men, feoƿertiʒ sciłł ʒebete.

xii. Be cyrliscre fæmnan onfēʒ.[3]

Gif mon on cirliscre fæmnan breost ʒefeo, mid[13] v sciłł hire ʒebete.

Gif he hie oferƿeorƿe 7 mid ne ʒ̄hæme, mid x sciłł ʒebete.

Gif he mid ʒ̄-

[1] á del. before be [2] v del. before ix [3] rubrics in left margin Nw2 [4] þe] be [5] þenne above þe sio Nw2 [6] fæderenmæʒū] fæd'e'renmæʒū [7] rubrics Nw2 [8] Gif] Gif ~~hiora~~ [9] ʒeo has iu over eo [10] equi siluestres above stodðeofe [11] hæme] hé'æ'me [12] hundteontiʒ] hund~~ƿe~~teontiʒ [13] mid] ~~mid~~ mid

ƿille. Gif he losige, ⁊ hine mon eft gefô, forgýlde he hine sýlfne be his ƿergýld, ⁊ ðone gýlt gebete, sƿa ƿere sƿa ƿite, sƿa he geƿýrht age.

Be ðam ðe nunnan of minster ût alædaþ.

8 Gif hƿa nunnan of mýnstre ût alæde butan cýninges leafe oþþe bisceopes, gesýlle hundtƿentig scill.: healf cýninge, healf bisceope ⁊ þær cýrice hlaforde ðe ða nunnan age. Gif heo leng libbe ðonne se ðe heo ut læde, nage heo ýrfes naƿiht. Gif heo bearn gestrýne, næbbe ꝥ ðær ýrfes na mare þonne seo modor. Gif mon hire bearn ofslea, gýlde cýning ðæra medra maga dæl; fædran mægum heora dæl mon agýfe.

Be ðon ðe mon ofslea bearn eacnend ƿif.

9 Gif mon ƿîf mid bearn ofslea, ðonne ꝥ bearn in hire sý, forgýlde ðone ƿif mon fullan gýlde, ⁊ ꝥ bearn be ðæs fædren cnosles ƿere healfan gýlde; â sý ꝥ ƿite sýxtig scill., oþ ꝥ angýlde arise to þrittigū scill.; Sýþþan hit to þæm arise ꝥ angýld, sýþþan sý ꝥ ƿite hund tƿelftig scill. Hƿilon ƿæs gold þeofe ⁊ stodþeof ⁊ beoþeof, ⁊ manig ƿitu, maran ðonne oþru; nu sýnd ealle gelice butan manðeof: hund tƿelftig scill.

[Ld 31v] Be forlegerum.

10 Gif mon hæme mid tƿelfhindes monnes ƿif, hund tƿelftig scill. gebete ðæm ƿere; Sýxhýndū men, hund teontig scill. gebete; Ceorliscum men, feoƿertigum scill.; And ꝥ sý on cƿýc æhtum feo godum ⁊ mon nænigne mon on ꝥ ne sýlle.[1]

11 Gif mon on ceorlisce fœmnan breost gefô, mid fif scill. hire gebete. Gif he hi ofer ƿeorpe ⁊ mid ne gehæme,[2]

Nw2 rubrics inserted into CN, including one for 11 which is absent from Ld [1] And ꝥ ... sýlle found here in Ld instead of in 18 [2] errata — Post gehæme interpone mid týn scill. gebete. Gif he mid gehæme

mid ȝehæme, mid lx sciłł ȝebete.

Gif oþer mon mid hire læȝe ǽr, sie be healfū þǣ þoñ sio bot.

Gif hie mon teo, ȝeladie hie be sixteȝū hida, oþþe þoliȝe be healfne þære bote.

Gif borenran (ƿifmen)[1] þis ȝelympe, ƿeaxe sio bot be þā ƿere.

xiii. Be ƿudubærnete.[2]

Gif mon oþres ƿudu bærneð oþþe heaƿeð unalifedne, forȝielde ælc ȝreat treoƿ mid v sciłł, 7 siþþan æȝhhẏlc[3] sie sƿa feala[4] sƿa hiora sie mid v peninȝū, 7 xxx sciłł to ƿite.

Gif mon oþre æt ȝemænan ƿeorce offylle unȝeƿealdes,[5] aȝyfe mon þā mæȝū ꝥ treoƿ, 7 hie hit hæbben ær xxx nihta of þā lande, oþþe hī fo to se þe þone ƿudu áȝe.

xiiii. Be dumbra monna dædū.[2]

Gif mon sie dumb oþþe deafe ȝboren, ꝥ he ne mæȝ sinna onsecȝan ne ȝeondettan, bete se fæder his misdæda.

xv. Be þam þe beforan biscepū feohtað.[2]

Gif mon beforan arcebisceope ȝfeohte oþþe ƿæpne ȝbrede, mid l scill 7 hundteonteȝū ȝbete.[6] Gif beforan oðrū bisceope oþþe ealdorm̄ þis ȝlimp, mid hundteonteȝū sciłł ȝbete.

Gif mon cú oþþe stodmẏran forstele, 7 folan oþþe cealf ofadryfe, forȝelde mid sciłł, 7 þa modor be heora ƿeorþe.

Gif hƿa oþrū his unmaȝa oþfæste, 7 he hine on þære fæstinȝe forferie, ȝetrioƿe hine facnes se þe hine fede, ȝif hine hƿa hƿelces teo.

xvi. Be nunnena onfēȝ.[7]

Gif hƿa nunnan mid hæmeðþinȝe oþþe on hire hræȝl[8] oþþe on hire breost butan hire leafe ȝfó, sie

[1] ƿifmen] "men" ƿif, underlined, with ƿifmen in right margin Nw2 [2] rubrics Nw2 [3] æȝhhẏlc] ẏ from i [4] feala] feala with moniȝ written above Nw2 [5] offylle unȝeƿealdes] offylle'ð' unȝeƿeal'l'des with casu above Nw2 [6] scill 7 hundteonteȝū ȝbete] sciłł "ȝbete" 7 hundteonteȝū [7] rubric in right margin Nw2 [8] hræȝl] hræȝlé

mid lx scill. gebete. Gif oþer man mid hire læge ær, sẏ be healfum þæm þonne seo bôt. Gif hi mon teo, geladige hi be sixtegū hidum, oþþe ðolige be healfre þære bote. Gif æþelborenran ƿifman ðis gelẏmpe, ƿeaxe seo bôt be ðæm ƿere.

Be ƿudu bærnette.

12 Gif mon oþres ƿudu bærneþ oþþe heaƿeþ unalẏfedne, forgẏlde ælc great treoƿe mid fif scill., ⁊ sẏþþan æghƿẏlc sẏ sƿa feala sƿa heora sẏ mid v peningum, ⁊ ðrittig scill. to ƿite.

Be ðon ðe mon oþerne offẏlle.

13 Gif mon oþerne æt gemænan ƿeorc offẏlleþ ungeƿealdes, agẏfe mon ðæm magum ꝥ treoƿe, ⁊ hi hit hæbben ær ðrittig nihta of ðæm lande, oþþe him fô to se þe þone ƿudu age.

[Ld 32v] Be dumbra manna dædum.

14 Gif mon sẏ dumb oþþe deaf geboren, ꝥ he ne mæge his sẏnna geondettan ne onsecgan, bete se sæder[1] his misdæda.

Be gefeohtum.

15 Gif mon beforan ærcebisceope gefeohte oþþe ƿæpne gebrede, mid fiftigum scill. ⁊ hund teontegum gebete. Gif beforan oþrum bisceop oþþe ealdorman ðis gelimpe, mid hund teontegum scill. gebete.

Be ðon ðe mon mẏre oþ cû forstele.

16 Gif mon cû oþþe mẏre forstele, ⁊ folan oþþe cealf of adrife, forgẏlde mid feorƿrtigum scill.; ⁊ ða modor be heora ƿẏrþe.

Be ðon ðe oþru his unmagum oþfæsteþ.

17 Gif hƿa oþrum his unmagum oþfæste, ⁊ he hine on ðere fæstinge forferie, getrẏƿige hine facnẏsse se ðe hine fede, gif hƿa hƿẏlces teo.

Be nunnena onfeng.

18 Gif hƿa nunnan mid hæmed ðinge oþþe on hire hrægl oþþe on hire breost butan hire læfe gefô, sẏ

CN rubrics all from Nw2 and not identical to those in Ld. CN/Nw2 no rubrics for Ld 13, 16, 17 (from B) [1] errata — sæder lege fæder ʒfo, sie hit tƿẏbete sƿa ƿe ær be lerdū men fúndon.

Gif beƿeddedu fæmne hie forlicȝe, ȝif hio sie cirlisc,[1] mid lx sciłł ʒbete þā birȝean;[2] 7 ꝥ sie on cƿicæhtū[3] feoȝodū, 7 mon næniȝne mon on ꝥ ne selle.

Gif hio þonne sie sixhindu, hundteontiȝ sciłł ȝeselle þā bẏrȝean.[4]

Gif hio sie tƿelfhyndu,[5] hundtƿelfti sciłł ʒbete þā byrȝean.

xvii. Be ƿæpn lænum.[6]

Gif hƿa his ƿæpnes oþrū onlæne, þæt he mon mid ofslea, hie moton hie ʒsōnian ȝif hie ƿillaþ to þǣ ƿere.

Gif hi hie ne ʒsōnien, ȝylde[7] se þæs ƿæpnes onláȝ þæs ƿeres þriddan dæl, 7 þæs ƿites þriddan dæl.

Gif he hine trieƿan ƿille ꝥ he to þære læne facn ne ƿiste, ꝥ he mot.

Gif sƿeordhƿita[8] oþres monnes ƿæpn to feormunʒ onfó, oþþe smið monnes andƿeorc, hie hit ȝesund beȝen aȝyfan, sƿa hit hƿæðer heora ær onfenȝe, buton hiora hƿæðer ær þinȝode ꝥ he hit anȝylde healdan ne þorfte.

xviii. Be þam þe munecū feoh aþ befæstað.[6]

Gif mon oþres monnes munuce feoh oþfæste butan þæs munuces hlafordes leofnesse,[9] 7 hit hī losiȝe, þoliȝe his se þe hit ær ahte.

xix. Be preosta ȝefeohte.[6]

Gif preost oþerne mon ofslea, ƿeorƿe mon to handa 7 eal ꝥ he hī mid hames bohte, 7 hine bisceop onhadie þoñ hine mon of þǣ mẏnstre aȝife, butan se hlaford þone ƿer forþinȝian ƿill.

xx. Be eofotes andetlan.[6]

Gif mon on folces ȝemote cyninȝes ȝerefan ȝeẏppe eofot,[10] 7 his eft ʒspican ƿille, ʒstæle on ryh-

[1] cirlisc] cir'l'isc, with s on top of one [2] marito above birȝean [3] cƿicæhtū] cƿicæ'h'htū [4] marito above byrȝoan [5] tƿelfhyndu] tƿelfh'y'ndu with y from i [6] rubrics Nw2 [7] ȝylde] ẇ ȝylde [8] sƿeordhƿita] sƿeorthƿita [9] leofnesse] le'o'fnesse Nw2 [10] eofot is underlined

ᵹeꝼô, ꞅẏ hıꞇ ꞇƿẏbôꞇ ꞅƿa ƿe æꞃ be læƿeꝺum men ꝼunꝺon.[1]

Be ðon ðe heoꞃa ƿæpne lænaþ ꞇo manꞅlıhꞇ.

19 Ᵹıꝼ hƿa hıꞅ ƿæpne oþꞃum læne, ꝥ he mıꝺ man oꝼꞅlea, hı moꞇon hı ᵹeꞅomnıan ᵹıꝼ hı ƿıllaþ ꞇo ðæm ƿeꞃe. Ᵹıꝼ hı hı ne ᵹeꞅomnıan, ᵹẏlꝺe ꞅe ðæꞅ ƿæpneꞅ [Ld 33v] on lænꝺe ðæꞅ ƿeꞃeꞅ þꞃıꝺꝺa ꝺæle. Ᵹıꝼ he hıne ꞇꞃẏƿıan ƿılle ꝥ he ꞇo þæꞃe læne ꝼacne nẏꞅꞇe, ꝥ he moꞇ; ᵹıꝼ ꞅƿeoꞃꝺ hƿıꞇa oþꞃeꞅ manneꞅ ƿæpne ꞇo ꝼeoꞃmunᵹe unꝺeꞃꝼô, oþþe ꞅmıþ manneꞅ anꝺƿeoꞃc, hı hıꞇ ᵹeꞅunꝺ beᵹen aᵹẏꝼen, ꞅƿa hıꞇ hƿæþeꞃ heoꞃa æꞃ unꝺeꞃꝼenᵹe, buꞇon heoꞃa hƿæþeꞃ æꞃ ðınᵹoꝺe ꝥ he hıꞇ anᵹẏlꝺe healꝺan ne ðoꞃꝼꞇe.

Be ðam ðe munecum ꝼeoh beꝼæꞅꞇaþ.

20 Ᵹıꝼ mon oþꞃeꞅ monneꞅ munuc ꝼeoh beꝼæꞅꞇ buꞇon þæꞅ munuceꞅ hlaꝼoꞃꝺeꞅ leaꝼe, ⁊ hıꞇ hım loꞃıᵹe, ðolıᵹe hıꞅ ꞅe ðe hıꞇ æꞃ ahꞇe.

Be ƿꞃeoꞅꞇa ᵹeꝼeohꞇe.

21 Ᵹıꝼ ƿꞃeoꞅꞇ oþeꞃne man oꝼꞅlea, ƿeoꞃþe mon ꞇo hanꝺa ealle ꝥ he mıꝺ hameꞅ bohꞇe, ⁊ hıne bıꞅceop unhaꝺıe ðonne hıne man oꝼ ðæm mẏnꞅꞇꞃe aᵹẏꝼe, buꞇon ꞅe hlaꝼoꞃꝺ ðone ƿeꞃe ꝼoꞃþınᵹıan ƿılle.

Be eoꝼeꞇeꞅ anꝺeꞇlan.

22 Ᵹıꝼ mon on ꝼolceꞅ ᵹemoꞇ cẏnınᵹeꞅ ᵹeꞃeꝼan ᵹeẏppe eoꝼoꞇ, ⁊ hıꞅ eꝼꞇ ᵹeꞅƿıcan ƿılle, ᵹeꞅꞇæle on ꞃıh-

Nw2 rubrics inserted into CN [1] Ld omits passage found in other MSS = CN Gif beƿeddedu ... byrᵹean

on rihtran hand ʒif he mæʒe; ʒif he ne mæʒe, þoliʒe his anʒyldes, (7 fo to þæm ƿite).[1]

xxi. Be hundes slyte.[2]

Gif hund mon toslite oþþe abite: æt forman misdæde[3] ʒ̄selle vi sciłł, ʒif he hī mete sylle, æt æftran cerre xii sciłł, æt þriddan xxx sciłł.

Gif æt þisse misdæda hƿelcre se hund losiʒ̄, ʒa þeos bót hƿæþere forþ.

Gif se hund ma misdæda ʒ̄ƿyrce, 7 he hine hæbbe, bete be fullan ƿere sƿa dolʒbote sƿa[4] he ƿyrce.

xxii. Be neatena misdædū.[5]

Gif neat mon ʒeƿundiʒe, ƿeorƿe þæt neat to honde oþþe foreþinʒie.

xxiii. Be ceorles mennenes nedhæmed.[6]

Gif mon ceorles mennen to nedhæmde ʒeþreatað, mid v sciłł ʒ̄selle þǣ ceorle 7 lx sciłł to ƿite.

Gif þeoƿmon þeoƿne to nedhæmde ʒ̄nede, bete mid his eoƿende.[7]

xxiiii. Be tƿyhyndum men æt hloðslyhte.[6]

Gif mon tƿihyndne mon unsynniʒne mid hloðe ofslea,[8] ʒylde se þæs sleʒes andeta sie ƿer 7 ƿite; 7 æʒhƿelc mon þe on siþe ƿære ʒ̄selle xxx sciłł to hloðbote.

xxv. Be syxhyndum men.[9]

Gif hit sie syxhẏnde mon, ælc mon to hloðbote sixti sciłł, 7 se slaʒa ƿer 7 ƿite.

xxvi. Be tƿelfhyndum.[10]

Gif he sie tƿelfhynde, ælc heora hundtƿelftiʒ sciłł,[11] se slaʒa ƿer 7 ƿite.

Gif[12] hloð þis ʒedo 7 eft oþsƿerian ƿille, teo hie ealle; 7 þoñ ealle forʒyltden þone ƿer ʒemænū hondū 7 ealle an ƿite, sƿa to þā ƿere belympe.

xxvii. Be unʒeƿintredes ƿifmonnes nedhæmeð.[10]

Gif mon unʒeƿintredne ƿifmon to nydhǣde ʒ̄þreatiʒe, sie ꝥ sƿa þæs ʒeƿintredan monnes bót.

[1] 7 fo to þæm ƿite] inserted before xxi Nw2 [2] xxi. Be hundes slyte] Be hund'es' slyte; rubric in right margin Nw2 [3] misdæde] e from a [4] dolʒbote sƿa] dolʒbote 'sƿa' with dolʒ underlined and sƿa added Nw2; dolh in right margin Nw2 [5] rubric with a of neat- from t Nw2 [6] rubrics mostly in right margin Nw2 [7] eoƿende] underlined, and in right margin testiculis Nw2 [8] ofslea] del. of þ before ofslea [9] rubric Nw2 [10] rubric in right margin Nw2 [11] sciłł] sħ sciłł [12] Gif] del. of ʒ before ʒif

on rihtran hand, gif he mæge; gif he ne mage, ðolige his angẏldes.

Be hundes slite.

23 Gif hund man to slite oþþe abîte: æt forman misdæde gesẏlle vj scill., gif he him mete sẏlle, Æt ðæm oþran cẏrre xij scill., æt ðriddan xxx scill. Gif æt ðissa misdæda hƿẏlcere se hund losige, [Ld 34V] ga ðeos bot ðeah hƿaþere forþ. Gif se hund ma misdæda geƿẏrce, ⁊ he hine hæbbe, bete be fullan ƿere sƿa dolg bôt oþþe sƿa hƿæt he geƿẏrce.

Be nẏtena misdædum.

24 Gif neat man geƿundige, ƿeorþe ꝥ neat to handa oþþe foreþingie.

Be nẏdhæmed.

25 Gif mon ceorles mennen to nẏdhæmede geþreataþ, mid fif scill. gebete ðæm ceorle ⁊ sẏxtig scill. to ƿite. Gif ðeoƿ man ðeoƿne to nẏdhæmed genẏde, gebete mid his eoƿende. Gif mon ungeƿintredne ƿifman to nẏdhæmede geþreatige, sẏ ꝥ sƿa ðæs geƿintredes mennes bôt.[1]

Be mansliht mid hloþe.

26 Gif mon tƿẏhẏndne man unsẏnnīgne mid hloþe ofslea, gẏlde se ðæs slæges andetta sẏ ƿere ⁊ ƿite; ⁊ ælc mon ðe on siþe ƿære gesẏlle ðrittig scill. to hloþ bôt. Gif hit sẏ sẏxhẏnde man, ælc to hloþebôt gesẏlle sẏxtig scill., ⁊ se slaga ƿere ⁊ ƿite. Gif he sẏ tƿelfhẏnde man, ælc heora hund tƿelftig scill. agẏfe, ⁊ se slaga ƿere ⁊ ƿite. Gif hlôþ ðis gedô ⁊ eft ofsƿerian ƿille, teo hi ealle; ⁊ ðonne ealle forgẏlden ðone ƿer gemænum handum ⁊ ealle anƿite, sƿa to ðæm ƿere to belimpe.

Nw2 rubrics inserted into CN; Ld has simply Be mansliht mid hloþe for 4 separate rubrics Nw2 [1]Ld Gif mon ... mennes bôt not in CN at this point, but after Ld 26 as separate item xxvii Be ungeƿintredes ƿifmonnes nedhæmeð

-nes bót.

Gif fædrenmaʒa mæʒleas mon ʒfeohte 7[1] mon ofslea, 7 þon̄ ʒif he[2] medrenmaʒas hæbbe, ʒylden þa[3] þæs peres þriddan dæl, (7 þriddan dæle þa ʒeʒildan, for þriddan dæle)[4] he fleo.

Gif he medrēmaʒas naʒ, ʒylden þa ʒʒyldan healfne, for healfne he fleo.

xxviii.

Gif mon spa ʒradne mon ofslea, ʒif he maʒas naʒ, ʒylde mon healfne cẏninʒe, healfne þǣ ʒʒyldan.

xxix. Be folcleas[5] ʒepyrhtū.[6]

Gif mon folcleasunʒ ʒpyrce 7 hio on hine ʒræsp[7] peorþe, mid nanū leohtran þinʒ ʒbete þon hī mon áceorf þa tunʒon óf, ꝥ hie mon na undeorran peorþe moste lesan þonne hie mon be þā pere ʒahtiʒe.

xxx. Be ʒodborʒum.[6]

Gif hpa oþerre ʒodborhes[8] oncunne, 7 teon pille, ꝥ he hpelcre ne ʒlæste þæra þe he hī ʒseald, aʒyfe þone foreað on feoper ciricū, 7 se oþer, ʒif he hine treopan pille, in xii ciricū do he ꝥ.

xxxi. Be ciepemonnum.[6]

Eac is ciepemonnū[9] ʒereht: þa men þa hie up mid hī læden, ʒbrenʒen beforan cẏninʒes ʒrefan on folcʒmote, 7 ʒerecce hu[10] maniʒe þara syn; 7 hie nimen þa men up[11] mid hī þe hie mæʒen eft to folcʒmote to rihte ʒbrenʒan. 7 þon̄e[12] hī þearf[13] sie ma manna up mid hī to hæbbanne on hiora fore, ʒcẏþe sẏmble spa oft spa hī þearfe sie in ʒmotes ʒpitnesse cẏninʒes ʒerefan.

xxxii. Be cyrlisces monnes byndulan.[14]

Gif mon cẏricliscne[15] mon ʒbinde unsyniʒne, ʒbete mid x sciƚƚ.

Gif hine mon bespinʒ, mid xx sciƚƚ ʒbete.

Gif he hine on henʒene alecʒe, mid xxx sciƚƚ ʒbete.

Gif he hine on bismor[16] to homolan

[1] 7] ~~on~~7 with 7 also in left margin Nw2 [2] ʒif he] ʒif 'he' Nw2 [3] þa] ~~þa~~'hio' Nw2 [4] dæl/ with 7 þriddan ... dæle (the words in brackets) in left margin Nw2 [5] second l of folcleas from t Nw2 [6] rubrics Nw2 [7] in left margin ʒerest Nw2 [8] ʒodborhes] ʒodborh'e'es with ʒodborʒes in left margin Nw2 [9] is ciepemonnū] ~~is~~'i's ciepemonnū with is ciepemonnū in left margin Nw2 [10] hu] u from e [11] nimen þa men up] nim̄ 'up' þa m̄ with niman and men^up in left margin. Nw2 [12] þon̄e] þon̄'e' Nw2 [13] þearf] r from f [14] rubric in left margin Nw2 [15] cẏricliscne] cẏricliscre with ẏ from i Nw2 [16] bismor] bismoré Nw2

[Ld 35^{v}] Be mægleasum monnum.

27 Gif fædren maga mægleas man gefeahte ⁊ man ofslea, ⁊ ðonne gif he mædren magas hæbbe, gýlden ða ðæs weres ðriddan dæl, ⁊ ðriddan dæl ðam gegýldan, ⁊ for ðriddan ðæl he fleo; gif he medren magas næbbe, gýlden ða gegýldan healfne, for healfne he fleo. Gif mon swa geradne man ofslea, gif he magas nage, gýlde man healf cýning, healfne ðæm gegýldan.

Be folc leasungum gewýrhtum.

28 Gif mon folc læsunge gewýrce ⁊ heo on hine gewæs weorþe, mid nanum leahtran ðinge ne gebete ðonne him mon aceorf ða tungan of, ꝥ hi mōna undeorran weorþe most lýsan, ðonne hi mon be ðæm were geahtige.

Be god borhgum.

29 Gif hwa oþerne godborges oncunne, ⁊ teon wille, ꝥ he hwýlcne ne gelæste ðæra ðe he gesealde, agýfe ðone foreaþ on feower cýricum, ⁊ se oþer, gif he hine treowian wille, innan twelf cýricum do he ꝥ.

Be cýpmannum.

30 Eac is ceapmannum geriht: ða men þe hi up mid heom lædaþ, gebringan beforan cýninges gerefan on folc gemote, ⁊ gerecce hu maniga ðæra sýn; ⁊ [Ld 36^{v}] hi nimen ða men mid heom ðe hig magon eft to folc gemote to rihte gebringan. ⁊ ðonne heom ðearf sý ma manna up mid heom to hæbbanne on heora fore, gecýþe sýmble swa oft swa þearf sý on gemotes gewitnýsse cýninges gerefan.

Be ceorlisces mannes bindelan.

31 Gif mon ceorliscne man gebinde unscýldigne, gebete mýd týn scill.; gif hine mon beswinge, mid tweontig scill. gebete. Gif he hine on hengene gebringe, mid ðrittig scill. gebete. Gif he hine on bismore to homelan

Nw2 rubrics inserted into CN; CN lacks Ld's rubric <u>Be mægleasum monnum</u> but has the number <u>xxvii</u> in the middle of Ld 27 homolan bescire, mid x sciłł ᵹbete.

Gif he hine to preoste[1] scyre unbundenne, mid xxx sciłł ᵹbete.

Gif he þone beard ofascire, mid xx sciłł ᵹbete.

Gif hine ᵹbinde, 7 þon̄ to preoste bescyre, mid lx sciłł ᵹbete.

xxxii. Be speres ᵹemeleasnesse.[2]

Eac is funden: ᵹif mon hafað spere ofer eaxle, 7 hine mon on asnæseð, ᵹyld þone ƿer butan ƿite.

Gif he foran eaᵹū asnase, ᵹylde þone ƿer; ᵹif hine man teo ᵹƿealdes on þære dæde,[3] ᵹtreaƿe hine be þā ƿite 7 mid þy ꝥ ƿite afylle,[4] Gif se ord sie ufor[5] (þryfinᵹre) þon̄ hīdeƿeard sceaft.

Gif hie sin bú ᵹelice, ord 7 hīdeƿeard sceaft, þæt sie butan ƿleo.

xxxiiii. Be boldᵹtæle.[6]

Gif mon ƿille of boldᵹtale[7] in oþer boldᵹtæl[8] hlaford secan, do ꝥ mid þæs ealdormannes ᵹƿitnesse þe he ær in his scire folᵹode.

Gif he hit butan his ᵹƿitnesse do, ᵹeselle se þe hine to men feormie cxx sciłł to ƿite: dæle he hƿæðere ꝥ, healfe cẏninᵹe in þa scire þe he ær folᵹode, healf in þa þe he oncymþ.

Gif he hƿæt ẏfla ᵹedon hæbbe þær he ær ƿæs, bete ꝥ se þe hine þonne to men onfo, 7 cẏninᵹe cxx sciłł to ƿite.

xxxv. Be ᵹefeohte beforan ealdormen.[6]

Gif mon beforan cyninᵹes ealdormon on ᵹmote ᵹfeohte, bete ƿer 7 ƿite sƿa hit riht sie; 7 beforan þā, cxx sciłł þā ealdormen to ƿite.

Gif he folcᵹemot mid ƿæpnes bryde arære, þā ealdormen hundtƿelftiᵹ sciłł to ƿite.

Gif þisses hƿæt beforan cyninᵹes ealdormonnes ᵹinᵹran ᵹlimpe, oþþe cẏninᵹes preoste, xxx[9] sciłł to ƿite.

xxxvi. Be ceorlisces monnes fletᵹefeohte.[6]

Gif hƿa on cyrlisces monnes flette ᵹfeohte, mid syx sciłł ᵹbete þā ceorle.

Gif he ƿæpne ᵹbrede 7 no fiehte, sie be healfū þā.

Gif syxhindū þissa hƿæþer

[1] to preoste] to preoste to preoste [2] rubric mostly in right margin Nw2 [3] dæde] dædá'e' Nw2 [4] ƿite 7 mid þy ꝥ ƿite afylle] ƿite '7' mid þy "ƿite" ꝥ afylle with mid ... afylle underlined and in right margin mid þẏ ꝥ ƿite afylle with y of afylle on top of e Nw2 [5] ufor] ufor/ with þryfinᵹre in left margin Nw2 [6] rubrics all in right margin Nw2 [7] boldᵹtale] has mansionem above [8] boldᵹtæl] has mansionem above, presumably, though it looks more like mansioes [9] preoste, xxx] preos'te' x̸xxx

homelan berscype, mid x scill. gebete. Gif he hine to preost berscype unbundenne, mid xxx scill. gebete. Gif he ðone bearde of ascyre, mid xx scill. gebete. Gif he hine gebinde, ⁊ ðonne to preost berscype, mid lx scill. gebete.

Be speres gymeleaste.

32 Eac is funden: gif mon hæfþ spere ofer eaxle, ⁊ hine mon onsnæseþ, gylde ðone wer buton wite. Gif he foran eagum asnære, gylde ðone wite; ⁊ gif hine mon teo gewealdes on ðære dæde, getreowie hine be ðæm wite ⁊ mid ðæm ꝥ wite afylle, gif se ord sy ufor þry fingere ðonne hindwearde sceafte. gif hi syn butu gelice, ord ⁊ hindweard sceaft, ꝥ sy buton pleoh.

[Ld 37v] Be boldgetæle.

33 Gif mon wille of boldgetæle in oþer boldgetæle hlaford secan, do ꝥ mid ealdormannes gewitnysse þe he ær on his scire folgode; gif he hit buton his gewitnysse dô, gesylle se ðe hine to men feormie hund twelftig scill. to wite: dæle he hwæþere ꝥ, healf ðæm cyning on ðæm scire ðe he ær folgode, healf on ðæm ðe he on cymþ; gif he hwæt to yfle gedôn hæfþ ðær he ær wæs, bete ꝥ se ðe hine ðonne to men underfo, ⁊ cyning mid hund twelftigum scill. to wite.

Be gefeohte beforan ealdormen.

34 Gif mon beforan cyninges ealdormen on gemote gefeohte, bete wer ⁊ wite swa hit riht sy; ⁊ beforan ðæm, hund twelftig scill. ðæm ealdormen to wite; gif hwa folces gemote mid wæpnes brygde arære, ðæm ealdormen cxx scill. to wite gesylle; gif ðisses hwæt beforan cyninges ealdormannes gingran gelimpe, oþþe cyninges preost, ðrittig scill. to wite gesylle.

Be cyrlisces monnes flette gefeohte.

35 Gif hwa on cyrlisces monnes flette gefeohte, mid syx scill. gebete ðæm ceorl. Gif he wæpne gebred ⁊ ne gefeohte, sy be healfum ðæm. Gif syxhyndum ðissa hwæþere

hƿæþer ȝelympe, þryfealdlice[1] (arise seo bote be ðære ceorliscan bote, tƿelfhindū men tƿifealdlic be þæs seoxhindan bote).

Be borhbryce.[2]

Cẏninȝes burȝbrẏce bið cxx sciƚƚ, arcebisceopes hundniȝontiȝ sciƚƚ, oþres bisceopes 7 ealdormonnes lx sciƚƚ, tƿelfhẏndes[3] monnes xxx sciƚƚ, syxhindes[4] xv sciƚƚ; ceorles edorbryce[5] v sciƚƚ.

Gif þisses hƿæt ȝlympe þenden fyrd ute sie, oþþe in Lenctenfæsten, hit sie tƿẏbote.

Gif mon in Lenȝten haliȝ ryht in folc butan leafe álecȝ,[6] ȝebete mid cxx sciƚƚ.

xxxvii. Be boclondū.[7]

Se mon se þe bocland hæbbe, 7 hī his maȝas læfdon, þon̄ setton ƿe ꝥ he hit ne moste sellan of his mæȝborhȝe, Gif ðær biþ ȝƿrit oþþe ȝƿitnes ðæt hit þara manna forbod ƿære þe hit on fruman ȝstryndon, 7 þara þe hit hi sealdon, ꝥ he sƿa ne mote. 7 ꝥ þonne on cẏninȝes 7 on bisceopes ȝƿitnesse ȝerecce beforan his maȝū.

xxxviii. Be feohte.[2]

Eac ƿe beodað: se mon se þe his[8] ȝfan hāsittende ƿite, ꝥ he ne feohte ær þā[9] he hī ryhtes bidde.

Gif he mæȝnes hæbbe, ꝥ he his ȝfán beride 7 inne besitte, ȝeheald hine vii niht inne 7 hine on ne feohte ȝif he inne[10] ȝþolian ƿille; 7 þonne ẏmb vii niht, ȝif he ƿille on hand ȝan 7 ƿæpenu sellan, ȝheald hine xxx nihta ȝesundne 7 hine his maȝū ȝbodie 7 his freondū.

Gif he circan þonne[11] ȝierne, sie þonne be þære circan are, sƿa ƿe ær bufan cƿædon.

Gyf he þonne þæs mæȝenes ne hæbbe, ꝥ hine inne besitte, ride to þā ealdormen,[12] bidde hine fultumes; Gif he hī fultumian ne ƿille, ride

[1] þryfealdlice] followed by del. of ~~be "syx hundan" þæs bote~~ and by the 14 words in brackets in top margin Nw2 [2] rubrics in left margin Nw2; xxxvii is wanting, but xxxviii is present [3] tƿelfhẏndes] ẏ from i [4] syxhindes] syxhindes ~~mon~~ Nw2 [5] edorbryce] edorbryce with eodor in right margin Nw2 and eodor, i(d est) semitas sepis in left margin Nw2; MS looks more like sūmitas sepis [6] álecȝ] alias: haliȝ rift butan rihte alecȝe, i(d est) sāctū velū sine recto deponat in left margin Nw2 [7] rubric mostly in right margin Nw2 [8] his] 'h'is [9] þā] þā ꝥ [10] inne] ~~hine~~ 'inne' Nw2 [11] circan þonne] ∮circan∮ þonne [12] ealdormen] e of -men on top of a

hƿæþere gelimp, ðrýfealdlic arise seo bote be þære ceorliscan bôt, tƿelfhýndū men tƿýfealdlic be ðæs sýxhýndum bôt.

[Ld 38V] Be burhbrýce.

36 Cýninges burhbrýce biþ hund tƿelftig scill., Ærcebisceopes burhbrýce hundnigontig scill., Oðres bisceopes ⁊ ealdormannes sýxtig scýll., tƿelfhýndes mannes ðrittig scill., Sýxhýndes mannes fiftýn scill.; Ceorles edorbrýce fif scill. Gif ðisses hƿat gelimp ðonne fýrd ut sý, oþþe in lenctene, sý hit tƿýbot. Gif mon on lencgtene haligrift on folc buton leafe alecge, gebete mid hund tƿelftigum scill.

Be boclande.

37 Se mon se ðe boclande hæbbe, ⁊ him his magas læfdon, ðonne setton ƿe ꝥ he hit ne moste sýllan of his mægeborh, Gif ðær biþ geƿrit oþþe geƿitnýsse ꝥ hit ðara manna forbôd ƿære ðe hit on fruman gestrindon, ⁊ ðara ðe hit him sealdon, ꝥ he sƿa ne mote. ⁊ ꝥ ðonne on cýmnges[1] ⁊ on bisceopes geƿitnýsse gerecce beforan his magum.

Be gefeohte.[2]

38 Eac ƿe beodaþ: se mon þe his gefân ham sittende ƿite, ꝥ he ne feohte ærþon he him rihtes bidde. Gif he mægnes hæbbe, ꝥ he his gefân beride ⁊ inne besitte, gehealde hine vii nihte inne ⁊ hine on ne feohte gif he inne geþolian ƿille; ⁊ ðonne ýmb seofon niht, gif he ƿille on hand gân ⁊ ƿæpnu sýllan, ge[Ld 39V]heald hine xxx nihta gesunde ⁊ hine his magum gebodie ⁊ his freondum. Gif he cýricean ðonne geýrne, sý ðonne be ðære cýricean are, sƿa ƿe ær bufan cƿædon. Gif he ðonne ðæs mægenes ne hæbbe, ꝥ he hine inne besitte, ride to ðæm ealdormen, bidde hine fultumes; Gif he him fultumian ne ƿille, ride

Nw2 rubrics inserted into CN [1] typographical error not noted Ld [2] margin — al. fæþe i. capitalibus inimicitiis; errata — In margine: fæþe lege fæhþe

ride to þā cẏninȝe, ær he feohte.

Eac ꝑelce ȝif mon becume on his ȝefán 7 he hine ær[1] hamfæstne ne ꝑite, Gif he ꝑille his ꝑæpen sellan, hine mon ȝhealde xxx nihta 7 hine his freondū ȝcyþe; ȝif he ne ꝑille his ꝑæpnu sellan, þonne mot he feohtan on hine. Gif he ꝑille on hond ȝan 7 his ꝑepnu sẏllan, 7 hꝑa ofer ꝥ on hī feohte, ȝylde ꝑa ꝑer ꝑa ꝑunde ꝑa he ȝeꝑyrce 7 ꝑite; 7 hæbbe his mæȝ forꝑorht.

Eac ꝑe cꝑædað ꝥ mon mot mid his hlaforde feohtan orꝑiȝe,[2] ȝif mon on þone hlaford feohte, ꝑa mot se hlaford mid þy men feohtan.

Æfter þære ilcan ꝑisan[3] mot mon feohtan mid his ȝborene mæȝe, Gif hine mon o ꝑoh onfeohteð,[4] buton ꝑiþ his hlaforde: þæt ꝑe ne lyfað.

7 mon mot feohtan orꝑiȝe, Gif he ȝmeteð oþerne æt his æꝑū ꝑife betinedū durū oþþe under anre reon, oþþe æt his dehter æꝑūborenre, oþþe æt his ꝑeoster[5] (æꝑum)borenre, oþþe æt his meder þe ꝑære to æꝑū ꝑife forȝyfen his fæder.

xxxix. Be mæssedaȝe freolse.[6]

Eallū frioū monnū þæs daȝas sien forȝyfene, butan þeoꝑū monnū 7 esneryhtū: xii daȝas on Ǵehhol, 7 þone dæȝ þe Crist þone deofol oferꝑiþde, 7 Scs Greȝorius ȝemynddæȝ, 7 vii daȝas to Eastron, 7 vii ofer, 7 an dæȝ æt Sce Petres tide 7 Sce Paules, 7 on hærfæste þa fullan ꝑucan ær Sca Marian mæssan, 7 æt Ealra Haliȝra ꝑeorþunȝe[7]

[1] ær] ær þā or ær þæ with þā or þæ del. [2] orꝑiȝe] in right margin orpite Nw2 [3] ꝑisan] ꝑ.san with i very faintly visible [4] onfeohteð] second e from a [5] ꝑeoster] ꝑeoster/ with æꝑum in right margin Nw2 [6] rubric mostly in right margin Nw2 [7] ꝑeorþunȝe] ꝑeorþu'n'ȝe

ride to ðæm cyning, ær he feohte. Eac sƿylce gif mon becume on his gefân ⁊ he hine ær hamfæstene ne ƿite, gif he ƿille his ƿæpne syllan, hine mon gehealde xxx nihta ⁊ hine his freondum gecyþe; gif he ne ƿille his ƿæpnu syllan, ðonne mot he feohtan on hine. Gif he ƿille on hand gân ⁊ his ƿæpnu syllan, ⁊ hƿa ofer ꝥ on him feohte, gylde sƿa ƿer sƿa ƿund sƿa he geƿyrce ⁊ ƿite; ⁊ hæbbe his mæg forƿorht. Eac ƿe cƿædaþ ꝥ mon mot mid his hlaford feahtan orƿite, gif mon on þone hlaforde feahte, sƿa mot se hlaford mid þy men feohtan; æfter ðær ylcan ƿisan mot mon feohtan mid his geborene mæge, gif hine mon on ƿoh onfeohtaþ, buton ƿiþ his hlaford: ꝥ ƿe ne lyfaþ. Eac mon mot feohtan orƿite, gif he gemeteþ oþerne æt his æƿum ƿife betynedum durum oþþe under anre reon, oþþe æt his dohtor æƿum borenre, oþþe æt his sƿeoster æƿum borenre, oþþe æt his meder ðe ƿære to æƿum ƿife forgyfen his fæder.

[Ld 40v] Be mæsse dæge freolse.

39 Eallum freoum mannum ðæs dægas syn forgyfene, butan ðeoƿum monnum ⁊ esne rihtum: xii dagas on gehol, ⁊ ðone dæg ðe crist ðone deofol ofersƿiþde, ⁊ Seintus Gregorius gemynde dæg, ⁊ vii dagas to eastron, ⁊ vii ofer, ⁊ an dæg æt Seint Petres tide ⁊ Seint Paules, ⁊ on hærfeste ða fullan ƿucan ær Sctā marian mæssan, ⁊ ealra haligra ƿeorþunge

ƿeorþunʒe ænne dæʒ. 7 iiii Ƿodnesdaʒas on iiii Ybrenƿicū[1] þeoƿū eallū syn forʒyfen, þā þe hī leofost sie to sellanne æʒhƿæt þæs þe hī æniʒ mon for Godes noman ʒselle, oþþe hie on ænezū[2] hiora hƿilsticū ʒeearnian mæʒen.

xl. Be ƿundum.[3]

Heafodƿunde to bote:[4] ʒif þa ban beoð butu þẏrel, xxx scill ʒeselle hī mon.
Gif þæt uterre ban biþ þyrel, ʒeselle xv scill to bote.

xli.[5]

Gif in feax biþ ƿund inces lanʒ, ʒeselle ænne scill to bote.
Gif beforan feaxe biþ ƿund inces lanʒ, tƿeʒen scill to bote.

xlii.[5]

Gif hī mon aslea oþere eare[6] of, ʒselle xxx scill to bote.
Gif se hlist oþstande þæt he ne mæʒe ʒehyran, ʒselle lx scill to bote.

xliii.[5]

Gif mon mennes[7] eaʒe ofaslea, ʒselle hī mon lx scill 7 sẏx scill 7 syx peninʒas 7 þriddan dæl peninʒes to bote.
Gif hit in þā heafde sie, 7 he noht ʒseon ne mæʒe mid, stande þriddan dæl þære bote inne.
Gif mon oþrū ꝥ neb ofaslea, ʒebete hī mid lx scill.
Gif mon oþrū þone toð onforan heafde ofaslea, ʒbete ꝥ mid viii scill.
Gif hit sie se ƿonʒtoð, ʒselle iiii scill to bote.
Monnes tux biþ xv scill ƿeorþ.
Gif monnes ceacan mon forslyhþ þæt hie beoþ forode, ʒbete mid xv scill.
Monnes cinban, ʒif hit biþ toclofen, ʒeselle mon xii to bote.
Gif monnes þrotbolla biþ þyrell, ʒbete mid xii scill.
Gif monnes tunʒe biþ of heafde[8] (mid)[9] oþres monnes dædū don, þæt biþ ʒlic 7[10] eaʒan bote.
Gif mon

[1] iiii Ybrenƿicū] iiii ~~Yberƿ~~ Ybrenƿicū [2] æneʒū] æf'n'eʒū Nw2 [3] rubric in left margin, xl in right margin Nw2 [4] bote] bot~~an~~'e' Nw2 [5] numeral in right margin Nw2 [6] oþere eare] oþere 'e'are Nw2 [7] mennes] men'nes' Nw2 [8] heafde] heasde—f not crossed [9] mid] in left margin Nw2 [10] 7 del. Nw2

ƿeoꞃþunᵹe an ꝺæᵹe. ⁊ ꝼeoƿeꞃ ƿoꝺneſꝺaᵹaſ on ꝼeƿeꞃ ẏmbꞃen ƿucum ðeoƿum eallum ſẏnꝺ ꝼoꞃᵹẏꝼen, ðæm ðe hī leoꝼoſꞇ ſẏ ꞇo ſẏllanne æᵹhƿæꞇ ðæſ ðe him mon ꝼoꞃ ᵹoꝺeſ naman ᵹeſẏlle, oþþe hi on æniᵹum heoꞃa hƿilſꞇẏccū ᵹeæꞃnian maᵹon.

Be ƿunꝺum.

40 Heaꝼoꝺ ƿunꝺe ꞇo bôꞇ: ᵹiꝼ ða bân biþ buꞇu ðẏꞃel, xxx ſcill. ᵹeſẏlle him mon. Ᵹiꝼ ꝥ uꞇꞇꞃe ban biþ ðẏꞃl, ᵹeſẏlle ꝼiꝼꞇẏne ſcill. ꞇo boꞇe. Ᵹiꝼ in ꝼeaxe biþ ƿunꝺ ẏnceſ lanᵹ, ᵹeſẏlle ænne ſcẏll. ꞇo boꞇe. Ᵹiꝼ hiꞇ beꝼoꞃan ꝼeaxe biþ ƿunꝺ ẏnceſ lanᵹ, ꞇƿeᵹen ſcill. ꞇo boꞇe; ᵹiꝼ him mon oꝼaſlea ꝥ oþeꞃ eaꞃe, ᵹeſẏlle him ðꞃiꞇꞇiᵹ ſcill. ꞇo boꞇe. Ᵹiꝼ ſe hlẏſꞇ oþſꞇanꝺe ꝥ he ne mæᵹe ᵹehẏꞃā, ᵹeſẏlle xxx[1] ſcill. ꞇo boꞇe. Ᵹiꝼ mon men eaᵹe oꝼaſlea, ᵹeſẏlle him [Ld 41v] mon ſẏxꞇiᵹ ſcill. ⁊ ſẏx ſcill. ⁊ ſẏx peninᵹaſ ⁊ ðꞃiꝺꝺan ꝺæl peninᵹeſ ꞇo boꞇe. Ᵹiꝼ hiꞇ in ðam hæꝼꝺe ſẏ, ⁊ he nochꞇ ᵹeſeon ne mæᵹe miꝺ, ſꞇanꝺ ðꞃiꝺꝺan ꝺæle ðæꞃe boꞇe inne. Ᵹiꝼ mon oþꞃum ꝥ neb oꝼ aſlea, ᵹebeꞇe him miꝺ lx ſcill.; ᵹiꝼ mon oþꞃū ðone ꞇoþe on ꝼoꞃan heaꝼꝺe oꝼaſlea, ᵹebeꞇe ꝥ miꝺ eahꞇa ſcill.; ᵹiꝼ hiꞇ ſẏ ſe ƿonᵹ ꞇoþ, ᵹeſẏlle ꝼeoƿeꞃ ſcill. ꞇo boꞇe; monneſ ꞇuſ biþ ſẏxꞇẏne ſcill. ƿeoꞃþe; ᵹiꝼ mon monneſ ceacan ꝼoꞃſlea ꝥ heo beoþ ꝼoꞃoꝺe, ꝼiꝼꞇẏne ſcill. ᵹebeꞇe. Manneſ cinn bân, ᵹiꝼ hiꞇ biþ ꞇocloꝼen, ᵹeſẏlle mon ꞇƿelꝼ ſcill. ꞇo boꞇe. Ᵹiꝼ manneſ ðꞃoꞇ bolla bẏþ ðẏꞃl, ᵹebeꞇe miꝺ ꞇƿelꝼ ſcill. Ᵹiꝼ monneſ ꞇunᵹe biþ oꝼ heaꝼꝺe miꝺ oþꞃeſ monneſ ꝺæꝺum ᵹeꝺon, ꝥ biþ ᵹelic ⁊ eaᵹum bôꞇ. Ᵹiꝼ mon

CN rubrics and numbers from Nw2; xli, xlii, xliii absent from Ld [1] margin — al. 60

Gif mon bið on axle ƿund, ꝥ þæt liþseaƿ[1] utfloƿe, ꝫbete mid xxx sciłł.

Gif se earm bið forad bufan elmboꝫan, þær sculon xv sciłł to bote.

Gif þa earmscancan beoð beꝫen forade, sio bot biþ xxx sciłł.

Gif se þuma biþ ofasleꝫen, þā sculon xxx sciłł to bote.

Gif se næꝫle biþ ofásleꝫen, þā sculon v sciłł (to bote).[2]

Gif se scẏtefinꝫer bið ofásleꝫen, sio bot biþ xv sciłł; his næꝫles biþ iii sciłł.

Gif se midlesta finꝫer sio ofásleꝫen, sio bot bið xii sciłł; 7 his næꝫles bot biþ ii scill.

Gif se ꝫoldfinꝫer sie ofasleꝫen, to þā sculon xvii sciłł to bote; 7 his næꝫles iiii sciłł to bote.

Gif se lytla finꝫer biþ ofásleꝫen, þā sceall to bote ix[3] scill; 7 an sciłł his næꝫles, ꝫif se sie ofásleꝫen.

Gif mon biþ on hrife[4] ƿund, ꝫselle hī mon xxx sciłł.

Gif he þurhƿund biþ, æt ꝫhƿæþerū muþe xx sciłł.

Gif monnes þeoh be þyrel, ꝫselle hī mon xxx sciłł.

Gif hit forad sy, sio bot eac biþ xxx sciłł.

Gif se sconca biþ þẏrel[5] beneoþan cneoƿe, þær sculon xii sciłł to bote.

Gif he forad sie beneoþan cneoƿe, ꝫselle hī xxx sciłł to bote.

Gif sio micele ta bið ofasleꝫen, ꝫselle hī xx sciłł to bote.

Gif hit sie sio æfterre ta, xv sciłł to bote ꝫselle hī mon.

Gif sio midleste ta sie ofasleꝫen, þær sculon ix sciłł to bote.

Gif hit biþ sio feorþe ta, þær sculon vi sciłł to bote.

Gif sio litle ta sie ofasleꝫen, ꝫselle hī v sciłł.

Gif mon sie on þa herþan[6] ƿund to þā sƿyþe ꝥ he ne mæꝫe bearn ꝫestrynan, ꝫebete hī mon ꝥ mid lxxx

[1] liþseaƿ] above, in a small hand, is iūctura — very difficult to read [2] sciłł / with to bote in left margin Nw2 [3] ix] x begun prematurely before ix, then del. [4] hrife] f rife with hrif ł rif, i(d est), ilia in right margin Nw2 [5] þẏrel] þẏrelł [6] MS has, in small hand above herþan, testiculis, which is repeated in left margin

Gif mon on eaxle biþ geƿundod, þ þ liþ seaƿe utfloƿe, gebete mid ðrittig scill. Gif se earme biþ forad bufan ðæm elmbogan, ðær sculon fẏftẏne scill. to bote. Gif ða earm scancan biþ begen forade, seo bote biþ xxx scill. Gif se ðuma biþ of aslagen, ðæm sculon xxx scill. to bote; gif se nægl biþ of aslagen, seo bot biþ fif scill.; gif se scẏte fẏnger biþ ofaslagen, seo bôte biþ fẏftẏne scill.; his nægl beoþ iiii scill.; gif se midlesta fingere sẏ ofaslagen, se bot biþ xii scill.; ⁊ his nægles ii scill.; gif se goldfinger biþ ofaslagen, to ðæm sculon seofontẏne scill. to bote; ⁊ his nægles iiii scill. Gif se lẏtla finger sẏ ofaslagen, ðæm [Ld 42v] sceal to bote nigon scill.; ⁊ ân scill. his nægles, gif hit sẏ ofaslagen. Gif mon biþ on hrif geƿundod, gesẏlle him mon xxx scill.; gif he ðurh ƿund biþ, æt ægþrum muþe treontig scill. Gif monnes ðeoh biþ ðẏrl, gesẏlle him mon xxx scill. to bote. Gif hit forod sẏ, seo bot biþ eac xxx scill. Gif se scanca biþ ðẏrl beneoþan cneoƿe, ðær sculon tƿelf scill.; gif he forad sẏ beneoþan cneoƿe, gesẏlle him xxx scill. to bote. Gif seo micele tâ biþ ofaslagen, gesẏlle him mon xx scill. to bote. Gif hit sẏ seo æftere tâ, fiftẏne scill. to bote. Gif seo midlesta tâ sẏ ofaslagen, ðær sculon nigon scill. to bote; gif hit sẏ seo feoƿerþe tâ, þær sculon vi scill. to bote. Gif se lẏtle tâ sẏ ofaslagen, gesẏlle him mon fif scill. to bote. Gif mon sẏ on ða hærþan to ðam sƿiþe geƿundod þ he ne mæge bearn gestrẏnan, gebete him þ mid lxxx

lxxx sciłł.

Gif men sie se earm mid honda mid ealle ofacorfen beforan elmboȝan, ȝbete ꝥ mid lxxx sciłł.

Æȝhƿelcere ƿunde beforan feaxe[1] 7 beforan sleafan[2] 7 beneoþan cneoƿe, sio bot biþ tƿysceatte[3] máre.

Gif sio lendenbræde biþ forsleȝen, þær sceal lx sciłł to bote.

Gif hio biþ onbestunȝen, ȝeselle xv sciłł to bote.

Gif hio bið þurhþẏrel, þoñ sceal þær xxx sciłł to bote, *Gif se mon cƿic sie.

Gif[4] mon biþ on[5] eaxle ƿund, ȝebete lxxx sciłł.

Gif mon oþrū þa hond utan forslea, ȝselle hī xx sciłł to bote, Gif hine mon ȝlacnian mæȝe.

Gif hio healfe onƿeȝ fleoȝe, þonne sceal[6] xl sciłł to bote.

Gif mon oþrū rib forslea binnan ȝhalre hyde, ȝselle x sciłł to bote.

Gif sio hide sie tobrocen 7 mon ban ofado, ȝselle xv sciłł to bote.

Gif monnes eaȝe hī mon ofaslea, oþþe his hand, oþþe his fot, þær ȝæþ ȝlic bot to eallū: vi peninȝas 7 vi sciłł 7 lx sciłł 7 þryddan[7] dæl peninȝes.

Gif monnes sconca biþ ofasleȝen ƿiþ þæt cneƿ, þær sceal lxxx sciłł to bote.

Gif mon oþrū þa sculdru[8] forslea, ȝselle hī mon xx sciłł to bote.

Gif hie mon inbeslea 7 mon bán ofadó, ȝselle mon þæs to bote xv sciłł.

Gif mon þa ȝreatan sinƿe forslea, ȝif hie mon ȝlacnian mæȝe ꝥ hio hal sie, ȝeselle xii sciłł to bote.

Gif se mon healt sie for þære sinƿe ƿunde, 7 hine mon ȝlacnian ne mæȝ, ȝselle xxx sciłł to bote.

Gif þa

[1] feaxe underlined, with f from s; in right margin feaxe Nw2 [2] sleafan] slieafan underlined, with in left margin sleafan, i(d est) mania Nw2 [3] tƿysceatte] ~~tƿysceastre~~ tƿysceatte [4] before Gif * indicates error; Gif se mon cƿic sie Nw2; in other MSS (but not Ld) Gif se mon cƿic sie follows lxxx sciłł [5] on] o from i [6] sceal] sceałł [7] þryddan] y from i [8] þa sculdru underlined, with d on top of þ; in left margin sculdru Nw2

lxxx scill. Gif men sẏ earme mid honda mid ealle of acorfan beforan elmbogan, gebete ꝥ mid lxxx scill. Æghƿẏlcere ƿunde beforan feaxe ⁊ beforan slẏfan ⁊ beneoþan cneoƿe, biþ tƿẏgẏlde mare; gif seo lenden breda biþ forslagen, ðær sceal sẏxtig scill. to bote; gif heo biþ on bestungen, fiftẏne scill. Gif heo biþ ðurh ðẏrl, ðonne sceal ðær xxx scil. to bote.[1] Gif mon biþ on eaxle geƿundod, gebete mid lxxx scill. Gîf mon oþrum ða hand uton forslea, gesẏlle him xx scill. to bote, gif hine mon [Ld 43^{v}] gelacniā mæge. Gif heo healfe on ƿege fleoge, þonne sceal sẏxtig scill. to bote. Gif mon oþrū ƿib forslea binnan gehalre hẏde, gesẏlle x scill. to bote; gif seo hẏde sẏ to brocen ⁊ mon bân of adô, gesẏlle fiftẏne scill.; gif mōnes eage him mon ofaslea, oþþe his hand, oþþe his fôt, ðær gæþ gelic bôt to eallum: sẏx peningas ⁊ sẏx scill. ⁊ sẏxtig scill. ⁊ ðriddan dæle peninges. Gif monnes sconca biþ ofaslagen ƿiþ ꝥ cneoƿe, ðære sceal lxxx scill. to bote. Gif mon oþrum þa sculdru forslea, gesẏlle him mon xx scill. to bote; gif hi mon inbeslea ⁊ mon bân ofadô, gesẏlle mon ðæs to bote fiftẏne scill. Gif mon ða greatan sinƿe forslea, gîf hine mon gelacnian mæge ꝥ he hâl sẏ, gesẏlle xii scill. to bote. Gif se mon healt sẏ for ðære sinƿe ƿunde, ⁊ hine mon gelacnian ne mæge, gesẏlle xxx scill. to bote. Gif ðæs

[1] Ld omits words found in other MSS = CN Gif se mon cpic sie from Nw2

Gif þa smalan sinpe man forslea, ȝ̄selle hī mon v sciłł to bote.

Gif mon oþrū þa ȝ̄peald[1] forslea uppe on þā speoran, 7 forpundie to þā spiþe ꝥ he naȝe þære ȝ̄peald, 7 hpæþere lifiȝe spa ȝescended, ȝeselle hī mon c sciłł to bote, buton hī pitan ryhtre 7 mare ȝ̄reccan.

THE LAW OF INE

xliiii.

Ic Ine, mid Godes ȝyfe[2] Ƿesseaxna cẏninȝ, mid ȝ̄þeahte 7 mid lare Cenredes mines fæder, 7 Heddes mines bisceopes, 7 Eorcenpoldes mines bisceopes, mid[3] eallū minū ealdormonnū, 7 þā ẏldestan piotū[4] minre þeode, 7 eac micelre ȝ̄somnunȝ̄ Godes þeopa, pæs smeaȝende be þære hælo urra sapla, 7 be þā staþole ures rices, ꝥte ryht æp 7 ryhte cẏnedomas þurh[5] ure folc ȝefæstnode[6] 7 ȝ̄trymed pæron, ꝥte næniȝ ealdormonna ne us underȝ̄þeodedra æfter þā pere apendende þæs ure domas.

xlv. Be Godes þeopena reȝole.[7]

Ærest pe beodað ꝥte Godes þeopas hiora ryhtreȝol on ryht healdan; Æfť þā pe bebeodað ꝥte ealles folces æp 7 domas þus syn 3healdene.

xlvi. Be cildum.[8]

Cild binnan þryteȝū nihta sie ȝ̄fulpad; ȝif hit spa ne sie, xxx sciłł ȝ̄bete.

Gif hit ðonne sie dead butan fulpihte, ȝebete mid eallū þā þe he aȝe.

xlvii. Be Sunnandæȝes peorcū.[9]

Gif þeopmon pyrce on Sunnandæȝ be his hlafordes hæse, sie he frioh, 7 se hlaford ȝeselle xxx sciłł to pite.

Gif þonne se þeopa butan his ȝ̄pitnesse pyrce, þoliȝe his hyde.

Gif þonne se fri-

[1] ȝ̄peald] ~~ȝ̄seald~~ ȝ̄peald [2] ȝyfe] y from i [3] mid] ~~7~~ 'mid' Nw2 [4] piotū] pi'o'tū Nw2 [5] þurh followed by del. of a second h Nw2 [6] ȝefæstnode] ȝewfæstť'n'ode Nw2 [7] rubric in right margin Nw2 [8] rubric Nw2 [9] rubric half in right margin Nw2

Gif ðæs smalan sineƿan mon for-
slea, gesylle him mon syx scill. to bote. Gif
mon oþrum ða geƿeald forslea up on þæm
sƿeore, ⁊ forƿundige to ðæm sƿiþe ꝥ he
nage ðær geƿeald, ⁊ ðeah hƿæþere li-
fige sƿa gescēde, gesylle him mon
hund scill. to bote, buton him
ƿitan rihtre ⁊ mare ge-
reccan.

[end of Ld 43^{V}]

Ines. æ[1]

[Ld 0^{V}] Ic Ine, mid godes gyfe ƿestseaxna cyning, mid geþeaht ⁊ mid lære cenredes mines fæder, ⁊ heddes mines biscepes, ⁊ eorcenƿoldes mines biscepes, ⁊ mid eallum minum ealdormannum, ⁊ þam yldestan ƿitan minre þeode, ⁊ eac mycelre somnunge godes þeoƿena, ƿæs smeagende be ðære hæle urra saƿla, ⁊ be ðam staþole ures rices, ꝥ ryht æƿ ⁊ ryhte cynedomas þurh ure folc gefæstenode ⁊ getrymmed ƿæron, ꝥ nænig ealdormanna ne us undergeþeodendra æfter ðæm ƿære aƿendende þas ure domas.

Be godes þeoƿena regole.

1 Ærest ƿe bebeodaþ ꝥ godes þeoƿas hiora ryht regole gyman ⁊ on ryht healdan; Æfter þam ƿe beodaþ ꝥ ealles folces æ[2] ⁊ domas þus synd gehealdene.

Be cildum.

2 Cild binnan þryttigum nihta sy gefulƿad; gif hit sƿa ne sy, xxx scillinges gebete. Gif hit þonne sy dead butan fulluhte, gebete he hit mid eallum þæm þe he age.

Be sunnan dæges ƿeorcum.

3 Gif [Ld 1^{V}] þeoƿ mon ƿyrce on sunnan dæg be his hlafordes hæse, sy he freo, ⁊ se hlaford sylle xxx scillinges to ƿite. Gif þonne se þeoƿa butan his geƿitnysse ƿyrce, þolige his hyde oþþe his hydgyldes.[3] Gif ðonne se fri-

Nw2 rubrics inserted into CN [1] rubric in Ld, not followed by xliiii as in CN [2] margin — alias æƿ, id est, nuptiarum fœdera [3] oþþe his hydgyldes not in CN but in B, H

se friȝea[1] þẏ dæȝe pẏrce butan his hlafordes hæse, þolie his freotes.

xlviii. Be cyricsceatū.[2]

Ciricsceatas syn aȝifene be sc̄e Martẏnes mæssan; ȝif hpa ꝥ ne ȝ̄læste, sie he scẏldiȝ lx sciŀŀ, 7 be[3] xiifealdū aȝyfe þone ciricsceat.

xvix. Be cyricsocnū.[4]

Gif hpa sie deaðes scyldiȝ, 7 he[5] cirican ȝeyrne,[6] hæbbe his feorh, 7 bete spa hī ryht pisiȝ̄.

Gif hpa his hyde forpyrce, 7 cirican ȝ̄yrne, sie hī sio spinȝelle forȝyfen.

l. Be ȝefeohtum.[4]

Gif hpa ȝ̄feohte on cyninȝes huse, sie he scyldiȝ ealles his ierfes, 7 sie on cẏninȝes dome hpæder he lif aȝe þe naȝe.

Gif hpa on mẏnsī ȝefeohte, cxx sciŀŀ ȝebete.

Gif hpa on ealdormannes huse ȝ̄feohte, oþþe on oþres ȝ̄þunȝenes pitan, lx sciŀŀ ȝebete he, 7 oþer syxtiȝ to pite.

Gif he[7] þon̄ on ȝafolȝyldan[8] huse oþþe on ȝ̄bures ȝ̄feohte, xxx sciŀŀ to pite ȝ̄selle, 7 þā ȝ̄bure vi sciŀŀ.

7 þeah hit sie on middan felda ȝ̄fohten,[9] cxx sciŀŀ to pite sie aȝifen.

Gif he[7] þonne on ȝ̄beorscipe hie ȝ̄ciden, 7 oþer hiora mid ȝ̄þylde hit forbere, ȝeselle se oþer xxx sciŀŀ to pite.

li. Be stale.[10]

Gif hpa staliȝe spa his pife nẏte 7 his bearn, ȝeselle lx sciŀŀ to pite.

Gif he þonne staliȝe on ȝ̄pitnesse ealles his heredes, ȝonȝen hie ealle on þeopot.

Tynpintre cniht mæȝ bion þiofþe[11] ȝ̄pita.

lii. Be ryhtes bene.[10]

Gif hpa hī ryhtes bidde beforan hpelcū sciremen

[1] friȝea] in left margin freo Nw2 [2] rubric half in right margin Nw2 [3] be] b'e' [4] rubric in left margin Nw2 [5] he] be [6] ȝeyrne] ȝeħyrne [7] Gif he] Gif 'he' Nw2 [8] ȝafolȝyldan] ȝafolȝyld'a'n with second a on del. of one Nw2 [9] ȝ̄fohten] e from a [10] rubric Nw2 [11] þiofþe] þi'o'fþe Nw2

se frigea ðy dæge ƿyrce butan his hlafordes hæse, þolige his freotes oþþe sixtig scillinges ⁊ ƿreost sy tƿyscildig.

Be cyricsceatte.

4 Cyric sceattas syn agifene be Seint martynes mæssan; Gif hƿa ꝥ ne gelæste, sy he scyldig feoƿertig scill., ⁊ be tƿelf fealdum agyfe ðone cyric sceat.

Be cyric socnum.

5 Gif hƿa sy deaþes scyldig, ⁊ he cyricean geyrne, hæbbe his feorh, ⁊ bete sƿa him riht ƿisige. Gif hƿa his hyde forƿyrce, ⁊ cyricean geyrne, sy him seo sƿingle forgyfen.

Be gefeohte.

6 Gif hƿa gefeohte on cyninges hus, sy he scyldig ealles his yrfes, ⁊ sy on cyninges dome hƿæðer he life age ðenage. Gif hƿa on mynster gefeohte, hund tƿelftig scill. gebete. Gif hƿa on ealdormannes hus feohte, oþþe on oþres geþungenes ƿitan, sixtig scill. gebete he, ⁊ oþer syxtig scill. gesylle to ƿite. Gif he ðonne on gefolgylden hus oþþe on gebures gefeohte, xxx scill. to ƿite gesylle, ⁊ ðæm gebure syx scill. And ðeah hit sy [Ld 2^{v}] on middan felda gefohten, hund tƿelftig scill. to ƿite sy agyfen. Gif ðonne on gebeorscipe hi geciden, ⁊ oþer heora mid geþylde hit forbere, gesylle se oþer xxx scillinges to ƿite.

Be stale.

7 Gif hƿa stalige sƿa his ƿif nyte ⁊ his bearn, gesylle syxtig scill. to ƿite. Gif he ðonne stalige on geƿitnysse ealles his hyredes, gāgen hi ealle on ðeoƿet; tynƿintre cniht mæg beon þeofþe geƿita.

Be rihtes bene.

8 Gif hƿa him rihtes bidde beforan hƿilcum scirmen

Nw2 rubrics inserted into CN

-men oþþe oþrū deman, 7 abiddan[1] ne mæʒe, 7 him ƿedd sellan nelle, ʒebete xxx sciłł, 7 binnan vii nihton ʒedó hine ryhtes ƿyrþne.

lii. Be þā ƿræcēdū, ær hī mon ryhtes bidde.[2]

Gif hƿa ƿrace dó ærþon he hī rhytes bidde, ꝥ he him onnime aʒyfe, 7 forʒylde 7 ʒebete mid xxx sciłł.

liiii. Be reaflace.[3]

Gif hƿa binnan þā ʒemærū ures rices reaflac[4] 7 nednæme[5] dó, aʒife he þone reaflac, 7 ʒeselle lx sciłł to ƿite.

lv.[6] Be þone þe his ʒelond bebycʒað.[7]

Gif hƿa his aʒenne ʒ̄leod[8] bebicʒʒe, þeoƿne oþþe fryʒne, þeah he scẏldiʒ sie ofer sæ, forʒylde hine he[9] his ƿere.

lvi. Be ʒefonʒenū þeofum.[7]

Gif þeof sie ʒefonʒen sƿelte[10] he deað, oþþe his lif be his ƿere man alyse.

lvii. Be þǣ þe heora ʒeƿitnesse beforan bisceop aleoʒað.[7]

Gif hƿa beforan bisceoƿe his ʒeƿitnesse 7 his ƿedd aleoʒe, ʒebete mid cxx sciłł.

lviii. Be hloðe.[11]

Þeofas ƿe hatað oð vii men; frō vii hloð oð xxxv; siþþan (bið here).[12]
Se þe hloðe betẏʒen sie, ʒesƿicne se hine be cxx hida oððe sƿa bete.

[1] abiddan] underlined with hæbban above Nw2 [2] rubric in right margin Nw2; underneath appears next rubric ~~Be reaflace~~, del. [3] rubrics in right margin Nw2 [4] in a small hand above reaflac appears latrociniū violēta captio, very difficult to read Nw2 [5] nednæme] first n from m; in right margin ne deme, i(d est) violēta captio Nw2 [6] l del. before lv [7] rubrics Nw2 [8] in a small hand above aʒenne ʒ̄leod is compatriota [9] he] be [10] spelte] spelt'e' Nw2 [11] lviii in right margin Nw2; further down right margin ~~lviii~~ Be hloðe Nw2 [12] bið here in right margin Nw2

lix.[13] Be heriȝe.[3]

Se þe hereteama betẏȝen sie, he hine be his ƿerȝylde alyse oþþe be his ƿere ȝspicne.
Se að sceal bion healf be huslȝenȝū.
Þeof, siþþan he bið on cẏninȝes bende, nah he þa spicne.

lx. Be þeofsleȝe.[3]

Se þe þeof ofslyhþ, se mot ȝcẏþan mid[14] aþe ꝥ he hine synniȝne ofslohȝe, nales þa ȝȝyldan.

lxi. Be forstolenū flæsc.[3]

Se þe forstolen flæsc findeð 7 ȝdyrneð,[15] ȝif he dear he mot mid aþe ȝecẏþan ꝥ he hit aȝe; se þe hit ofspireð, he ah ꝥ meldfeoh.[16]

lxii. Be cyrliscū þeof ȝefanȝenū.[3]

Cyrlisc[17] mon ȝif he oft betẏȝen ƿære, ȝif he æt siþestan sie ȝfonȝen, slea mon hond of oþþe fote.[18]
Cyninȝes[19]

[13] ~~lx~~ del. before lix [14] mid from nied [15] ȝdyrneð has crossbar of ð del. and in right margin ȝedyrned, i(d est) celatā Nw2 [16] in right margin i(d est) pecūias indicationē ł delaturā regis Nw2 [17] Cyrlisc] C from G [18] in bottom left oþþe fote in green ink Nw2 [19] in bottom right cyninȝes with ~~oþþe fot~~ del. above it

-men oþþe oþꞃum ꝺeman, ⁊ hebban ne mæᵹ, ⁊ him ƿeꝺꝺ mon ꞅẏllan nẏlle, ᵹebeꞇe xxx ꞅcill., ⁊ binnan ꞅeoꝼon nihꞇe ᵹeꝺô hine ꞃihꞇeꞅ ƿẏꞃþe.

Be þam ƿꞃæcenꝺan.

9 Ᵹiᵹ hƿa ƿꞃæce ꝺo æꞃþon he him ꞃihꞇeꞅ biꝺꝺe, ꝥ he him on nime aᵹẏꝼe, ⁊ ꝼoꞃᵹẏlꝺ ⁊ ᵹebeꞇe xxx ꞅcill.

Be ꞃeaꝼlace.

10 Ᵹiꝼ hƿa binnan ðam ᵹemæꞃum uꞃeꞅ ꞃiceꞅ ꞃeaꝼlâc ⁊ nẏꝺnæme ꝺô, aᵹẏꝼe he ðone ꞃeaꝼlâc, ⁊ ᵹeꞅẏlle ꞅẏxꞇiᵹ ꞅcill. ꞇo ƿiꞇe.

Be leoꝺ bẏᵹene.

11 Ᵹiꝼ hƿa hiꞅ aᵹenne leoꝺan bebicᵹe, þeoƿne oþþe ꝼꞃiᵹe, þeah he ꞅcẏlꝺiᵹ ꞅẏ, ⁊ oꝼeꞃ ꞅæ ꞅenꝺe, ꝼoꞃᵹẏlꝺ hine be hiꞅ ƿæꞃe ⁊ ƿiþ ᵹoꝺ ꝺeoplice beꞇe.[1]

[Ld 3v] Be ðam þe heoꞃa ᵹeƿiꞇnẏꞅꞅe ᵹeleoᵹaþ.

12 Ᵹiꝼ hƿa beꝼoꞃan biꞅceoƿe hiꞅ ᵹeƿiꞇnẏꞅꞅe ⁊ hiꞅ ƿeꝺ aleoᵹe, ᵹebeꞇe miꝺ hunꝺ ꞇƿelꝼꞇiᵹ ꞅcill.

Be ᵹeꝼanᵹenum þeoꝼum.

13 Ᵹiꝼ þeoꝼ ꞅẏ ᵹeꝼonᵹen ꞅƿelꞇ he ꝺeaþe, oþþe hiꞅ liꝼ be hiꞅ ƿeꞃe mon alẏꞅe. Þeoꝼaꞅ ƿe haꞇaþ oþ ꞅeoꝼon men; ꝼꞃom ꞅeoꝼon hloþ oþ ꝼiꝼ ⁊ þꞃiꞇꞇiᵹ; ⁊ ꞅẏþþan heꞃe.

Be hloþum.

14 Se þe hloþ be ꞇoᵹen ꞅẏ, ᵹeꞅƿicne ꞅe hine be hunꝺ ꞇƿelꝼꞇiᵹum hẏꝺa oþþe ꞅƿa ᵹebeꞇe.

CN rubrics all Nw2; Ld 12 & 13 are in reverse order to that of other MSS; Ld 13's second sentence precedes rubric to 14 in Ld alone [1] ⁊ ƿiþ ᵹoꝺ ꝺeoplice beꞇe not in CN or other MSS, added later in margin in B

Be herge.

15 Se þe herteama betogen sy, he hine be his wergyld alyse oþþe be ðam geswicne. Se aþ sceal beon healf be huslgengum.[2] Þeof, syþþan he beoþ on cyninges bendum, nah he ða geswicne.

Be þeofslæge.

16 Se ðe ðeof ofslihþ, se mot gecyþan mid aþe ꝥ he hine scyldig ofslôge, ⁊ na les ða gegyldan.

Be forstolenum flæsce.

17 Se ðe forstolen flæsc findeþ ⁊ gedyrneþ, gif he dear he mot mid aþe gecyþan ꝥ he hit age; Se ðe hit ofspyraþ, he ah ꝥ meld feoh.

Be ceorliscum þeofum gefangenum.

18 Cyrlisc [Ld 4v] mon gif he oft betogen wære, gif he æt syþestan sy gefangen, slea mon hand oþþe fôt of.

Cyninges

CN rubrics all Nw2 [2] margin – huselgengum sonat etiā Catechumenos

lxiii. Be cyninʒes ʒeneat.[1]

Cẏninʒes ʒeneat, ʒif his ƿer bið tƿelfhund sciłł, he mot sƿerian for syxtiʒ hida ʒif he biþ huslʒenʒa.

lxiiii. Be feorran cumenū butan ƿæʒ ʒ̄mettū.[2]

Gif feorcund mon oþþe frēde butan ƿeʒe ʒeond ƿudu ʒonʒe, 7 ne[3] hrime ne horn blaƿe, for[4] þeof he biþ to þrouianne: oþþe to sleanne oþþe to alisanne.

lxv.

Gif mon þonne þæs ofsleʒenan ƿeren[5] bidde, he mot ʒ̄cẏþan ꝥ he hine for þeof ofsloʒe; nalles þæs ofsleʒenan ʒ̄ʒyldan ne his hlaford.

Gif he hit þon dyrneð, 7 ƿeorðeð[6] ȳb lonʒ ẏppe, þonne rimeð he þā deadan to þā aþe ꝥ hine moton his maʒas unsynʒian.[7]

lxvi. Be þoñ þe monnes ʒeneat staliʒe.[2]

Gif þin ʒeneat staliʒe 7 losiʒe þe, ʒif þu hæbbe byrʒean, mana þone þæs anʒyldes; ʒif he næbbe, ʒyld þu þæt anʒylde 7 ne sie hī to no þy þinʒodre.

lxvii. Be elþeodiʒes monnes sleʒe.[8]

Gif mon elþeodiʒne ofslea, se cyninʒ ah tƿædne dæl ƿeres, þriddan dæl sunu oþþe maʒas.

Gif he þonne mæʒleas sie: healf cẏninʒe, healf se siþ.

Gif hit þonne abbod sie oþþe abbodesse, dælen on þa ẏlcan ƿisan ƿiþ þone kẏninʒ.

Ƿealh ʒafolʒylda cxx sciłł, his sunu c, þeoƿne lx, somhƿelcne fifteʒū; Ƿealas hẏd[9] tƿelfū.

lxviii. Be ƿiteþeoƿes monnes sleʒe.[2]

Gif ƿiteþeoƿ[10] Enʒliscmon hine forstaliʒe, ho hine mon 7 ne ʒylde his hlaforde.

Gif hine mon ofslea, ne ʒylde hine mon his maʒū Gif hie hine on tƿelf monþū ne alysden.

Ƿealh, ʒif he hafað v hida,[11] he byð sẏxhẏnde.

Gif

[1] rubric in top margin Nw2 [2] rubrics in left margin Nw2 [3] 7 ne] 7 ~~hƿ~~ ne [4] for] fo'r' and in left margin for Nw2 [5] ƿeren] ~~þeræр~~ del. with ƿeren written above Nw2 [6] ƿeorðeð] ƿeordeð—first ð not crossed [7] unsynʒian] uns/'y'nʒian Nw2; the caret covers original i [8] rubric mostly in left margin Nw2 [9] hyd] ~~hẏð~~ hẏd with ẏ of hẏd from i Nw2 [10] ƿiteþeoƿ] ƿite~~þeor~~þeoƿ [11] hida] ħ hida

Be cẏninᵹeſ ᵹeneaꞇ.

19 Cẏninᵹeſ ᵹeneaꞇ, ᵹiꝼ hiſ ƿeꞃ biþ ꞇƿelꝼ hunꝺ ſcill., he moꞇ ſƿeꞃian ꝼoꞃ ſixꞇiᵹ hẏða ᵹiꝼ he beoþ huſlᵹenᵹa.

Be ꝼeoꞃꞃan cumenum men.

20 Ᵹiꝼ ꝼeoꞃ cuman man oþþe ꝼꞃemꝺe buꞇan ƿeᵹe ᵹeonꝺ ƿuꝺu ᵹonᵹe, ⁊ ne hꞃẏme ne hoꞃn blaƿe, ꝼoꞃ ðeoꝼ he biþ ꞇo þꞃoꝼianne: oþþe ꞇo alẏſanne. Ᵹiꝼ mon ðonne ðæſ oꝼſlæᵹenan ƿæꞃeſ biꝺꝺe, he moꞇ ᵹecẏþan ꝥ he hine ꝼoꞃ þeoꝼ oꝼſlôᵹe; na læſ þæſ oꝼſlæᵹenan ᵹeᵹẏlꝺan ne hiſ hlaꝼoꞃꝺ. Ᵹiꝼ he hiꞇ þonne ꝺẏꞃneþ, ⁊ ƿeoꞃꝺeþ emb lonᵹ ẏppe, ðonne ꞃẏmeþ he þæm ꝺeâꝺan ꞇo ðam aþe ðe hine moꞇon hiſ mæᵹaſ unſẏnᵹian.

Be ðon ðe monneſ ᵹeneaꞇ ſꞇaliᵹe.

21 Ᵹiꝼ ðin ᵹeneaꞇ ſꞇaliᵹe ⁊ loſiᵹe ðe, ᵹiꝼ þu hæbbe boꞃᵹaſ, mana ðone ðæſ anᵹẏlꝺeſ; ᵹiꝼ he næbbe, ᵹẏlꝺ ðu ꝥ anᵹẏlꝺe ⁊ ne ſẏ him na ðe ᵹeþinᵹoꝺꞃe.

Be ælþeoꝺiᵹeſ manneſ ſlæᵹe.

22 Ᵹiꝼ mon ælþeoꝺiᵹne mon oꝼſlea, ſe cẏninᵹ ah ꞇƿeᵹen ꝺælaſ þæſ ƿeꞃeſ, þꞃiꝺꝺan ꝺæl ſunu oþþe maᵹaſ. [Ld 5^{V}] Ᵹiꝼ he ðonne mæᵹleaſ ſẏ: healꝼ cẏninᵹ, healꝼ ſe ᵹeꞃiþ. Ᵹiꝼ hiꞇ ðonne abbuꝺ ſẏ oþþe abbuꝺiſſe, ꝺœlon on ða ẏlcan ƿiſan ƿiþ ðone cẏnninᵹ; ƿealh ᵹaꝼolᵹẏlꝺa hunꝺ ꞇƿelꝼꞇiᵹ ſcill., Ꝺiſ ſunu hunꝺ, Neꝺ þeoꞃne ſixꞇiᵹ ſcill., ſomhƿẏlcne miꝺ ꝼiꝼꞇeᵹum; ƿealeſ hẏꝺe miꝺ ꞇƿelꝼum; ƿealh, ᵹiꝼ he hæꝼþ ꝼiꝼ hẏꝺa, he biþ ſẏx hẏnꝺe.[1]

Be ƿiꞇe þeoƿum.

23 Ᵹiꝼ ƿiꞇe ðeoƿ enᵹliſc mon hine ꝼoꞃſꞇaliᵹe, hô hine mon ⁊ ne ᵹẏlꝺe hiſ hlaꝼoꞃꝺe. Ᵹiꝼ hine mon oꝼſlea, ne ᵹẏlꝺe hine mon hiſ maᵹum ᵹiꝼ hi hine on ꞇƿelꝼ monþum ne alẏſꝺon.

Ᵹiꝼ

Nw2 rubrics inserted into CN [1] ƿealh ... ſẏx hẏnꝺe found in other MSS at end of lxviii as in CN lxix. Be cyƿemonna forefenʒ uppe on lond.[1]

Gif cyƿemon uppe on folce ceapie, do ꝥ beforan ʒ̄ƿitnessū.

Gif þyfefeoh mon æt ciepan befo, 7 he hit næbbe beforan ʒodū ƿitū ʒ̄ceapod, ʒecẏþe hit be ƿite ꝥ he ne ʒeƿita ne ʒ̄stala nære, oþþe ʒyld to ƿite vi 7 xxx sciłł.

lxx. Be fundenes cildes fostre.[2]

To fundenes cẏldes fostre, þẏ forman ʒeare ʒ̄selle vi sciłł, þẏ æftran ʒeare xii, þy þriddan xxx, siþþan be his ƿlite.

lxxi. Be dearnunʒa bearn ʒestryñ.[2]

Se þe dearnenʒa bearn ʒestrineð 7 ʒ̄heleð, nah he his deaðes ƿer, ac his hlaford[3] 7 se cẏninʒ.

lxxii. Be þeofes onfenʒ æt þeofðe.[2]

Se þeof ʒefehð, ah x sciłł, 7 se cyninʒ þone þeof; 7 þa maʒas hī sperian aþas unfehða.[4]

Gif he þoñ oðyrne 7 oriʒe ƿeorþe, þoñ bið he ƿites scyldiʒ; ʒif[5] he onsacan ƿille, do he ꝥ be þā feo 7 be þā ƿite.

lxxiii. Be sƿeordes onlæne oðres þeoƿe.[2]

Gif mon sƿeordes onlǽne oþres esne 7 he losiʒe, ʒyld he hine þriddan dæl; Gif mon sƿere selle, healfne; ʒif he horses onlǽne, ealne he hine ʒylde.

lxxiiii. Be þon þe cyrlisc mon fleomanfeormiʒe.[6]

Gif mon cyrliscne[7] monnan fliemanfeormiʒ̄ teo, be his aʒnū ƿer ʒeladiʒe he hine. Gif he ne mæʒe, ʒyld hine his aʒne ƿere; 7 se ʒesiþmon sƿa be his ƿere.

lxxv. Be þon þe mon ƿif ʒebycʒe 7 þoñ seo ʒift tostande.[2]

Gif mon ƿif ʒ̄bicʒe, 7 sio ʒyft forð ne cume, aʒyfe þæt feoh 7 forʒylde 7 ʒ̄bete þā byrʒean sƿa his borʒbryce sie.

lxxvi. Be Ƿylisces monnes londhæfene.[2]

Gif Ƿẏlisc[8] mon hæbbe hyde londes, his ƿer bið[9] cxx sciłł; Gif he þoñe healfes hæbbe, lxxx sciłł; ʒif he næniʒ hæbbe, lx sciłł.

lxxvii. Be cyninʒes horsƿeale.[2]

Cyninʒes horseƿealh, se þe hī mæʒe ʒ̄ærendian, þæs ƿerʒild biþ cc sciłł.

[1] rubric in top margin Nw2 [2] rubrics mostly in right margin Nw2 [3] del. of -es(?) after hlaford Nw2 [4] above unfehða, factionem ł iuramētū, almost illegible [5] ʒif] i from e [6] rubric in right margin Nw2 [7] cyrliscne] cyrliscre [8] Ƿylisc] y from i [9] ƿer bið] ƿer 'bið' Nw2

Be cẏpmanna on lande.

24 Gif cẏpeman uppe on folc ceapige, dô ꝥ beforan geƿitnisse. Gif þẏfefeoh[1] mon æt cẏpmen befô, ⁊ he hit næbbe beforan godum ƿittum geceapod, gecẏþe hit be ƿite, ꝥ he ne geƿita ne gestala ƿære, oþþe gẏlde to ƿite sẏx ⁊ xxx scill.

Be fundenes cildes fostre.

25 To fundenes cildes fostre, þẏ forman geare gesẏlle sẏx scill., þẏ æfteran geare tƿelf, þẏ þriddan xxx, sẏþþan be his ƿlite.

[Ld 6v] Be ðeofes onfeng.

26 Se ðe þeof gefehþ, he ah tẏn scill., ⁊ se cẏning þone þeof; ⁊ þa magas him sƿerian aþas unfæhþa. gif he ðonne oþẏrne ⁊ ƿerige ƿeorþe, þonne biþ he ƿites scẏldig; Gif he ætsƿacan ƿille, dô he ꝥ be ðam feo ⁊ be þam ƿite.

Be ðam ðe dearnunga bearn strẏneþ.

27 Se ðe deornunga bearn gestreonaþ ⁊ geheleþ, nah se his deaþes ƿere, ac his hlaford ⁊ se cẏng.

Be ðam ðe his ƿæpnu onlæne.

28 Gif mon sƿeordes onlæne oþrum esne ⁊ he losige, be ðriddan dæle he hine gẏlde; Gif mon sƿere sẏlle, healfne; Gif mon hors onlæne, ealne he hine gilde.

Be ðam ðe flẏman feormige.

29 Gif mon cẏrlisne mannan flẏman feorminge teo, be his agenum ƿere geladige he hine. Gif he ne mæge, gẏlde he hine be his agenum ƿere; ⁊ se gesiþman eac sƿa be his ƿere.

Be ðon ðe mon ƿif bicge.

30 Gif mon ƿif gebẏcge, ⁊ seo gẏft forþ ne cume, agẏfe ꝥ feoh ⁊ forgẏld ⁊ gebete ðæm bẏrgean sƿa his borhbrẏce.

[Ld 7v] Be ciplisces monnes land hæfene.

31 Gif ƿilisc man hæbbe hẏde landes, his ƿere biþ hund tƿelftig scill.; Gif he ðonne healfe hæbbe, eahtatig scill.[2]

Be cẏninges hors ƿealh.

32 Cẏninges hors ƿealh, se ðe him mæg geærendian, þæs ƿergẏld biþ tƿa hund scill.

Nw2 rubrics inserted into CN; Ld's 26 & 27 in reverse order to that of other MSS, including CN

[1] margin — al. forstolen quod idem est [2] errata — interpone post eahtatig scill. hæc verba: Gif he næbbe nân land 60 scill.

Be monslyhte.[1]

Se þe on þære fore pære þæt mon monnan ofsloʒe,[2] (ʒetreoþe)[3] hine þæs sleʒes 7 þa fore ʒ̄bete be þæs ofsleʒenan perʒylde.

Gif his perʒield sie cc sciłł, ʒebete mid l sciłł; 7 þẏ ẏlcan ryhte do man be þā deorborenran.

lxxix. Be þeofslyht.[4]

Se þe þeof slyhð, he mot aðe ʒecẏþan þæt he hine fleondne for þeof sloʒe, 7 þæs deadan maʒas hī sperian unceases að;[5] ʒif he hit þoñe dyrne 7 sie eft ẏppe, þoñe forʒylde he hine.

Gif mon to ðā men feoh ʒeteme þe his ær oðsparen[6] hæfde, 7 eft oðsperian pille, oðsperiʒe[7] be þā pite 7 be þæs feos peorþe; ʒif he oþsperian[8] nẏlle, ʒebete þone mænan að[9] tpẏbote.

lxxx. Be þeofes onfenʒ.[4]

Se þe þeof ʒefehð, oððe hine mon ʒ̄fonʒenne aʒyfþ, 7 he hine þoñe alæte oþþe þa þyfðe ʒ̄dyrne, forʒylde þone þeof his pere.

Gif he ealdorman sie, þoliʒe his scire butan hī cẏninʒ arian pille.

lxxxi. Be cyrlisces monnes ontyʒenes æt þyfþe.[4]

Se ceorlisca[10] mon, se þe oft betẏʒen pære þifþe, 7 þoñe æt siþestan sẏnniʒne ʒefó in ceape oþþe elles æt openre scylde, slea hī mon hond oþþe fot.

lxxxii. Be bearna[11] fostre þoñ se pere ʒepite.[4]

Gif ceorl 7 his pif bearn hæbben ʒemæne, 7 fere se ceorl forð, hæbbe sio modor hire bearn 7 fede; aʒyfe hire mon vi sciłł to fostre, cú on sumera, oxan on pintra; healden[12] þa maʒas þone frumstol oþ þæt hit ʒepintred sie.

Gif hpa

[1] no numerals; rubric in top margin Nw2 [2] ofsloʒe] ~~ofslelʒe sleʒe~~ with ofsloʒe written above Nw2 [3] ʒetreoþe] ʒtrye with in left margin ʒetreoþe Nw2 [4] rubrics in left margin Nw2 [5] unceases að] in left margin uncorene að, i(d est) sine electiōe Nw2 [6] oðsparen] ~~oð~~sparen with oð del. and æt above in faint brown ink Nw2 [7] oðsperiʒe] /'on'~~oð~~/'on'speriʒe with second / and 'on' in faint brown ink Nw2 [8] oþsperian] e from a [9] above mænan að, p(er)iurium [10] ceorlisca] ce'or'l'isca with in left margin ceorlisca Nw2 [11] bearna] ~~ceorla~~ bearna [12] healden] second e from a

Be manslýhte.

33 Se ðe on ðære fore wære ðær mon man ofsloge, getrýwie hine be his were þæs slæges oþþe fore gebete be ðæs ofslagenan wergýlde. Gif his wergýlde sý twa hund scill., gebete mid fiftig scill.; And ða ýlcan riht dô man be ðem deorborenran.

Be ðeofslýhte.

34 Se ðe ðeof slýhþ, he mot mid aþe gecyðan, ꝥ he hine fleondne for ðeof sloge, ⁊ þæs deadan magas him swerian unceases aþ; Gif he hit þonne dýrne ⁊ sý eft ýppe, þonne forgýld he hine.

35 Gif mon to ðæm menn feoh geteme, þe his ær aþ ætswopen hæfd, ⁊ eft aþ ætswerian wille, swerige be ðam wite ⁊ be ðæs feos wýrþe; [Ld 8^{V}] Gif he oþswerian nýlle, gebete þone mænan aþe twýgbote.

Be ðon ðe mon þeof forlæte.

36 Se ðe ðeof gefehþ, oþþe him mon gefongene agýfþ, ⁊ he hine þonne alæte oþþe ða ðýfþe gedýrne, forgýlde ðone ðeof be his were. Gif he ealdorman sý, þolige his scire butan him cýning arian wille.

Be cýrlisces monnes betogennýsse.

37 Se cýrlisce man, se ðe oft betogen wære ðýfðe, ⁊ þonne æt siþestan sýnnigne gefô in ceape oþþe elles æt openre scýlde, slea him mon handa of oþþe fôt.

Be ðon ðe riht gehiwan bearn hæbban.

38 Gif ceorl ⁊ his wif bearn hæbben gemane, ⁊ fære se ceorl forþ, hæbbe se modor hire bearn ⁊ fede; agýfe hire mon sýx scill. to fostre, cû on sumera, oxan on wintran; Healdan ða magas ðone frumstol oþ ꝥ hit gewintrod sý.

Gif hwa

Nw2 rubrics inserted into CN

lxxxiii. Be unalyfedū fare frā hlaford.[1]

Gif hƿa fare unalifed frō his hlaforde, oþþe on oþre scire[2] hine bestele, 7 hine mon ȝ̄ahsiȝe, fare þær he ær[3] ƿæs 7 selle his hlaforde lx scilł.

lxxxiiii. Be ceorles ƿeorþiȝe.[4]

Ceorles ƿorðiȝ sceal beon ƿintres 7 sumeres betẏned; Gif he biþ untẏned, 7 recþ his neahȝebures ceap in on[5] his aȝen ȝeat, nah he æt þā ceap nan ƿuht ah:[6] adrife hine ut 7 þoliȝe æfƿerdlan.[7]

lxxxv. Be borȝes onsace.[4]

Borȝes mon mot oþsacan, ȝyf he ƿat,[8] ꝥte he ryht deð.[9]

lxxxvi. Be ceorles ȝærstun.[4]

Gif ceorles ȝærstun hæbben ȝemænne[10] oþþe oðer ȝedalland to tẏnanne, 7 habban sume ȝ̄tẏned hiora dæl[11] sume nabban, 7 etten hiora ȝ̄mænan æceras oþþe ȝærs, ȝán þa þon̄e þe þæt ȝeat aȝan 7 ȝebete þā oþrū þe hiora dæl ȝ̄tynedne hæbben,[12] ðone æƿerdlan[13] þe þær ȝ̄don sie; abidden hī æt þā ceap sƿẏlc ryht sƿẏlce hit cyn[14] sie.

Gif þonne hryðera[15] hƿilce sie þe heȝas brece 7 ȝa in ȝehƿær, 7 se hit nolde ȝ̄healdan se hit aȝe, oþþe ne mæȝe, nime se hit on his æcere mete 7 ofslea; 7 nime se aȝenfriȝea his fel 7 flæsc,[16] 7 þoliȝe þæs oþres.

lxxxvii. Be ƿudubærnete.[17]

Ðonne mon beame on ƿuda forbærne, 7 ƿeorðe yppe on þone þe hit dede, ȝylde he fulƿite: 7 ȝeselle lx scilł forþā þe fyr bið þeof.

Gif mon afelle on ƿuda ƿæl moneȝa[18] treoƿa, 7 ƿyrð eft undyrne, forȝylde iii[19] treoƿu ælc mid xxx scilł; ne þearf he hiora ma ȝeldan, ƿære hiora sƿa feala sƿa hiora ƿær, forþon sio æsc̄[20] bið melda nalles[21] þeof.

Gif mon

[1] rubric in top margin Nw2 [2] oþre scire] oþres scire [3] fare þær he ær] fare "he" þær ær [4] rubrics in right margin Nw2 [5] in on] mon [6] nan ƿuht ah] ~~þā þuht~~ 'nan ƿuht ah' and in right margin nan ƿuht ꝥ ah Nw2 [7] in right margin dānū (= dampnum) [8] ȝyf he ƿat] ȝyf he ꝥ ƿat [9] ꝥte he ryht deð] ꝥte 'he' ryht 'he' deð Nw2 [10] ȝemænne] first e from æ [11] hiora dæl] hiora ~~hi~~ dæl [12] hæbben] hæbbá'e'n [13] above æƿerdlan, dānū [14] above cyn, congruū [15] above hryðera, aīal (= animal) [16] flæsc] f from s [17] rubric half in right margin Nw2 [18] moneȝa] mon'e'ȝa Nw2 [19] del. of i after forȝylde in anticipation of iii [20] æsc̄ underlined and in right margin ælc, oplnor Nw2; Nowell is mistaken, for the intended meaning is axe [21] nalles] milles

Be unalýfedum fære fram his hlaford.

39 Gif hƿa fare unaleafed fram his hlaforde, oþþe on oþre scire hine bestele, ⁊ mon hine geacsige, fare þær he ær ƿæs ⁊ gýlde his hlaford sixtig scill.

Be ceorles ƿeorþige.

40 Ceorles [Ld 9^{V}] ƿeorþig sceal beon ƿintres ⁊ sumeres betýned; Gif he biþ untýned, ⁊ recþ his nehgebures ceap mon his agen geat, nah he æt ðæm ceape nân ƿiht: ac adrife hine ût ⁊ ðolige ðone æfƿýrdlan.

Be borges onsæce.

41 Borges mon mot ætsacan, gif he ƿat, ꝥ he riht deþ.

Be ceorla gemænum land.

42 Gif ceorlas hæbban gærstun gemænne oþþe oþer gedale land to týnanne, ⁊ hæbben sume getýned heora dæle sume næbben, ⁊ etten heora gemænan æcceras oþþe gærs, gân ða ðonne ðe ꝥ geat agon ⁊ gebeten þæm oþrum ðe heora dæle getýned hæbben, ðone æfƿýrdlan ðe ðære gedôn sý; ⁊ abidden him æt ðæm ceape sƿýlc riht sƿýlc cýn sý. Gif ðonne hrýþera hƿýlc sý þe hegas brece ⁊ ga in gehƿær, ⁊ se hit nolde gehealdan se hit age, oþþe ne mæge, nime se þe hit on his æcere gemete ⁊ ofslea; ⁊ nime se agen frigea his flæsc, ⁊ ðolige ðæs oþres.

Be ƿudu[1] bærnete.

43 Ðonne mon beam on ƿuda forbærne, ⁊ ƿýrþ ýppe on ðone ðe hit dýde, gýlde he fulƿite: ⁊ gesýlle sýxtig scill. for ðam ðe fýr biþ ðeof. [Ld 10^{V}] Gif mon afýlle on ƿuda ƿel manega treoƿu, ⁊ ƿýrþ ꝥ eft undýrne, forgýlde ðreo treoƿa ælc mid þrittig scill.; Ne ðearf he ma gýldan, ƿære heora sƿa feola sƿa heora ƿære, forþan seo eax biþ melda na læs ðeof.

Gif mon

Nw2 rubrics inserted into CN [1] errata — in titulo capitis: ƿudu, lege ƿudu lxxviii. Be ƿuda onfenȝ buta leafe.[1]

Gif mon þonne aceorfe an treoƿ þæt[2] mæȝe xxx sƿina underȝstandan,[3] 7 ƿirþ undirne, ȝeselle lx sciłł.

Gafolhƿitel sceall bion æt hiƿisce[4] vi peninȝa ƿeorþ.

lxxxix. Be burhbryce.[5]

Burhbryce mon sceal betan cxx sciłł kẏninȝes 7 bisceopes þær his ric[6] bið; ealdormonnes lxxx sciłł; cẏninȝes þeȝnes lx sciłł; ȝsiþcundes monnes landhæbbendes xxxv; 7 bi ðon ansacan.

xc. Be stæletyhtlan.[7]

Þonne mon monnan betẏhð, ꝥ he ceaƿ forstæle oþþe forstollenne ȝformie, þonne sceal he be lx hida[8] onsacan þære þyfþe, Gif he aðƿyrðe bið.[9]

Gif þonne Enȝlisc onstal ȝa forþ, onsace þoñe be tƿyfealdū; Gif hit þoñe bið Ƿilisc onstal, ne bið se að na þy mara.

Ælc mon mot onsacan frȳþe[10] 7 ƿærfæhþe,[11] ȝif he mæȝ oþþe dear.

xci. Be forstolene ceaƿ befanȝene.[7]

Gif mon[12] forstolenne ceaƿ befehð, ne mot hine mon tieman to þeoƿū men.

xcii. Be ƿiteþeoƿū men.[7]

Gif hƿelc mon biþ ƿiteþeoƿ niƿan ȝþeoƿad, 7 hine mon betẏhþ ꝥ he hæbbe ær ȝþyfed, ær hine mon ȝþeoƿode, þonne ah se teond ane sƿinȝellan æt hī; bedryfe hine to sƿinȝū be his ceƿe.

xciii. Be unaliefedes mæstines onfenȝ.[13]

Gif mon on his mæstenne unalyfed sƿin ȝemete,[14] ȝnime þoñe vi sciłł ƿeorð ƿed; ȝif hie þonne þær næren oftor þonne æne, ȝselle sciłł se aȝenfriȝea, 7 ȝcẏþe ðæt hie þær oftor ne comon be þæs ceaƿes ƿeorðe.

Gif hie þær tuƿa ƿæren, ȝselle tƿeȝen sciłł.

Gif mon nime æfæsne[15]

[1] rubric in top margin Nw2 [2] blot in MS, but þæt is clear enough [3] underȝstand'a'n with second a replacing e Nw2 [4] ȝafolhƿitel ... hiƿisce underlined and in left margin quid Nw2 [5] rubric Nw2 [6] his ric] his 'ric' Nw2, with ric repeated in left margin Nw2 [7] rubrics in left margin Nw2 [8] be lx hida underlined and in left margin i(d est), cū 60 hominibus Nw2 [9] del. of one after bið Nw2 [10] above frȳþe, firmationem [11] above ƿærfæhþe, perefactionē [12] Gif mon] Gif 'mon' Nw2 [13] rubric partly in right margin Nw2 [14] ȝemete] ȝemiete [15] in left margin æbesne, alias Nw2

44 Gif mon ðonne aceorfe ænne treoƿe ꝥ mæge þritig sƿina understandan,[1] ⁊ ƿẏrþ undẏrne, gesẏlle sixtig scill.

45 Gafol hƿitel æt hiƿisce sceal beon sẏx peninga ƿẏrþ.

Be burhbrẏce.

46 Burhbrẏce mon sceal betan mid hund tƿelftigum scill. Cẏninges ⁊ bisceopes þær his rice biþ; Ealdormannes mid eahtatig scillinges; Cẏninges ðegnes sẏxtig scill.; Gesiþcundes mannes landhæbbendes fif ⁊ xxx scill.; And be ðam onsacan.

Be stal tẏhtlan.

47 Ðonne mon monnan betẏhþ, ꝥ he ceap forstæle oþþe forstolenne gefeormige, þonne sceal he be sẏxtig hẏda ætsacan ðær ðeofþe, gif he aþ ƿẏrþ biþ. Gif ðonne englisc mon stalaþ ga forþ, ætsace be tƿẏfealdum; Gif hit ðonne biþ ƿilisc on stal, ne biþ se aþ na ðe mare. Ælc mon mot onsacan frẏmþe ⁊ ƿærsæhþe, gif he mæge oþþe [Ld 11^{V}] dearr.

Be forstolene ceap befangene.

48 Gif mon forstolene ceap befeþ, ne mot hine mon tẏman to ðeoƿum men.

Be ƿite ðeoƿum mannum.

49 Gif hƿẏlc mon biþ ƿite ðeoƿe niƿan geþeoƿod, ⁊ hine mon betẏh ꝥ he hæbbe ær geþeofad, ær hine mon geþeoƿad, ðonne ah se teond ane sƿingelan æt him; bedrife hine to sƿinglum be his ceape.

Be unalẏfedes mæstenes onfeng.

50 Gif mon on his mæstene unalẏfed sƿin gemete, genime ðonne sẏx scill. ƿẏrþ ƿed; Gif hi ðonne ðær næron oftor ðonne æne, gesẏlle ænne scill. se agen friga, ⁊ gecẏþe ꝥ hi ðær oftor ne comon be ðæs ceapes ƿẏrþe. Gif hi ðær tƿa ƿæron, gesẏlle tƿegen scill. Gif mon nime æbesne[2]

Nw2 rubrics inserted into CN; Ld does not share Nw2's rubric before 44, but B has Be wude andfenge

[1] errata — underſtandan lege understandân [2] margin — al. æfesne

æfesne on ƿinū: æt þryfinᵹrū ꝥ ðrydde, æt tƿyfinᵹrū ꝥ feorþe, æt þẏmelū ꝥ fifte.

xciiii. Be siþcundes mōnes ᵹeþinᵹe.[1]

Gif ᵹesiðcund[2] mon þinᵹað ƿiþ cẏninᵹ oþþe ƿiþ cẏninᵹes ealdormannan for his inhiƿan, oþþe[3] ƿiþ his hlaford for þeoƿe oþþe for friᵹe, nah he ðær nan ƿíterædene, se ᵹesið, forþon he hī nolde ǽr ẏfles ᵹ̄stiran æt hā.

xcv. Be þon þe ᵹ̄siðcund[4] mon fyrd forƿitie.[1]

Gif ᵹesiþcund[5] mon landaᵹende forsitte fyrd, ᵹ̄selle cxx sciłł 7 þoliᵹe his landes; unlandaᵹende lx sciłł; cyrlisc xxx sciłł to fyrdƿite.

lxcvi. Be dyrnum ᵹeðinᵹe.[6]

Se þe diernū ᵹeþinᵹū betoᵹen[7] sie, ᵹ̄sƿicne hine be cxx hida þara ᵹ̄þinᵹea,[8] oþþe ᵹeselle cxx[9] sciłł.

Be forstolenes mannes fore foreᵹesitte.[1]

Gif mon forstolenne man befo æt oþrū, 7 sie sio hond acƿolen[10] sio hine sealde þā men þe hine mon ætbefenᵹ, tieme þonne þone mon to þæs deadan byrᵹelse, sƿa oþer fioh sƿa hit sie, 7 cẏþe on þā aðe be lx hida ꝥ sio deade hond hine hī sealde. Þoñe hæfð he ꝥ ƿite afylled mid þy aðe; aᵹyfe þā aᵹendfrio þone monnan.

Gif he þonne ƿite hƿa þæs deadan ierfe hæbbe, tieme þoñe to þǣ ierfe, 7 bidde þa hond þe ꝥ ierfe hafað ꝥ he hī ᵹedó ðone ceap unbeceasne,[11] oþþe ᵹ̄cyþe þæt se deada næfre þæt yrfe ahte.

xcviii. Be ƿerfehð tyhtlan.[1]

Se þe bið ƿærfæhþe[12] betoᵹen, 7 he onsacan ƿille[13] þæs sleᵹes mid aðe; þoñe sceal bion on þære hyndene[14] an cẏninᵹæþe be xxx hyda, sƿa be ᵹesiþcundū men sƿa be cyrliscū, sƿa hƿæðer

[1] rubrics in right margin Nw2 [2] se cyninᵹ is marked for deletion and the ᵹe- of ᵹesiðcund is written above cyninᵹ Nw2 [3] oþþe] oþþ [4] ᵹ̄siðcund] 'ᵹ̄'siðcund [5] ᵹesiþcund has u on top of one [6] rubric half in right margin Nw2 [7] betoᵹen] be~~tƿiᵹu~~'toᵹen' Nw2 [8] in right margin ðara ᵹ̄þunᵹera, alias with del. of one after the e Nw2 [9] oþþe 'ᵹeselle' cxx Nw2 [10] acƿolen] ~~oð~~ 'a'cƿolen Nw2 [11] in right margin unbecappane, alias Nw2 [12] above ƿærfæhþe is homicidium [13] ƿille] altered from ƿelle [14] above hyndene is societate

æberne on swinum: æt ðrýfingrum swic þ ðridde, æt twýfingrum þ feorþ, æt ðýmelum þ fifte.

Be riþcundes monnes geþinge.

51 Gif geriþcund mon ðingaþ wiþ cýning oþþe wiþ cýninges ealdormannum for his inhiwan, oþþe wiþ his hlaford for ðeowe oþþe for frige, nah he þær nane wite rædene, se geriþ, forþon he nolde him ær ýfeles gestýran æt ham.

[Ld 12^{v}] Be ðon ðe geriþcund mon fýrd forsitte.

52 Gif se riþcundman land agende fýrde forsitte, gesýlle hund twelftig scill. ⁊ þolige his landes; unlandagende sýxtig scill.; ceorlisc ðrittig scill.

Be dýrnum geþinghe.

53 Se ðe dýrnum geþinghum betogen sý, geswicne[1] hine be cxx hýda ðæra ðinga, oþþe hund twelftig scill. gesýlle.

Be forstolenes mannes forfenge.

54 Gif mon forstolene man befô æt oþrum, ⁊ sý seo hand acwolen ðe hine sealde ðam men ðe hine mon æt befeng, týme ðonne ðone man to ðæs ðeadan býrgenne, swa oþer feoh swa hweþer swa hit sý, ⁊ cýþe on ðæm aþe be feowertig hida þ seo deade hand hine him sealde. Ðonne hæfþ he þ wite afýlled mid ðý aþe; agýfe ðam agend freo ðone man. Gif he ðonne wite hwa ðæs deadan ýrfe hæbbe, týme ðonne to ðæm ýrf, ⁊ bidde ða hond ðe þ ýrfe hafaþ þ he him gedô ðone ceape unbesacene, oþþe gecýþe þ se deade næfre þ ýrfe ahte.

Be wærfæhþe týhtlan.

55 Se ðe biþ werfæhþe betogen, ⁊ he ætsacan wille ðæs slæges mid aþe; ðonne sceal beon on ðære hýndene ân cýning aþe be ðrittig hýda, swa be geriþcundum [Ld 13^{v}] men swa be cýrliscum, swa hwæþer

Nw2 rubrics inserted into CN [1] margin — al. geclænsie

hpæðer spa hit sie.

Gif hine mon ȝylt, þonne mot he ȝesellan on þara hẏndena ȝ̄hpelcere monnan 7 bẏrnan 7 speord on þ perȝyld, ȝif he þyrfe.

Ƿiteþeopne monnan Ƿẏliscne mon sceal bedrifan be xii hidū spa þeopne to spinȝū; Enȝliscne be feoper 7 xxx hida.

xcix. Be epes peorðe.[1]

Epo bið mid hire ȝiunȝe sceape scitt peorð oþþæt xiiii[2] niht ofer Eastran.

c. Be ȝ̄hpelces[3] ceapes anȝylde.[1]

Gif mō hpelcne[4] ceap ȝ̄biȝð, 7 he þoñe onfinde hī hpelce unhælo on binnan xxx nihta, þonne peorpe þone ceape to honda; oþþe speriȝ̄ þæt he hī nane facn on nẏste þa he hine hī sealde.

ci. Be ceorlisces monnes stale.[1]

Gif ceorl ceap forstelð 7 bereð into his erne,[5] 7 befehð hine[6] þærinne mon, þoñe bið[7] se his dæl scyldiȝ[8] butan þā pife anū, forþon hio sceal hire ealdor hyran. Gif hio dear mid aþe ȝ̄cẏþan þæt hio þæs forstolenan ne onbyte, nime hire þriddan sceat.

cii. Be neata horn.[1]

Oxan horn biþ x peninȝa peorþ.

Cuu horn biþ tpeȝea peninȝa. Oxan tæȝl biþ[9] scitt peorð, cus[10] bið fifa. Oxan eaȝe bið v peninȝa peorþ, cus biþ scitt peorþ.

ciii.[11]

Mon sceall symble to bereȝafole aȝyfan æt anū pyrhtan vi pæȝa.

ciiii. Be hyrȝeoc.[12]

Se ceorl se þe hæfð oþres ȝ̄oht ahyred, ȝif he hæbbe ealle on fodre[13] to aȝyfanne, ȝ̄sceapiȝ[14] mon, aȝyfe ealle; Gif he næbbe, aȝyfe healf on fodre, healfe on oþrū ceape.

cv. Be cyricsceat.[1]

Ciricsceat[15] mon sceal aȝyfan to þā healme[16] 7 to þā heorþe,[17] þe se mon on bið to middū pintra.

Þonne

[1] rubrics in left margin Nw2 [2] xiiii] xii'ii' Nw2 [3] ȝ̄hpelces] 'ȝ̄'hpelces Nw2 [4] hpelcne] hpelcre [5] above erne, secretū [6] 7 befehð hine] 7 befehð 'hine' Nw2 [7] þoñe bið] þoñe 'bið' Nw2 [8] scyldiȝ] ~~sinniȝ~~ del. with scyldiȝ written above Nw2 [9] biþ] biþ'~~ciii~~'—ciii is the numeral for the next law [10] cus] s from f [11] numeral in left margin Nw2; there is a ¶ mark in the text, and the original numeral was out of place—see 9 above [12] rubric in left margin Nw2; above -ȝeoc is ȝ̄oc, i(d est) iugū in left margin Nw2 [13] above fodre, annona [14] ȝ̄sceapiȝ̄] del. of one after i [15] Ciricsceat] initial G del. and C supplied in left margin Nw2 [16] above healme, culmine [17] heorþe] ~~eorþ~~ heorþe with, above heorþe, mansione

hƿæþer sƿa hit sy. Gif hine mon gylt, ðonne mot he gesyllan on ðæra hyndena gehƿylcre monnan ⁊ byrnan ⁊ sƿeord on ꝥ ƿergyld, gif he ðurfe. Ƿite ðeorne monnan ƿyliscne man sceal bedrifan be tƿelf hydum sƿa ðeorne to sƿingum; engliscne be feoƿer ⁊ ðrittig hyda.

Be eoƿes ƿyrþe.

56 Eoƿu biþ mid hire geonge sceape scill. ƿeorþ oþ ꝥ feoƿertyn niht ofer eastron.

57 Gif mon hƿylcne ceape gebygeþ, ⁊ he ðonne on finde him hƿylcne unhælo binnan ðrittig nihta, ðonne ƿeorpe ðone ceape to handa ðam syllende; oþþe sƿerige ꝥ he him nân facn on nyste ða he hine him sealde.

Be cyrlisces monnes stale.

58 Gif ceorle ceap forstylþ ⁊ bereþ into his ærne, ⁊ befehþ hit ðær inne mon, ðonne biþ se his dæle scyldig butan ðæm ƿîf anum, forþon heo sceal hire ealdre hyran. Gif heo dear mid aþe gecyþan ꝥ heo ðæs forstolenan ne onbite, nime hire ðæne ðriddan dæle ðære æhta.

Be oxan.

59 Oxan horn biþ tyn pening ƿyrþe.
Cû horn tƿega peninga ƿyrþe.
Oxan tægl biþ iiij peninga ƿyrþe,
Cûs tægl biþ fif peninga ƿirþe.
Oxan [Ld 14V] eage biþ fif peninge ƿyrþe,
Cûs eage biþ scill. ƿyrþe.

60 Man sceal symle to beregafol agyfan at anum ƿyrþan six pund ƿæga.—[1]

Be hyre Geôc.

61 Se ceorl se ðe hæfþ oþres geoc ahyred, Gif he hæbbe ealle on fodre to agyfanne, gesceapige mon, agyfe ealle; gif he næbbe, agyfe healf on fodre, healf on oþrum ceape.

Be cyric sceatte.

62 Cyric sceatte mon sceal agyfan to ðæm hælme ⁊ to ðæm heorþe, ðe se man on biþ to middan ƿintra.
Ðonne

Nw2 rubrics inserted into CN; CN has rubric for c. where Ld has none for 57 [B = Be ȝehwylces ceapes wyrðe]; Ld has no rubric but the number 60 because rubric list gave CN ciii to Be cuus horne — the number ciii is in CN but Nw2 seems to be altering and has omitted the rubric [1] margin — desyderatur nonnihil — but in Liebermann E, H and B have nothing further

cvi.[1] Be þon þe mon to ceape fordrife.[2]

Þonne mon bið tẏhlan betẏʒen, 7 hine mon bedryfeð to ceape, nah þonne self nane ƿiht to sellane[3] beforan ceape;[4] þonne ʒæð oþer mon seleþ his ceape for sƿa þe þoñe Ʒþinʒian maƷ, on ða rædenne þe he hī ʒa to honda, oþ ꝥ he his ceap hī Ʒinnian mæʒe; þoñe betyhð hine mon eft oþre siþe 7 bedryfð[5] to ceape; Gif hine forþ nele forstandan se þe hī ær ceap foresealde, 7 he hine þonne forfehð, þoliʒe þoñe his ceapes se, þe he hī ær foresealde.

cvii.[6] Be ʒesiðcundes monnes fære.[7]

Gif ʒesiþcund mon fare, þoñe mot he habban his Ʒrefan mid hī 7 his smiþ 7 his cildfestran.

cviii. Be londhæbbendū.[8]

Se þe hæfð xx hida, se sceal tæcnan xii hida Ʒsettes landes þoñe he[9] faran ƿille.

cix.

Se þe hæfð x hida, se sceal tæcnan vi hida Ʒsettes landes.

cx.

Se þe hæbbe þreora hida, tæcne oþres healfes.

cxi.

Gif mon Ʒþinʒað ʒyrde londes oþþe mare to rædeʒofole 7 hereð, ʒif se hlaford hī ƿile ꝥ land arǽran to ƿeorce 7 to ʒafole, ne þearf he hī onfon ʒif he hī nan botl ne selð; 7 þolie þara æcra.

cxii. Be siðcundes monnes dræfe of lond.[10]

Gif mon Ʒsiðcundne monnan adryfe, þy botle, næs þære setene.

cxiii. Be sceapes ʒonʒ mid his fleose.[11]

Sceap sceal ʒonʒan mid his flise oð midne sumor, oþþe ʒylde ꝥ flise mid tƿā peninʒū.

cxiiii. Be tƿyhyndum ƿære.[10]

Æt tƿẏhindū ƿere mon sceal syllan to monbote xxx sciłł; æt syxhindū, lxxx sciłł; æt xiihindū, cxx sciłł.

Æt[12] tynhindū to fostre:[13] x fa-

[1] numeral in left margin Nw2 [2] rubric in top margin Nw2 [3] sellane] selllane [4] ceape] ceaƿ'c'e Nw2 with in right margin ceace, glossed certamē [5] bedryfð] s for f [6] cvii] second i Nw2 [7] rubric half in right margin Nw2 [8] rubric in right margin, cviii repeated in left margin Nw2 [9] he] be [10] rubric mostly in right margin Nw2 [11] rubric in right margin Nw2 [12] Æt] æ't' [13] to fostre] to foftre

Be ðon ðe mon ꞇo ceape ꝼoꞃðꞃæꝼe.

63 Ðonne mon biþ ꞇẏhꞇlaꝺ beꞇoᵹen, ⁊ hine mon beꝺꞃiꝼþ ꞇo ceape, nah ðonne ꞅẏlꝼ nân ƿihꞇ ꞇo ꞅẏllanne beꝼoꞃan ceace; ðonne ᵹaþ oþeꞃ man ꞅẏllaþ hiꞅ ceap ꝼoꞃe ꞅƿa he ðonne ᵹeþinᵹian mæᵹe, on ða ꞃæꝺꝺene ðe him ᵹa ꞇo hanꝺa, oþ ꝥ he hiꞅ ceap him ᵹeinnian mæᵹe; Ðonne beꞇẏhþ hine mon eꝼꞇ oþꞃe ꞅiþe ⁊ beꝺꞃiꝼþ ꞇo ceape; Ᵹiꝼ he hine ꝼoꞃþ nẏlle ꝼoꞃꞅꞇanꝺan ꞅe ðe him æꞃ ceap ꝼoꞃe ꞅealꝺe, ⁊ he him ðonne ꝼoꞃeꝼehþe, þoliᵹe ðonne hiꞅ ceapeꞅ ꞅe, ðe he him æꞃ ꝼoꞃꞅealꝺe.

Be ᵹeꞅiþcunꝺeꞅ monneꞅ ꝼaꞃe.

64 Ᵹiꝼ ᵹeꞅiþcunꝺ man ꝼaꞃe, ðonne moꞇ he habban hiꞅ [Ld 15^{v}] ᵹeꞃeꝼan miꝺ him ⁊ hiꞅ ꞅmiþ ⁊ hiꞅ cilꝺ ꝼoꞅꞇꞃan.

Be lanꝺ hæbbenꝺum.

65 Ꞅe ðe hæꝼþ ꞇƿenꞇiᵹ hẏꝺa lanꝺeꞅ, ꞅe ꞅceal ꞇæcan ꞇƿelꝼ hẏꝺa ᵹeꞅeꞇꞇeꞅ lanꝺeꞅ ðonne he ꝼaꞃan ƿille. Ꞅe ðe hæꝼþ ꞇẏn hẏꝺa, ꞅe ꞅceal ꞇæcan ꞅẏx hẏꝺa ᵹeꞅeꞇꞇeꞅ lanꝺeꞅ. Ꞅe ðe hæꝼþ ðꞃeo hẏꝺa, ꞇæce oþꞃeꞅ healꝼeꞅ.

66 Ᵹiꝼ mon ᵹeþinᵹaþ ᵹẏꞃꝺelanꝺeꞅ oþþe mæꞃe ꞇo ꞃæꝺe ᵹaꝼole ⁊ ᵹeeꞃæþ, ᵹiꝼ ꞅe hlaꝼoꞃꝺ him ƿille ꝥ lanꝺ aꞃæꞃan ꞇo ƿeoꞃce ⁊ ꞇo ᵹaꞃole,[1] ne ðeaꞃꝼ he him onꝼon ᵹiꝼ he him nan boꞇle ne ꞅẏlþ; ⁊ ne ðoliᵹe ðæꞃa æcꞃa.

Be ᵹeꞅiþcunꝺeꞅ monneꞅ ꝺꞃæꝼe oꝼ lanꝺe.

67 Ᵹiꝼ mon ᵹeꞅiþcunꝺne monnan aꝺꞃẏꝼe,[2] ðẏ boꞇle, næꞅ ðæꞃ ꞅeꞇene.

Be ꞅceapeꞅ ᵹanᵹe miꝺ ꝼleoꞅ.

68 Ꞅceape ꞅceal ᵹonᵹan miꝺ hiꞅ ꝼlẏꞅe oþ miꝺne ꞅðmoꞃ,[3] oþþe ᵹẏlꝺ ꝥ ꝼleoꞅ miꝺ ꞇƿam peninᵹum.

Be ƿeꞃum.

69 Æꞇ ꞇƿẏhẏnꝺum ƿeꞃe mon ꞅceal ꞅẏllan ꞇo monboꞇe xxx ꞅcill.; ⁊ æꞇ ꞅẏxhẏnꝺum, eahꞇaꞇiᵹ ꞅcill.; æꞇ ꞇƿelꝼhẏnꝺum, hunꝺ ꞇƿelꝼꞇiᵹ.

Be ꝼoꞅꞇꞃe.

70 Æꞇ ꞇẏn hẏꝺum ꞇo ꝼoꞅꞇꞃe: ꞇẏn ꝼa-

Nw2 rubrics inserted into CN; CN assigns the numbers cviii, cix and cx to Ld's single 65; for CN cxi Ld has 66, and neither CN nor Ld has a rubric; Ld has a separate number 70 and the rubric Be ꝼoꞅꞇꞃe where CN continues cxiiii without a break [1] errata — ᵹaꞃole lege ᵹaꝼole [2] margin — al. ꝼoꞃðꞃiꝼe [3] errata — ꞅðmoꞃ lege ꞅomoꞃ

x fata hunizes,[1] ccc hlafa, xii ambra Ƿilisces ealað,[2] xxx hlutres,[3] tƿa ealðe hriþeru oþþe x ƿederas, x zees, xx henna, x cysas, amber fulne buteran, v leaxas,[4] xx pundƿæza fodres, 7 teontiz æla.[5]

cxv. Be ƿertyhtlan.[6]

Gif mon sie ƿertyhtlan[7] betozen 7 he hit þonne zeondette[8] beforan aðe, 7 onsace ær, bide mon mid þære ƿiterædenne oð ðæt se ƿer z̄zolden sie.

cxvi.[9] Be ƿerzyldþeofe.[10]

Gif mon ƿerzyldþeof z̄fehþ, 7 he losize ðẏ dæze þā monnū þe hine zefoð, þeah hine mon z̄fo ẏmb niht, nah hī mon mare æt þoñ fulƿite.

cxvii.[9] Be anre nihte þyfðe.[10]

Gif hit biþ nihteald þyfþ, zebeten þa þone zyld þe hine zefenzon, sƿa hie zeþinzian mæzen ƿiþ cyninz 7 his z̄refan.

cxviii. Be þoñe þe þeoƿƿealh[11] fraone forslihð.[10]

Gif þeofƿealh Enzliscne monna ofslihð, þoñe sceal se þe hine ah ƿeorƿan hine to honda hlaford 7 mazan, oþþe lx scill̶ zesellan ƿið his feore.

Gif he þoñe þone ceap nelle forezesellan, þoñe mot se hlaford hine zefreozean; zylden siþþan his mazas þone ƿer, Gif he mæzborz hæbbe freo; zif he næbbe, heden[12] his þa zefan.

Ne þearf se frize mid þā þeoƿan mæz zyldan, buton he hī ƿille fæhþe ofaceaƿian; ne se þeoƿa mid þy frizean.

cxix. Be forstolenes ceapes forfonz.[13]

Gif mon ceap befehð forstollenne, 7 sio hond tẏmþ þoñ sio hine mon[14] ætbefehð to oþrū m̄, zif se mon hine þoñ onfon ne ƿille,[15] 7 sezþ[16] ꝥ he hī næfre ꝥ ne seald, ac seald oþre, þoñe mot se ze-

[1] hunizes] huni'z'es Nw2 [2] in left margin ealað, i(d est), ceruisiae [3] hlutres underlined [4] above, salmones [5] above, anguillae [6] rubric Nw2 [7] above, homicidii [8] zeondette] zeonde dette [9] numeral in right margin Nw2 [10] rubrics in left margin Nw2 [11] þeoƿƿealh] þeoƿ'ƿealh' [12] heden] hed~~en~~ [13] rubric in body of text below the numerals Nw2 [14] mon] mon is underlined, then nan is added above it and del. Nw2 [15] ne ƿille] ꝥ'n'ille Nw2 [16] sezþ] ~~seh~~ sezþ

tẏn fata huniges, [Ld 16^{v}] ðreo hund hlafa, twelf ambra ƿẏlisces ealoþ, ðrittig hluttres, twa eald hrẏþeru oþþe[1] tẏn cẏsas, amberfulne buteran, fif leaxas, twentig pund ƿaga fodres, ⁊ hundteontig[2] æla.

Be ƿertẏhtlan.

71 Gif mon sẏ ƿertẏhtlan betogen ⁊ he hit ðonne geandette beforan aþe, ⁊ onsace ær, abide mon mid ðære ƿite rædenne oþ ꝥ se ƿere gegolden sẏ.

Be ƿergẏld ðeofes forefeng.

72 Gif mon ƿergẏld ðeof gefehþ, ⁊ he losige ðẏ dæge ðæm mannum ðe hin[3] gefoþ, ðeah hine man gefô ẏmb niht, nah him mon mare æt ðonne fulƿite. Gif hit biþ niht eald ðẏfþe, gebeten ða þone gẏlt ðe hine gefengon, swa hig geþingian magon ƿiþ cẏning ⁊ his gerefan.

Be ðon ðe ðeoƿ ƿealh frigne man ofslea.

73 Gif ðeoƿe ƿealh engliscne man ofslihþ, ðonne sceal se ðe hine ah ƿeorþan hine to handa hlaforde ⁊ magum, oþþe sẏxtig scill. gesẏllan ƿiþ his feorh. Gif he ðonne ðone ceap nelle fore gesẏllan, ðonne mot se hlaford hine gefreogan; gẏldan sẏþþan his magas ðone ƿere, Gif he mæg[Ld 17^{v}]borh hæbbe; Gif he næbbe, heden his ða gefan. Ne ðearf se frigea mid ðeoƿan men gẏldan, buton he him ƿẏlle fæhþe of aceaƿian; ne se ðeoƿa mid ðæm frigean.

Be forstolenes ceapes forfeng.

74 Gif mon ceap befehþe forstolene, ⁊ seo hand tẏmþ ðonne seo hine mon æt befehþ to oþrum men, gif mon hine onfôn nẏlle, ⁊ sægþ ꝥ he him næfre ꝥ ne sealde, ac sealde oþer, ðonne mot se ge-

Nw2 rubrics inserted into CN; Ld 72 corresponds to CN cxvi and cxvii and has only one rubric for the two in Nw2

[1] errata — post oþþe interpone hæc verba: tẏn ƿeþeras, tẏn gees, treontig henna [2] Ot has hu...,so this is CN's error [3] typographical error not noted Ld

se ʒecẏþan se þe hit temeð[1] to þære honda, ꝥ he hī nan oþer ne seald butan ꝥ ẏlce.

cxx. Be þon þe mon oðres ʒodsunu ofslea.[2]

Gif hƿa oþres ʒodsunu slea oþþe his ʒodfæder, sie sio mæʒbot[3] 7 sio manbot ʒlic; ƿeaxe sio bot be þā ƿere, sƿa ilce sƿa sio manbot deð þe þā hlaford sceal.

Gif hit þon̄ne[4] kyninʒes ʒodsunu sie, bete be his ƿere þā cẏninʒe, sƿa ilce sƿa þære mæʒþe.

Gif he þon̄e on þone ʒeonbyrde þe hine sloh, þonne etfealle[5] sio bot þǣ ʒodfæder, sƿa ẏlce sƿa[6] ꝥ ƿite þā hlaford deð.

Gif hit biscsunu sie, sie be halfū þā.[7]

[1] temeð] nēþ'temeð' with nēþ underlined Nw2 [2] rubric in right margin Nw2 [3] mæʒbot] mæʒbot ~~ʒelic ƿeax~~ [4] þone] þonne [5] del. of h before etfealle Nw2 [6] sƿa ẏlce sƿa] sƿa ẏlce ~~sƿa illce~~ Nw2 [7] MS has a line across the page after the text and in right margin finis legm̄ Inae

ꞅe ᵹecẏþan, ꞅe ðe hıꞇ ꞇẏmþ ꞇo ðaꞃa hanꝺa, ꝥ he hım nan oþeꞃ ne ꞅealꝺ buꞇan ꝥ ẏlce.

Be ᵹoꝺꝼæꝺeꞃeꞅ oþþe ᵹoꝺꞅuneꞅ ꞅlẏhꞇ.

Gıꝼ hƿa oþꞃeꞅ ᵹoꝺꞅunu ꞅlea oþþe hıꞅ ᵹoꝺꝼæꝺeꞃ,
ꞅẏ ꞅeo mæᵹboꞇ ⁊ ꞅeo manboꞇ ᵹelıc; ƿeaxe ꞅeo boꞇ
be ðæm ƿeꞃe, ꞅƿa ılce ꞅƿa ꞅeo manboꞇ ꝺeþ ðe ðæm
hlaꝼoꞃꝺ ꞅceal. Gıꝼ hıꞇ ðonne cẏnınᵹeꞅ ᵹoꝺ-
ꞅunu ꞅẏ, beꞇe be hıꞅ ƿeꞃe ðæm cẏnınᵹ, ꞅƿa
ꞅame ılce ꞅƿa ðæꞃe mæᵹþe. Gıꝼ he ðonne
on þone ᵹeonbẏꞃꝺe þe hıne ꞅloh, þon-
ne æꞇ ꝼealle ꞅeo boꞇ þæm ᵹoꝺꝼæ-
ꝺeꞃ, ꞅƿa ꞅame ẏlce ꞅƿa ꝥ ƿıꞇe
þæm hlaꝼoꞃꝺe ꝺeþ. Gıꝼ hıꞇ
bıꞅceop ꞅunu ꞅẏ, ꞅẏ be
halꝼum ðæm.

Appendix

In the list that follows, some of the significant manuscript variants in the laws of Alfred and Ine have been noted for comparison in the hope of casting some light on the relationships between the surviving texts of the laws of the Anglo-Saxons. Complete lists of the variants are to be found in the thesis of Richard Dammery, to whose work I am, as ever, heavily indebted. The majority of the variants concern the rubrics, and the list follows the order of appearance of the variants in the preceding edition of CN. Suspensions and contractions have been silently expanded, and word-division is editorial.

LIST OF RUBRICS

CN 236^{v}	7	circan	CN
		circ'e'n'e'	Nw2
		circan	E
		cyricena	G
		circean	H
		... can	Ot
		[cẏꞃıcena]	Ld
	xii	cirliscre	E
		cyrliscre	G
		cierliscre	H
		.irilscre	Ot
		cirilscre	CN
		ci'o'rl'i'scre	Nw2
		[om.]	Ld
	xxii	nietena	E Ot CN
		nytena	G H
		netena	Nw2 (first minim del.)
		[nẏꞇena]	Ld
	xxiii	niedhæmede	E B H Ot
		niedhæmde	G
		niedhemeðe	CN
		'nid'h'æ'meðe	Nw2
		[nẏꝺhæmeꝺ]	Ld
	xxvii	ƿifmonnes	E
		ƿifmannes	G
		mannes	H
		monnes ƿif	Ot CN
		'ƿif monnes'	Nw2
		[om.]	Ld

CN 237^{r}	xlv	ðeoƿa	E G H Ot CN
		þeoƿ'en'a	Nw2
		[þeoƿena]	Ld
	lxii	cirliscum	E
		ciorlisum	CN
		cyrliscum	G
		ci'e'rliscum	H
		ci'o'rliscum	Nw2
		[ceoꞃlıꞅcum]	Ld
CN 237^{v}	lxxxii	ryhtȝesamhiƿan	E
		rih't'ȝesamhiƿon	G
		rihtȝesamhiƿan	H
		ȝerihtsimhiƿan	CN
		ȝeriht'ȝe'simhiƿan	Nw2
		[ꞃıhꞇ ᵹehıƿan]	Ld
	xcv	forsitte	E G H
		forsytte	CN
		forƿitie	Nw2
		[ꝼoꞃꞅıꞇꞇe]	Ld

BIBLICAL PROLOGUE

CN 238^{v}	mid sƿelce hræȝle	E
p. 94, l. 17	mid sƿilce hræȝle	G CN
	mid sƿylce reafe	H
	mid sƿ'i'lce hræȝle	Nw2 (corrected from hwelce)
	mid hƿilce hræȝle	Nw3
	Mıꝺ ꞅƿẏlce hꞃæᵹle	Ld
CN 239^{r}	læte hie freo	E CN
p. 96, l. 3	læte hie faran freo	G
	læte hy friȝe	H
	læte hie 'faran' freo	Nw2
	læte hie faran freo	Nw3
	læꞇe hı ꝼaꞃan ꝼꞃeo	Ld
p. 96, l. 11	hƿa	E G H 'Nw2' Nw3
	sƿa	CN
	hƿa	Ld

p. 96, l. 22	on cease	E
	on ceaste	GH
	on ceast	CN Nw3
	on ceast'e'	Nw2
	on ceaꞅꞇ	Ld
CN 239v	ꝫereccen	E
p. 98, l. 1	ꝫetæcan	G
	ꝫereccan	H
	ꝫerecꝫan	CN
	'ce' above ꝫan	Nw2 (ꝫetæcan in lighter ink above)
	betæcan	Nw3
	ᵹeꞇæcan	Ld
p. 98, l. 4	ðeoƿenne	E G Nw3
	þeoƿene	H CN
	þeoƿe'n'ne	Nw2
	ꝺ̃eoƿenne	Ld
p. 98, l. 6	ofƿorƿod	E G CN
	oftorfod	H
	ofƿ'e'orƿod	Nw2
	of'ƿeorƿod'	Nw3
	oꝼƿeoꞃƿoꝺ	Ld
p. 98, l. 8	inne	E Nw3
	[om.]	G
	innan	H
	hine	CN
	'inne'	Nw2
	ınne	Ld
p. 98, l. 11	ðeoƿmennen	E Nw3
	þeoƿmennen	CN
	ðeoƿne mennen	G
	þeoƿene mennen	H
	'þeoƿne *al.*'	Nw2
	ꝺ̃eoƿemennen	Ld
p. 98, ll. 11-12	se oxa	E CN
	se oxa sie	G
	sy se oxa	H
	se oxa 'sie'	Nw2
	ꞅe oxa ꞅẏ	Ld

p. 98, l. 16	pisse	E CN
	piste	GH
	pis't'e	Nw2
	pist	Nw3
	pıſτ	Ld
CN 240^{r}	Gif	E H Nw2
p. 100, l. 3	ʒyf	G
	Gif he	CN
	Ᵹıᵹ	Ld
p. 100, l. 6	ðæt	E G H Nw2 Nw3
	þæt þæt	CN
	þæτ	Ld
p. 100, l. 8	cucu	E H CN Nw3
	cpicu	G
	'cpicu'	Nw2
	cucu	Ld
p. 100, l. 10	ʒetriepe	E
	ʒetrype	G Nw3
	ne sy	H
	ʒetrype	CN
	'eo' above ʒetrype	Nw2 ('ʒetrype' in margin)
	ᵹeτꞃẏpıᵹe	Ld
p. 100, l. 14	netene	E Nw3
	nietene	G
	nytene	H
	nietene	CN
	'netene'	Nw2
	nẏτene	Ld
p. 100, l. 15	ʒodʒeldum	E CN Nw3
	ʒodʒyldum	G
	ʒodʒyltum	H
	'ʒold' above ʒod	Nw2
	ᵹoꝺᵹelꝺum	Ld
p. 100, l. 17	Þa pudupan	E Nw2 Nw3
	Þa pydpan	G
	Þa pydepan	H
	þu pudupan	CN
	puꝺupan	Ld

CN 240^{v}	niedlinʒ, 7 ne ʒehene	E
p. 102, l. 4	niedlinʒ, 7 ʒehere	CN
	niedlinʒ ʒehyne	G
	nydlinʒ 7 ʒehyn	H
	niedlinʒ 7 ʒehere; 'nid'linʒ 'ne ʒehine'	Nw2
	niedlinʒ ne ʒehine	Nw3
	nıꝺlınᵹ	Ld
p. 102, l. 13	ʒeclysp	E
	ʒeclæsp	G
	ʒeclebs	H
	ʒeclips	CN
	ʒecl'ep's	Nw2
	ʒeclefs	Nw3
	ᵹeclepꞅ	Ld
p. 102, l. 14	7 ðæs	E H
	7 on þæs	G Nw3
	7 þæs	CN
	7 'on' þæs	Nw2
	7 on ꝺæꞅ	Ld
p. 102, l. 16	Dem ðu spiðe emne	E
	Dem þu spiþe emne	CN
	Dem ðu spiðe rihte 7 spiðe emne	G
	Dem ðu spiþe rhytne dom '7'	H
	Deme þu spiþe riht 7 spiþe emne	Nw2
	Deme þu spiðe emne	Nw3
	Deme þu ꞅpıþe ꞃıhꞇe 7 ꞅpıþe emne	Ld
p. 102, l. 24	cleopien ʒe	E
	clypiʒen ʒe	G
	clipien ʒe	H
	cleopinʒum	CN
	cleop'piʒe ʒe'	Nw2
	cleopiʒe ʒe	Nw3
	cleopıᵹe ᵹe	Ld
CN 241^{r}	hefiʒran pisan budon	H Nw3
p. 46, l. 12	hefiʒran	E
	hefiʒran pisan budan	G
	hefiʒran	CN
	hefiʒran 'pisan budan'	Nw2
	heꝼıᵹꞃan pıꞅan buꝺon	Ld

p. 104, l. 17		ƿeorðien	E
		ƿeorþien	CN
		ƿeorðian	G
		ƿurðian	H
		ƿeorþi'ʒ'en	Nw2
		ƿeorðiʒen	Nw3
		ƿeoꞃþıᵹen	Ld
CN 241v		þara þe me ne licodon	E
p. 104, l. 15		þara þe me ne lycodon	H
		[om.]	CN
		þa þe me ne licodon	'Nw2' Nw3 Nw4
		ðа þe me lıcoꝺon	Ld

THE LAW OF ALFRED

CN 242v	iii	no rubric	E H CN
		Be cyrecena socnūm	'Nw2' Nw3
		Be ciricena socnum	Nw4
		Be cẏꞃıcena ꞅocnum	Ld
p. 110, l. 8		7 næbbe his aʒne forfonʒen	E
		7 hæbbe his aʒen forfanʒen	H
		7 næbbe his aʒene forfonʒen	CN
		7 'hæbbe' his aʒene forfonʒen	Nw2
		7 hæbbe his aʒene forfonʒen	Nw3
		[om.]	Nw4 Ld
	iiii	no rubric	E B H CN
		Be borhbryce	'Nw2' Nw3 Nw4
		Be boꞃhbꞃẏce	Ld
p. 110, l. 10		abrece	EH
		brece	CN Nw4
		'a'brece	Nw2
		bryce	Nw3
		bꞃece	Ld
	v	no rubric	E H CN
		Be cyninczes sƿicdome	B
		Be 'hlafordsyrƿe'	Nw2
		Be hlaford syrƿunʒum	Nw3
		Be hlafordꞅearƿe	Nw4
		Be hlaꝼoꞃꝺ ꞅẏꞃƿe	Ld

	vi	no rubric	E H CN
		Be ciricene friðe	B
		Be cyrccena friþe	Nw2
		Be cyrecena fryðe	Nw3
		Be ciricena friþe	Nw4
		Be cẏꞃıcena ꝼꞃẏþe	Ld
CN 243[r] p. 112, l. 10		ðone halʒan þunresdæʒ	E B H Nw4
		'þone dæʒ halʒan þunres'	CN
		þone halʒan 'þunresdæʒ'	Nw2
		ðone halʒan þu'n'resdæʒe	Nw3
		ðone halᵹan ðunꞃeꞅ ꝺæᵹe	Ld
	vii	no rubric	E H CN
		Be ðam ðe steleð ciricean	B
		'Be cyrecena stale'	Nw2
		Be cyrecyna stæle	Nw3
		Be ciricena stale	Nw4
		Be cẏꞃıcena ꞅꞇale	Ld
	viii	no rubric	E H CN
		Be ðam þæt man feohteð on kyninʒes healle	B
		Be þonne þe mon on cyninʒes healle ʒefeoht	'Nw2' Nw3
		Be þam þe on cyninʒes healle feoht	Nw4
		Be ðon ðe mon on cẏnınᵹeꞅ healle ᵹeꝼeohꞇe	Ld
CN 243[v]	ix	no rubric	E CN
		Be ðam þe nunnan of mynstre ut alæðeð	B
		Be nunnan hæmede	'Nw2' Nw3 Nw4
		Be ðam ðe nunnan oꝼ mınꞅꞇeꞃ uꞇ alæꝺaþ	Ld
	x	no rubric	E H CN
		Be ðam ðæt man ofslea ƿif mid cilde	B
		Be bearneacum ƿife ofsleʒenum	'Nw2' Nw4
		Be bearneacum ƿife ofsliʒenum	Nw3
		Be ðon ðe mon oꝼꞅlea beaꞃn eacnenꝺ ƿıꝼ	Ld
	xi	no rubric	E H CN
		Be hæmedðinʒum	B
		'Be forleʒerum'	Nw2
		Be forliʒerum	Nw3
		Be tƿelfhindes monnes ƿife forliʒerum	Nw4
		Be ꝼoꞃleᵹeꞃum	Ld
	xii	no rubric	E H CN Ld
		Eft	B
		Be cyrliscre fæmnan onfenʒ	'Nw2' Nw3
		Be ceorliscre fæmnan onfenʒ	Nw4

CN 244r	xiii	no rubric	E H CN Nw4
		Be ƿudebernete, 7 ʒif man afylled bið onʒemænum ƿeorce	B
		'Be ƿudubærnete'	Nw2
		Be ƿudubærnette	Nw3
		Be ƿuꝺu bæꞃneꞇꞇe	Ld
p. 116, l. 7		sƿa fela	E
		sƿa feola	B
		sƿa moniʒ	H
		sƿa feala	CN Nw3 Nw4
		sƿa 'moniʒ'	Nw2
		ꞅƿa ꝼeala	Ld
	xiiii	no rubric	E H CN
		Be dumbra manna dædum	B Nw4
		Be dumbra monna dædum	'Nw2' Nw3
		Be ꝺumbꞃa manna ꝺæꝺum	Ld
	xv	no rubric	E H CN
		Be ðam þæt man toforan bisceoƿe feohteð	B
		'Be þam þe beforan bisceƿum feohtað' (bisceoƿum Nw3; þæm Nw4)	Nw2
		Be ᵹeꝼeohꞇum	Ld
	xvi	no rubric	E H CN Nw3
		Be nunnena andfencʒum	B
		'Be nunnena onfenʒ'	Nw2
		Be þam þe nunnan mid hæmedþinʒað	Nw4
		Be nunnena onꝼenᵹ	Ld
CN 244v	xvii	no rubric	E H CN
		Be þam þe heore ƿeƿna lænað to manslihte	B
		'Be ƿæƿn lænum'	Nw2
		Be ƿæƿna lænum	Nw3
		Be þæm þe heora 'ƿæƿna' oðru t'o' monslyht lænað	Nw4
		Be ꝺon ꝺe heoꞃa ƿæƿne lænaþ ꞇo manꞅlıhꞇ	Ld
	xviii	no rubric	E H CN
		Be þam þe munecan heore feoh befæstað	B
		Be þam þe munecum feoh aþ befæstað	'Nw2' Nw3
		Be þæm þe munecum heora feoh butan leafe befæstað	Nw4
		Be ꝺam ꝺe munecum ꝼeoh beꝼæꞅꞇaþ	Ld

p. 118, l. 16		lefnesse	E
		hleafe	B
		leafe	H
		lefnesse	CN
		le'o'fnesse	Nw2
		leofnesse	Nw3 Nw4
		leaꝼe	Ld
	xix	no rubric	E H CN
		Be preosta ʒefeohte	B 'Nw2' Nw3 Nw4
		Be ƿꞃeoꞅꞇa ᵹeꝼeohꞇe	Ld
	xx	no rubric	E H CN B Nw4
		Be cyninczʒes ʒerefan ðyfðe	B
		Be eofotes andetlan	'Nw2' Nw3
		Be eoꝼeꞇeꞅ anꝺeꞇlan	Ld
CN 245^{r}		anʒyldes	E B CN
p. 120, l. 1		anʒildes and fo to ðam ƿite	H
		anʒyldes '7 fo to þæm ƿite'	Nw2
		anʒyldes 7 fo to ðam ƿite	Nw3
		anʒyldes 7 fo to þæm ƿite	Nw4
		anᵹẏlꝺeꞅ	Ld
	xxi	no rubric	E H CN
		Be hundes slihte	B
		'Be hund'es' slyte'	Nw2
		Be hundes slyte	Nw3
		Be hundes to slyte	Nw4
		Be hunꝺeꞅ ꞅliꞇe	Ld
	xxii	no rubric	E H CN
		Be nytena misdædum	B
		Be neatena misdædum	'Nw2' Nw3
		Be netena misdædum	Nw4
		Be nẏꞇena miꞅꝺæꝺum	Ld
	xxiii	no rubric	E H CN Nw4
		Be ceorles mennenes nydhemede	B
		'Be ceorles mennenes nedhæmed'	Nw2
		Be ceorles mennenes nedhæmeð	Nw3
		Be nẏꝺhæmeꝺ	Ld

	xxiiii	no rubric	E H CN Nw4
		Be tpyhyndum men æt hloðslihte	B
		'Be tpyhyndum men æt hloðslyhte'	Nw2
		Be tpyhindum men æt hloðeslyhte	Nw3
		Be manꞅlıhꞇ mıꝺ hloþe	Ld
	xxv	no rubric	E H CN Nw4 Ld
		Be sixhyndum men	B
		Be syxhyndum men	'Nw2' Nw3
	xxvi	no rubric	E H CN Nw4 Ld
		Be tpylfhendum men	B
		Be tpelfhyndum	'Nw2' Nw3
	xxvii	no rubric	E H CN Ld
		Be unʒepintredes pifmannes slaʒe	B
		'Be unʒepintredes pifmonnes nedhæmeð'	Nw2
		Be unʒepyntredes pifmonnes nedhæmde	Nw3
		Be unʒepintredes pifmonnes nedhæmðe	Nw4
CN 245^{v}		7 ðriddan dæl ða ʒeʒyldan, for ðriddan dæl om.	E CN
p. 122, l. 3		'7' for ðriddan dæl	B
		ðriddan dæl ða ʒeʒyldan, for ðriddan dæl	H
		'7 þriddan dæle þa ʒeʒildan, for þriddan dæle'	Nw2
		7 þryddan dæl þa ʒeʒyldan for þryddan dæl	Nw3
		7 þriddan dæl þa ʒeʒildan for þriddan dæle	Nw4
		7 ðꞃıꝺꝺan ꝺæl ðam ꝫeꝫẏlꝺan	Ld
	xxix	no rubric	E H B CN
		'Be folcleas ʒepyrhtum'	Nw2
		Be folcleas'e' ʒepyrhtum	Nw3
		Be folcleasunʒ ʒepyrhtum	Nw4
		Be ꝼolc leaꞅunꝫum ꝫeꝩẏꞃhꞇum	Ld
p. 122, l. 9		ʒeresp peorðe	E
		ʒeræf peorðe	B
		peorðe ʒeræf	H
		ʒeræsp peorðe	Nw4
		ʒeræsp peorþe	CN
		'ʒerest'	Nw2
		ʒeræs'ʒ' peorðe (p del.)	Nw3
		ꝫeꞃæꞅ	Ld

	xxx	no rubric	E H CN
		Be ʒodborhʒum	B
		'Be ʒodborʒum'	Nw2
		Be ʒodborʒum	Nw3
		Be ʒodborhum	Nw4
		Be ᵹoꝺ boꞃhᵹum	Ld
p. 122, l. 13		ʒodborʒes	E B H Nw3
		ʒodborh'e'es	CN
		'ʒodborʒes'	Nw2
		ʒodborhes	Nw4
		ᵹoꝺboꞃᵹeꞅ	Ld
	xxxi	no rubric	E H CN
		Be cypmannum	B
		'Be ciepemonnum'	Nw2
		Be ciepmonnum	Nw3
		Be ceapmonnum	Nw4
		Be cẏpmannum	Ld
p. 122, l. 16		Eac is ciepemonnum	E
		Eac is cypemonnum	B
		Eac is cypemannum	H
		Eac 'is' ciepemonnum	CN
		'is ciepemonnum'	Nw2
		Eac is ceapmonnum	Nw3
		Eac is ceapemonnum	Nw4
		Ɛac ıꞅ ceapmannum	Ld
p. 122, l. 17		nimen þa men	E B CN
		nimen ða men up	H
		nimen 'up' þa men	Nw2 (margin: 'nimen men up')
		nimen up þa men	Nw3 Nw4
		nımen ða men	Ld
	xxxii	no rubric	E H CN
		Be ceorlisces mannes bindelan	B
		Be cyrlisces monnes byndulan	'Nw2'
		Be cyrlisces monnes byndelan	Nw3 Nw4
		Be ceoꞃlıꞅceꞅ manneꞅ bınꝺelan	Ld
CN 246r	xxxiii	no rubric	E H CN
		Be speres ʒymeleaste	B
		Be speres ʒemeleasnesse	'Nw2' Nw4
		Be speres ʒymeleasnesse	Nw3
		Be ꞅpeꞃeꞅ ᵹẏmeleaꞅꞇe	Ld

p. 124, l. 9		sie ufor	E CN
		s'i' ufor	B
		sy þreofinȝre ufor	H
		sie ufor 'þryfinȝre'	Nw2 Nw4
		sie ufor þryfinȝra	Nw3
		ꞅẏ uꝼoꞃ þꞃẏ ꝼinᵹeꞃe	Ld
	xxxiiii	no rubric	E H CN Nw3
		Be boldȝetale	B
		Be boldȝetæle	'Nw2' Nw4
		Be bolꝺᵹeꞇæle	Ld
	xxxv	no rubric	E H CN
		Be ðam ðe beforan aldormen on ȝemote feohte	B
		'Be ȝefeohte beforan ealdormen'	Nw2
		Be þam þe beforan ealdormen on ȝemote ȝefeohte	Nw4
		Be ᵹeꝼeohꞇe beꝼoꞃan ealꝺoꞃmen	Ld
	xxxvi	no rubric	E H CN
		Be cyrlisces monnes fletteȝefeohte	B
		'Be ceorlisces monnes fletȝefeohte'	Nw2
		Be ceorlisces monnes flette ȝefeohte	Nw4
		Be cẏꞃliꞅceꞅ :monneꞅ ꝼleꞇꞇe ᵹeꝼeohꞇe	Ld
CN 246^{V}		arise be ðære cierliscan bote; tƿelfhyndum men tƿyfealdlice	H
p. 126, l. 1		[om.]	E CN
		arise bæ ðære cyrliscan bote; tƿelfhyndum men tƿifealdlice	B
		arise seo bote be ðære ceorliscan bote tƿelfhindum men tƿifealdlic	'Nw2' Nw4
		aꞃiꞅe ꞅeo boꞇe be þæꞃe ceoꞃliꞅcan bôꞇ, ꞇƿelꝼhẏnꝺum men ꞇƿẏꝼealꝺlic	Ld
p. 126, l. 3		no rubric	E H CN
		Be burhbryce	B
		'Be borhbryce'	Nw2
		Be burȝbryce	Nw4
		Be buꞃhbꞃẏce	Ld
p. 126, l. 5		edorbryce	E Ot CN
		'eoderbryce'	B
		edorbrice	H
		'eodor'	Nw2
		eodorbryce	Nw4
		eoꝺoꞃbꞃẏce	Ld
p. 126, l. 7		haliȝ ryht	E H CN
		haliȝ riht	B
		'*alias* haliȝ rift butan rihte alecȝe'	Nw2
		haliȝ ryht 'ryft *al.*' (margin)	Nw4
		haliᵹꞃiꝼꞇ	Ld

	xxxvii	no rubric	E H Ot CN
		Be boclande	B
		'Be boclondum'	Nw2
		Be boclandum	Nw4
		Be boclanꝺe	Ld
	xxxviii	no rubric	E H Ot CN
		'Be feohte'	Nw2
		Be fæhþe	Nw4
		Be ᵹeꝼeohꞇe	Ld
p. 126, l. 19		ðonne ciricen	E
		þonne cir'i'cean	H
		⸿circan⸿ þonne	CN
		circan þonne	Nw4
		cẏꝛıcean ꝺonne	Ld
CN 247r		orpiʒe	E CN
p. 128, l. 6		onpiʒe	H
		.rpiʒe	Ot
		orpite	'Nw2' Nw4
		oꝛpıꞇe	Ld
p. 128, l. 11		'oððe æt his spistær borenre'	E
		'oððe mid his spister æpumborenre'	H (margin)
		....................speos.........borenre	Ot
		oððe æt his speoster borenre	CN
		'æpum' Nw2; om. Nw4	
		oþþe æꞇ hıꞅ ꞅpeoꞅꞇeꝛ æpum boꝛenꝛe	Ld
	xxxix	no rubric	E H Ot CN
		Be mæssedaʒe freolse	'Nw2'
		Be mæssedæʒe freolse	Nw4
		Be mæꞅꞅe ꝺæʒe ꝼꝛeolꞅe	Ld
CN 247v	xl	no rubric	E H CN
		Be heafodpunde 7 oðre liman	B
		Be pundum	'Nw2' Nw4
		Be punꝺum	Ld
p. 130, l. 24		of heafde	EBH
		of heasde	CN
		of heasde 'mid'	Nw2
		of heafde mid	Nw4
		oꝼ heaꝼꝺe mıꝺ	Ld

CN 248^{r}	hrif	E Nw4
p. 132, l. 11	rif'e'	B
	hrife	H
	frife	CN (f del.Nw2)
	hrif *alias* rif	Nw2
	hꞃıꝼ	Ld
CN 248^{v}	sliefan	E
p. 134, l. 3	slefan	B
	slyfan	H
	slieafan	CN
	sleafan	'Nw2' Nw4
	ꞅlẏꝼan	Ld
p. 134, l. 7	Gif	E H
	Gyf	B
	Gif se mon cƿic sie	Nw2
	Gif*	CN (asterisk indicating error)
	[om.]	Ld
p. 134, l. 16	ða sculdru	E B H
	þa sculdru	CN
	'sculdru'	Nw2
	þæs sculdru	Nw4
	þa ꞅculꝺꞃu	Ld

THE LAW OF INE

CN 249^{r}	mid	E B H
p. 136, l. 8	7	CN
	'mid'	Nw2
	mıꝺ	Ld
p. 136, l. 9	ure	E B H
	hure	CN
	ure	Nw2
	uꞃe	Ld
p. 136, l. 9	ȝefæstnode	E B H
	ȝefæstrode	CN
	ȝefæst'n'ode	Nw2
	ᵹeꝼæꞅꞇenoꝺe	Ld
xlv	no rubric	E B Bu H CN
	'Be ȝodes þeoƿena reȝole'	Nw2
	Be ᵹoꝺeꞅ þeoƿena ꞃeᵹole	Ld

	xlvi	no rubric	E B Bu H CN
		'Be cildum'	Nw2
		Be cılꝺum	Ld
	xlvii	no rubric	E B Bu H CN
		'Be sunnandæȝes ƿeorcum'	Nw2
		Be ꞅunnan ꝺæᵹeꞅ ƿeoꞃcum	Ld
	xlviii	no rubric	E Bu H CN
		Be ciricsceatte	B
		'Be cyricsceatum'	Nw2
		Be cıꞃıcꞅceaꞇꞇe	Ld
CN 249^{v}	xvix	no rubric	E Bu H CN
		Be ciricsocnum	B
		'Be cyricsocnum'	Nw2
		Be cẏꞃıc ꞅocnum	Ld
	l	no rubric	E Bu H CN
		Be ȝefeohtum	B 'Nw2'
		Be ᵹeꝼeohꞇe	Ld
p. 138, l. 22		ðiefðe	E
		þyfðe	B
		þeofðe	Bu
		ðyfðe	H
		þifþe	CN
		þi'o'fþe	Nw2
		þeoꝼþe	Ld
	lii	no rubric	E Bu H CN
		Be rihtes bene	B
		'Be ryhtes bene'	Nw2
		Be ꞃıhꞇeꞅ bene	Ld
CN 250^{r}		abiddan	E B H CN
p. 140, l. 1		.biddan	Bu
		'hæbban'	Nw2
		hebban	Ld
	lii	no rubric	E Bu H CN
		Be þam ƿrecendan	B
		'Be þam ƿræcendum ær him mon ryhtes bidde'	Nw2
		Be þam ƿꞃæcenꝺan	Ld
	liiii	no rubric	E Bu H CN
		Be reaflace	B 'Nw2'
		Be ꞃeaꝼlace	Ld

	lv	no rubric	E Bu H CN
		Be landbyʒene ('leodan' above land)	B
		'Be þone þe his ʒelond bebycʒað'	Nw2
		Be leoꝺ bẏᵹene	Ld
	lvi	no rubric	E Bu H CN
		Be ʒefanʒenum ðeofum	B
		'Be ʒefonʒenum þeofum'	Nw2
		Be ᵹeꝼanᵹenum þeoꝼum	Ld
	lvii	no rubric	E Bu H CN
		Be þam þe heore ʒeƿitnesse ʒeleoʒað	B
		'Be þæm þe heora ʒeƿitnesse beforan bisceop aleoʒað'	Nw2
		Be ꝺam þe heoꞃa ᵹeƿıꞇnẏꞅꞅe ᵹeleoᵹaþ	Ld
	lviii	no rubric	E Bu H CN Ld
		Be hloðe	B
		'Be hloðe'	Nw2
	lix	no rubric	E Bu H CN
		Be herʒe	B
		'Be heriʒe'	Nw2
		Be heꞃᵹe	Ld
	lx	no rubric	E Bu H CN
		Be ðeofslæʒe	B
		'Be þeofsleʒe'	Nw2
		Be þeoꝼꞅlæᵹe	Ld
	lxi	no rubric	E Bu H CN
		Be forstolenum flæsce	B
		'Be forstolenum flæsc'	Nw2
		Be ꝼoꞃꞅꞇolenum ꝼlæꞅce	Ld
	lxii	no rubric	E Bu H CN
		Be ceorliscum ðeofum ʒefanʒenum	B
		'Be cyrliscum þeof ʒefanʒenum'	Nw2
		Be ceoꞃlıꞅcum þeoꝼum ᵹeꝼanᵹenum	Ld
CN 250^{v}	lxiii	no rubric	E Bu H CN
		Be cinʒes ʒeneate	B
		'Be cyninʒes ʒeneat'	Nw2
		Be cẏnınᵹeꞅ ᵹeneaꞇ	Ld
	lxiiii	no rubric	E Bu H CN
		Be feorran cumenan men	B
		'Be feorran cumenum butan ƿæʒ ʒemettum'	Nw2
		Be ꝼeoꞃꞃan cumenum men	Ld

p. 142, l. 8		peres	E B Bu H
		perær	CN
		'peren'	Nw2
		pæꞃeꞅ	Ld
	lxvi	no rubric	E Bu H CN
		Be ðam þe mannes ᵹeneat staliᵹe	B
		'Be þon þe monnes ᵹeneat staliᵹe'	Nw2
		Be ðon ðe monneꞅ ᵹeneaꞇ ꞅꞇaliᵹe	Ld
	lxvii	no rubric	E Bu H CN
		Be ælðeodiᵹes mannes slæᵹe	B
		'Be elþeodiᵹes monnes sleᵹe'	Nw2
		Be ælþeoꝺiᵹeꞅ manneꞅ ꞅlæᵹe	Ld
	lxviii	no rubric	E B H CN
		'Be piteþeopes monnes sleᵹe'	Nw2
		Be piꞇe þeopum	Ld
CN 251^{r}	lxix	no rubric	E H CN
		Be cypmanna fare uppe land	B
		'Be cypemonna forefenᵹ uppe on lond'	Nw2
		Be cẏpmanna on lanꝺe	Ld
	lxx	no rubric	E H CN
		Be fundenes cildes fostre	B 'Nw2'
		Be ꝼunꝺeneꞅ cilꝺeꞅ ꝼoꞅꞇꞃe	Ld
	lxxi	no rubric	E H CN
		Be ðam þe dearnunᵹe bearn stryneð	B
		'Be dearnunᵹa bearn ᵹestryne'	Nw2
		Be ðam ðe ꝺeaꞃnunᵹa beaꞃn ꞅꞇꞃẏneþ	Ld
p. 144, l. 9		hlaford	E B H CN
		hlafordes	Nw2
		hlaꝼoꞃꝺ	Ld
	lxxii	no rubric	E H CN
		Be ðeopes mannes onfenᵹe æt ðyfðe	B
		'Be þeofes onfenᵹ æt þeofðe'	Nw2
		Be ðeoꝼeꞅ onꝼenᵹ	Ld
	lxxiii	no rubric	E H CN
		Be ðam þe his speord alæne oðres ðeopan	B
		'Be speordes onlæne oðres þeope'	Nw2
		Be ðam ðe hiꞅ pæpnu onlæne	Ld

	lxxv	no rubric	E H CN
		Be þam þe man ƿif bycȝe 7 seo ȝift ƿiðstande	B
		'Be þon þe mon ƿif ȝebycȝe 7 þonne seo ȝift tostande'	Nw2
		Be ꝺon ꝺe mon ƿıꝼ bıcᵹe	Ld
	lxxvi	no rubric	E H CN
		Be ƿylisces mannes landhæfene	B
		'Be ƿylisces monnes londhæfene'	Nw2
		Be cıꞃlıꞅceꞅ monneꞅ lanꝺ hæꝼene	Ld
	lxxvii	no rubric	E H CN
		Be cininc ȝes horsƿale	B
		'Be cyninȝes horsƿeale'	Nw2
		Be cẏnınᵹeꞅ hoꞃꞅ ƿealh	Ld
CN 251^{v}	(lxxviii)	no rubric	E H CN
		Be manslihte	B
		'Be monslyhte'	Nw2
		Be manꞅlẏhꞇe	Ld
p. 146, l. 2		ofsloȝe	E B H
		ofslelȝe sleȝe	CN
		'ofsloȝe'	Nw2
		oꝼꞅloᵹe	Ld
	lxxix	no rubric	E H CN
		Be ðeofslihte	B
		'Be þeofslyht'	Nw2
		Be ꝺeoꝼꞅlẏhꞇe	Ld
p. 146, l. 7		unceases að	E B CN
		unceastes	H
		'uncorene að'	Nw2
		unceaꞃeꞅ aþ	Ld
p. 146, l. 8		oðsparen	E H
		ætsporen	B
		oðsparen	CN
		'æt'sparen	Nw2
		æꞇꞅpoꞃen	Ld
	lxxx	no rubric	E H CN
		Be ðeofes andfenȝe 7 hine sƿa forlæte	B
		'Be þeofes onfenȝ'	Nw2
		Be ꝺon ꝺe mon þeoꝼ ꝼoꞃlæꞇe	Ld

	lxxxi	no rubric	E H CN
		Be ceorlisces monnes betoȝenesse	B
		'Be cyrlisces monnes ontyȝenes æt þyfþe	Nw2
		Be cẏꞃlıꞅceꞅ monneꞅ beꞇoᵹennẏꞅꞅe	Ld
	lxxxii	no rubric	E H CN
		Be ðam ðe rihtȝesamhiƿan bearn habban	B
		'Be bearna fostre þonne se ƿere ȝeƿite'	Nw2
		Be ꝺon ꝺe ꞃıhꞇ ᵹehıƿan beaꞃn hæbban	Ld
CN 252r	lxxxiii	no rubric	E H CN
		Be unalyfedum fare fram his laforde	B
		'Be unalyfedum fare fram hlaford'	Nw2
		Be unalẏꝼeꝺum ꝼæꞃe ꝼꞃam hıꞅ hlaꝼoꞃꝺ	Ld
	lxxxiiii	no rubric	E H CN
		Be ceorles ƿorðiȝe	B
		'Be ceorles ƿeorþiȝe'	Nw2
		Be ceoꞃleꞅ ƿeoꞃþıᵹe	Ld
p. 148, l. 6		nan ƿuht	E
		nan ƿiht	B
		nan ƿuht	H
		þa þuht	CN
		'nan ƿuht ah'	Nw2
		nân ƿıhꞇ	Ld
	lxxxv	no rubric	E B H CN
		'Be borȝes onsace'	Nw2
		Be boꞃᵹeꞅ onꞅæce	Ld
	lxxxvi	no rubric	E H CN
		Be ðam þæt ceorlas habbað land ȝemæne 7 ȝærstunas	B
		'Be ceorles ȝærstun'	Nw2
		Be ceoꞃla ᵹemænum lanꝺ	Ld
	lxxxvii	no rubric	E H CN
		Be ƿudebærnete	B
		'Be ƿudubærnete'	Nw2
		Be ƿuꝺu bæꞃneꞇe (ƿuꝺu corrected in errata)	Ld
p. 148, l. 21		æsc	E CN
		eax	B
		æx	H
		'ælc *opinor*'	Nw2
		eax	Ld

CN 252^{v}	lxxxviii	no rubric	E H CN Ld
		Be ƿude andfenȝe	B
		'Be ƿuda onfenȝ buta leafe'	Nw2
p. 150, l. 2		underȝestandan	E H
		understandan	B
		underȝestanden	CN
		underȝestand'a'n	Nw2
		unꝺeꞃꝼꞇanꝺan (ꝼ corrected in errata)	Ld
	lxxxix	no rubric	E H CN
		Be burhbryce	B 'Nw2'
		Be buꞃhbꞃẏce	Ld
	xc	no rubric	E H CN
		Be staltihlan	B
		'Be stæletyhtlan'	Nw2
		Be ꞅꞇal ꞇẏhꞇlan	Ld
	xci	no rubric	E H CN B
		'Be forstolene ceap befanȝene'	Nw2
		Be ꝼoꞃꞅꞇolene ceap beꝼanᵹene	Ld
	xcii	no rubric	E H CN
		Be ƿiteðeoƿum mannum	B
		'Be ƿiteþeoƿum men'	Nw2
		Be ƿıꞇeðeoƿum mannum	Ld
	xciii	no rubric	E H CN
		Be unalefedum mæstenum andfencȝe	B
		'Be unaliefedes mæstines onfenȝ'	Nw2
		Be unalẏꝼeꝺeꞅ mæꞅꞇeneꞅ onꝼenᵹ	Ld
CN 253^{r}		æfesne	E
p. 152, l. 1		æfæsne [252^{v}], æfesne [253^{r}]	CN
		æbesne	B H
		'æbesne *alias*'	Nw2
		æbeꞅne (*alias* æꝼeꞅne margin)	Ld
	xciiii	no rubric	E H CN
		Be ȝesiðcundes mannes ȝeðinȝe	B
		'Be siþcundes monnes ȝeþinȝe'	Nw2
		Be ꞅıþcunꝺeꞅ monneꞅ ᵹeþınᵹe	Ld

	xcv	no rubric	E H CN
		Be þam þe ȝesiðcund man fyrde forsitte	B
		'Be þon þe 'ȝe'siðcund mon fyrð forƿitie'	Nw2
		Be ðon ðe ꝿeſiþcunꝺ mon ꝼẏꞃꝺ ꝼoꞃſıꞇꞇe	Ld
	lxcvi	[*sic*] no rubric	E H CN
		Be dyrnunȝe þincðe	B
		'Be dyrnum ȝeðinȝe'	Nw2
		Be ꝺẏꞃnum ꝿeþınꝿþe	Ld
p. 152, l. 10		betyȝen	E
		betoȝen	B H
		betƿiȝum	CN
		be'toȝen'	Nw2
		beꞇoꝿen	Ld
p. 152, l. 10		þara ȝeðinȝea	E
		þara ȝeþinȝea	CN
		ðara ðinȝa	B
		ðæra ȝeþinȝa	H
		'ðara ȝeþunȝera *alias*'	Nw2
		ðæꞃa ðınꝿa	Ld
	(xcvii)	no rubric	E H CN
		Be forstolenes mannes forfenȝe	B
		'Be forstolenes mannes fore foreȝesitte'	Nw2
		Be ꝼoꞃſꞇoleneſ manneſ ꝼoꞃꝼenꝿe	Ld
p. 152, l. 18		unbeceasne	E CN
		unbesacene	B H
		'unbecappane *alias*'	Nw2
		unbeſacene	Ld
	xcviii	no rubric	E H CN
		Be ƿerfæhðe tyhlan	B
		'Be ƿerfehð tyhtlan'	Nw2
		Be ƿæꞃꝼæhþe ꞇẏhꞇlan	Ld
CN 253^v	xcix	no rubric	E H CN
		Be eoƿe ƿyrðe	B
		'Be eƿes ƿeorðe'	Nw2
		Be eƿes ƿeorð	Nw3
		Be eoƿeſ ƿẏꞃþe	Ld

	c	no rubric	E H CN Ld
		Be ȝehƿylces ceapes ƿyrðe	B
		'Be 'ȝe'hƿelces ceapes anȝylde'	Nw2
		Be ȝehƿelces ceapes anȝyld	Nw3
	ci	no rubric	E H
		Be cyrlisces mannes stale	B
		Be ceorlisces monnes stale	'Nw2' Nw3
		Be cẏꞃlıꞅceꞅ monneꞅ ꞅꞇale	Ld
p. 154, l. 13		synniȝ	E
		synniȝ ('scyldiȝ' above; different hand)	B
		scyldiȝ	H Nw3
		sinniȝ	CN
		'scyldiȝ'	Nw2
		ꞅcẏlꝺıᵹ	Ld
	cii	no rubric	E H CN B
		'Be neata hora'	Nw2
		Be neatum	Nw3
		Be oxan	Ld
	ciiii	no rubric	E H CN
		Be hyr oxan	B
		'Be hyrȝeoc'	Nw2
		Be hyrȝeoht	Nw3
		Be hẏꞃe Ᵹeôc	Ld
	cv	no rubric	E H CN
		Be ciricsceatte	B
		Be cyricsceat	'Nw2' Nw3
		Be cẏꞃıc ꞅceaꞇꞇe	Ld
CN 254r		no rubric	E H CN
		Be þam þe man to ceace fordræfe	B
		Be þon þe mon to ceape fordrife	'Nw2' Nw3
		Be ðon ðe mon ꞇo ceape ꝼoꞃꝺꞃæꝼe	Ld
	cvii	no rubric	E H CN
		Be ȝesiðcundes mannes fare	B
		Be ȝesiðcundes monnes fære	'Nw2' Nw3
		Be ᵹeꞅıþcunꝺeꞅ monneꞅ ꝼaꞃe	Ld
	cviii	no rubric	E H CN
		Be ðam þe hafð .xx. hida	B
		'Be londhæbbendum'	Nw2
		Be lanꝺ hæbbenꝺum	Ld

	cxii	no rubric	E H Ot CN
		Be ȝesiðcundes mannes drafe of lande	B
		'Be siðcundes monnes dræfe of lond'	Nw2
		Be ȝesiðcundes monnes dræfe of lond	Nw3
		Be ᵹeꞅıþcunꝺeꞅ monneꞅ ꝺꞃæꝼe oꝼ lanꝺe	Ld
	cxiii	no rubric	E H Ot CN
		Be sceapes ȝanȝe	B
		'Be sceapes ȝonȝ mid his fleose'	Nw2
		Be sceapes ȝanȝ mid his fleose	Nw3
		Be ꞅceapeꞅ ᵹanᵹe mıꝺ ꝼleoꞅ	Ld
	cxiiii	no rubric	E H Ot CN
		Be tƿyhindum ƿere	B
		Be tƿyhyndum ƿære	'Nw2' Nw3
		Be ƿeꞃum	Ld
CN 254^{v} p.158, l.1		hunies	E B
		huniȝes	H Nw3
		hunies	CN
		huni'ȝ'es	Nw2
		hunıᵹeꞅ	Ld
	cxv	no rubric	E H CN
		Be ƿertyhlan	B
		Be ƿertyhtlan	'Nw2' Nw3
		Be ƿeꞃꞇẏhꞇlan	Ld
	cxvi	no rubric	E H CN
		Be ƿerȝildðeofes forefenȝe	B
		'Be ƿerȝyldþeofe'	Nw2
		Be ƿerȝyldþeof	Nw3
		Be ƿeꞃᵹẏlꝺ ðeoꝼeꞅ ꝼoꞃeꝼenᵹ	Ld
	cxvii	no rubric	E H CN Nw3 Ld
		Be anre nihte ðyfte	B
		'Be anre nihte þyfðe'	Nw2
	cxviii	no rubric	E H Ot CN
		Be þam þe ðeoƿƿalh friȝne man ofslea	B
		'Be þonne þe þeoƿ'ƿealh' freone forslihð'	Nw2
		Be þonne þe þeoƿƿealh freone forslyhð	Nw3
		Be ðon ðe ðeoƿ ƿealh ꝼꞃıᵹne man oꝼꞅlea	Ld

	cxix	no rubric	E H CN
		Be forstolene ceape	B
		'Be forstolenes ceapes forfonʒ'	Nw2
		Be forstolenes ceapes forfonʒe	Nw3
		Be ꝼoꞃꞅꞇoleneꞅ ceapeꞅ ꝼoꞃꝼenᵹ	Ld
CN 255[r]	cxx	no rubric	E H Ot CN
		Be ʒodfæderes oððe ʒodsunes slæhte	B
		Be þon þe mon oðres ʒodsunu ofslea	'Nw2' Nw3
		Be ᵹoꝺꝼæꝺeꞃeꞅ oþþe ᵹoꝺꞅuneꞅ ꞅlẏhꞇ	Ld

Select Bibliography

Adams, Eleanor N. *Old English Scholarship in England from 1566-1800*. Yale diss. Yale Studies in English 55. New Haven: Yale University Press, London: Humphrey Milford, and Oxford: Oxford University Press, 1917.

Attenborough, Frederick L., ed. and trans. *The Laws of the Earliest English Kings (Æthelberht I to Æthelstan)*. Cambridge: Cambridge University Press, 1922; reissued New York: Russell and Russell, 1963.

Baron, John. *Report on the Anglo-Saxon Documents in Wilkins's Concilia*. Oxford, 1859.

Berkhout, Carl T. "The Pedigree of Laurence Nowell the Antiquary." *English Language Notes* 23 (1985), 15-26.

Black, Pamela M. "Laurence Nowell's 'disappearance' in Germany and its bearing on the whereabouts of his *Collectanea* 1568-1572." *English Historical Review* 92 (1977), 345-53.

———. "Some New Light on the Career of Laurence Nowell the Antiquary." *Antiquaries Journal* 62 (1982), 116-23.

Blockley, Mary. "Addenda and Corrigenda to N. R. Ker's 'A supplement to *Catalogue of Manuscripts Containing Anglo-Saxon*.'" *Notes and Queries*, n.s. 29 (1982), 1-3.

The British Museum Catalogue of Additions to the Manuscripts 1931-1935. London: The Trustees of the British Museum, 1967.

Campbell, Alistair, ed. *The Battle of Brunanburh*. London: William Heinemann Ltd., 1938.

Casaubon, Meric. "De lingua Anglica vetere, sive Saxonica, ejusque cum Graeca cognatione" in *De Quatuor Linguis Commentationis Pars prior*. London, 1650, pp. 127-418.

Chadwick, Henry Munro. *Studies on Anglo-Saxon Institutions*. Cambridge, 1905.

Cook, Albert S. *Extracts from the Anglo-Saxon Laws*. New York, 1880.

Crone, G.R. *Early Maps of the British Isles, A.D. 1000-A.D. 1579*. London, 1961.

Dammery, Richard. *The law code of King Alfred the Great.* Cambridge diss. Cambridge, 1990. Vol. 1 deals with the manuscripts, the textual transmission, the structure of the law-code, and bibliography; vol. 2 is an edition of the law-code. Dr. Dammery's planned facsimile of Lambarde's *Archaionomia* is to appear in the series *Early Studies in Germanic Philology*, published in Leiden and ed. Rolf Bremmer.

———. "Editing the Anglo-Saxon Laws: Felix Liebermann and Beyond." This paper was delivered at a conference on the editing of Old English texts held at the Manchester Centre for Anglo-Saxon Studies, University of Manchester, 25-27 May 1990 and published in *The Editing of Old English*, Cambridge: D.S. Brewer, 1994, pp. 251-61.

Dobbie, Elliott van Kirk, ed. *The Anglo-Saxon Minor Poems*. The Anglo-Saxon Poetic Records 6. New York: Columbia University Press; London: Routledge and Kegan Paul, 1942, 1958.

Dunkel, Wilbur Dwight. *William Lambarde, Elizabethan Jurist, 1536-1601.* New Brunswick, N.J.: Rutgers University Press, 1965. Contains article by Catherine Drinker Brown, "Historians Courageous", as preface.

Eckhardt, Karl August. *Leges Anglo-Saxonicum 601-925 (Gesetze der Angelsachsen, 601-925).* Germanenrechte, neue Folge, Abteilung Westgermanisches Recht, vol. 4. Göttingen: Munsterschmidt, 1958.

Edwards, Francis. *The Lambarde Catalogue of Early Printed Books*. London, 1909.

Flower, Robin. "Laurence Nowell and the Discovery of England in Tudor Times." *Proceedings of the British Academy* 21 (1935), 46-73.

———. "Laurence Nowell and a Recovered Anglo-Saxon Poem." *British Museum Quarterly* 8 (1933-34), 130-32.

———. "The Text of the Burghal Hidage." *London Medieval Studies* 1 (1937), 60-4.

Gneuss, Helmut, ed. "A preliminary list of manuscripts written or owned in England up to 1100." *Anglo-Saxon England* 9 (1981), 1-60.

Grant, Raymond J.S. "A Note on 'The Seasons for Fasting.'" *Review of English Studies*, n.s. 23, no. 91 (August, 1972), 302-04.

———. "Laurence Nowell's transcript of BM Cotton Otho B. xi." *Anglo-Saxon England* 3 (1974), 111-24.

———. *The B Text of the Old English Bede: A Linguistic Commentary*. Amsterdam and Atlanta: Editions Rodopi B.V., 1989.

Haddan, Arthur and William Stubbs, eds. *Councils and Ecclesiastical Documents Relating to Great Britain and Ireland, Edited after Spelman and Wilkins*. 3 vols. Oxford, 1869-78.

Hahn, Thomas. "The Identity of the Antiquary Laurence Nowell." *English Langauge Notes* 20, nos. 3-4 (March/June, 1983), 10-18.

Harvey, P.D.A. *Maps in Tudor England*. London: The Public Records Office and the British Library, 1993.

Hearne, Thomas. *Textus Roffensis*. Oxford, 1720.

Hetherington, M.S. "Sir Simonds D'Ewes and Method in Old English Lexicography." *Texas Studies in Language and Literature* 17 (1975), 75-92.

Holdsworth, Sir William S. *A History of English Law*. 3rd ed. London, 1923.

James, Montague Rhodes. *A Descriptive Catalogue of the Manuscripts in the Library of Corpus Christi College, Cambridge*. 2 vols. Cambridge: Cambridge University Press, 1912, 1. 81-5.

Kennett, White. "Life of Mr. Somner" in *A Treatise of Gavelkind, Both Name and Thing. Shewing the True Etymologie and Derivation of the One, the Nature, Antiquity, and Original of the Other*. 2nd ed. London, 1726.

Ker, Neil Ripley. *Catalogue of Manuscripts Containing Anglo-Saxon*. Oxford: Clarendon Press, 1957; repr. with supplement 1990.

———. "A supplement to *Catalogue of Manuscripts Containing Anglo-Saxon*." *Anglo-Saxon England* 5 (1976), 121-31.

———. *Medieval Libraries of Great Britain*. London, 1941; 2nd ed. London, 1964.

Lambarde, Brigadier-General Fane. "William Lambarde's Pedigree Notes." *Archaeologia Cantiana* 39 (1927), 131-33.

Lambarde, Multon. "The Lambarde Diary." *Miscellanea Genealogica et Heraldica* 2 (1876), 99-114. These are extracts from the Lambarde family diary (London, Drapers' Company, H./Add. 27).

Lambarde, William. *A Perambulation of Kent: Conteining the description, Hystorie, and Customes of that Shyre. Written in the yeere 1570. First published in the yeere 1576 and now increased and altered after the authors owne last copie*. Pp. 307-12, 357-62, 364-66 contain excerpts from the *Textus Roffensis*. London: E. Bollifant, 1576; 2nd ed. London, 1596; repr. Bath, England: Adams & Dart, 1970.

———. *An Alphabetical Description of the Chief Places in England and Wales*. London, 1730.

———, ed. and trans. *Archaionomia, sive De priscis Anglorum legibus libri, sermone anglico, vetustate antiquissimo, aliquot abhinc seculis conscripti, atq: nunc demum, magno iurisperitorum, & amantium antiquitatis omnium commodo, è tenebris in lucem vocati*. London: Ex officina Joannis Daij, 1568. Rev. ed. by Abraham Wheloc, Cambridge 1644. [With Latin trans.]

———. *Archeion or, a Discourse upon the High Courts of Justice in England*. Charles H. McIlwain and Paul L. Ward, eds. Cambridge, Massachusetts: Harvard University Press, 1957.

———. *The Duties of Constables, Borsholders, Tythingmen, and such other low and lay Ministers of the Peace*. 16th ed. London, 1640; repr. Amsterdam, Theatrum Orbis Terrarum and New York, Da Capo Press, 1969.

———. *The duty and office of high constables of hundreds, petty constables, tythingmen, and such inferior ministers of the peace with the several duties and offices of churchwardens, overseers, and collectors for the poor, of surveyors for amending the high ways, and distributors of the provision for the destruction of noisom fowl and vermin*. London: G. Sawbridge, T. Roycroft, and W. Rawlins, the assigns of R. Atkins and E. Atkins, 1677.

———. *Eirenarcha, or of the Office of the Justices of the Peace*. 12th ed. London, 1619; repr. London: Professional Books, 1972.

———. *William Lambarde's Notes on the procedures and privileges of the House of Commons (1584)*. House of Commons Library document no.10. London: H.M. Stationery Office, *c*. 1977.

Lee, S.D. "Two Fragments from Cotton MS. Otho B. x." *British Library Journal* 17 (1993), 83-87.

Leslie, Roy F. "Textual Notes on *The Seasons for Fasting*." *Journal of English and Germanic Philology* 52 (1953), 555-58.

Liebermann, Felix, ed. and trans. *Die Gesetze der Angelsachsen*. 3 vols. Halle, 1903-16; repr. Aalen, 1960. Vol. 1 *Text und Übersetzung* (texts and German trans.); vol. 2 part 1 *Wörterbuch* (glossary), part 2 *Rechts- und Sachglossar* (commentary); vol. 3 *Einleitung zu jedem Stück; Erklärungen zu einzelnen Stellen* (introduction and notes).

———. "Ist Lambardes Text der Gesetze Æthelstans neuzeitliche Fälschung?" *Anglia Beiblatt* 35 (1924), 214-18. [Reply to Sisam's first article]

———. "Angelsächsische Gesetztext gefälscht?" *Anglia Beiblatt* 36 (1925), 345-47. [Reply to Sisam's second article]

———. "Notes on the *Textus Roffensis.*" *Archaeologia Cantiana* 23 (1898), 101-12.

———, ed. *Quadripartitus, ein englisches Rechtsbuch von 1114*. Halle, 1892.

Lutz, Angelika, ed. *Die Version G der Angelsächsischen Chronik*. Texte und Untersuchungen zur Englischen Philologie 11, ed. Helmut Gneuss and Wolfgang Weiss, München, 1981.

Maitland, Frederic William. "The Laws of the Anglo-Saxons." *Quarterly Review* 200 (1904), 139-57.

Marckwardt, Albert H. "An Unnoted Source of English Dialect Vocabulary." *Journal of English and Germanic Philology* 46 (1947), 177-82.

———, ed. *Laurence Nowell's Vocabularium Saxonicum*. University of Michigan Publications in Language and Literature 25. Ann Arbor: University of Michigan Press, 1952.

———. "Nowell's *Vocabularium Saxonicum* and Somner's *Dictionarium*." *Philological Quarterly* 26 (1947), 345-51.

———. "The Sources of Laurence Nowell's *Vocabularium Saxonicum*." *Studies in Philology* 45 (1948), 21-36.

Miller, Thomas, ed. *The Old English Version of Bede's Ecclesiastical History of the English People*. 4 vols. Vol. 1. 1, London: Oxford University Press, 1890, repr. 1959, repr. New York, 1976; vol. 1. 2, London: Oxford University Press, 1891, repr. 1959, repr. New York, 1976; vols. 2. 1 and 2, London: Oxford University Press, 1898, repr. 1963. Early English Texts Society, o.s., nos. 95, 96, 110 and 111.

Mone, Franz Joseph. "Zur Geschichte und Kritik der angelsächsische Gesetze." *Quellen und Forschungen zur Geschichte der teutschen Literatur und Sprache* 1 (Aachen 1830), 482-548, 562.

Page, Raymond I. *Matthew Parker and his Books*. Kalamazoo, Michigan: Medieval Institute Publications, Western Michigan University, 1993.

Parkes, Michael B. "The palaeography of the Parker manuscript of the *Chronicle*, laws and Sedulius, and historiography at Winchester in the late ninth and tenth centuries." *Anglo-Saxon England* 5 (1976), 149-71.

Plucknett, T.F.T. *A Concise History of the Common Law*. 4th ed. London, 1948.

Plummer, Charles, ed. *Two of the Saxon Chronicles Paralleled.* Oxford, 1892-99; repr. with additions by Dorothy Whitelock 1952.

Pollock, Sir Frederick, and Frederic William Maitland. *The History of English Law*. 2nd ed. Cambridge, 1923.

Randolph, John. "Memoirs of William Lambarde." *Bibliotheca Topographica Britannica* 1, ed. John Nichols (1790), 493-530.

Read, Conyers C., ed. *William Lambarde and Local Government: His "Ephemeris" and Twenty-nine Charges to Juries and Commissions*. Ithaca, N.Y.: Cornell University Press, 1962. Preface for Folger Shakespeare Library by Giles E. Dawson, pp. v-xi.

Richards, Mary P. "The Manuscript Contexts of the Old English Laws: Tradition and Innovation" in Paul E. Szarmach, ed. *Studies in Earlier Old English Prose: Sixteen Original Contributions*. Albany, 1986, pp. 171-92.

Robertson, Agnes J., ed. *The Laws of the Kings of England from Edmund to Henry I.* Cambridge: Cambridge University Press, 1925; repr. New York: AMS Press, 1974.

Rosier, James L. "A new Old English glossary: Nowell upon Huloet." *Studia Neophilologica* 49 (1977), 189-94.

Schipper, William. "The Early Dictionaries of Old English and the Worcester Tremulous Scribe." *International Christian Univerity Language Research Bulletin* 4, 379-96.

Schmid, Reinhold. *Die Gesetze der Angelsächsische. In der Ursprache mit Übersetzung und Erläuterungen. I. Teil, den Text nebst Übersetzung enthaltend.* Leipzig, 1832; 2nd rev. and enlarged ed. 1858.

Sisam, Kenneth. "The Authenticity of Certain Texts in Lambard's *Archaionomia, 1568.*" From a review in *Modern Language Review* 18 (1923), 98-104, of Attenborough, and from *Modern Language Review* 20 (1925), 253-69, both repr. and expanded in *Studies in the History of Old English Literature*, Oxford: Clarendon Press, 1953; repr. 1962, pp. 232-58.

Smith, Thomas. *Catalogus Librorum Manusciptorum Bibliothecæ Cottonianæ*. Oxford, 1696.

Somner, William. *Dictionarium Saxonico-Latino-Anglicum. Voces, phrasesque præcipuas Anglo-Saxonicas... Accesserunt Ælfrici Abbatis Grammatica Latino-Saxonica, cum Glossario suo ejusdem generis*. Oxford: William Hall, 1659. Abridged edition, ed. Thomas Benson, 1701, following specimen copies issued in 1690 and 1699. 1659 edition repr. in facsimile Menston, England: The Scolar Press Ltd., 1970.

———. *Dictionarium Saxonico-Latino-Anglicum 1659*, ed. R.C. Alston. English Linguistics 1500-1800. A collection of facsimile reprints, no. 247. Menston, England: The Scolar Press Ltd., 1970.

———. "Glossarium: in quo obscuriora quæque vocabula, quæ toto hoc opere continentur copiose explicantur" in R. Twysden's *Historiae anglicanæ scriptores X* ... London, 1652.

Spelman, Henry. *Concilia, decreta, leges, constitutiones, in re ecclesiarum orbis Britannici.* Vol.1 (London, 1639), from the introduction of Christianity to the Norman Conquest, by Spelman alone; vol. 2, from the Norman Conquest to the reign of Henry VIII, ed. William Dugdale (London, 1664). [With Latin trans.]

Starnes, D.T. *Renaissance Dictionaries*. Austin, 1954.

Stearns, John M. *The Germs and Developments of the Laws of England, Embracing the Anglo-Saxon Laws Extant... as Translated into English uneder the Royal Record Commission... with Notes and Comments*. New York, 1889.

Thorpe, Benjamin, ed. and trans. *Ancient Laws and Institutes of England; comprising Laws enacted under the Anglo-Saxon Kings from Æthelbirht to Cnut, with an English Translation of the Saxon... also, Monumenta Ecclesiastica Anglicana from the Seventh to the Tenth Century*. 2 vols. London, 1840. Vol. 1 Secular Laws; vol. 2 Ecclesiastical Laws. [Thorpe completed an edition of the Anglo-Saxon Laws under preparation by Richard Price for the Commissioners on the Public Records after Price's death in 1833.]

Torkar, Roland, ed. *Eine Altenglische Übersetzung von Alcuins "De Virtutibus et Vitiis," Kap. 20.* Texte und Untersuchungen zur Englischen Philologie 7, ed. Helmut Gneuss and Wolfgang Weiss, München, 1981.

Turk, Milton Haight, ed. *The Legal Code of Alfred the Great.* Leipzig diss. Halle, 1890.

———, ed. *The Legal Code of Alfred the Great.* Halle and Boston, 1893.

Tyake, S. and J. Huddy. *Christopher Saxton and Tudor Mapmaking.* British Library Series, no. 2. London, 1980.

Wallace-Hadrill, J. M. *Early Germanic Kingship in England and on the Continent.* Oxford: Clarendon Press, 1971.

Wanley, Humphrey. *Antiquæ Literaturæ Septentrionalis liber alter. seu Humphredi Wanleii Librorum Vett. Codd. Septentrionalium, qui in Angliæ Bibliothecis extant, nec non multorum Vett. Codd. Septentrionalium alibi extantium Catalogus Historico-Criticus, cum totius Thesauri Linguarum Septentrionalium sex Indicibus.* Oxford: Sheldonian Theatre, 1705; reprinted New York, 1970. [This is the second volume of George Hickes's *Linguarum Vett. Septentrionalium Thesaurus Grammatico-Criticus et Archæologicus.*]

Ward, Paul L. "William Lambarde's Collections on Chancery." *Harvard Library Bulletin* 7 (1953), 271-98.

Warnicke, Retha M. "Note on a Court of Requests Case of 1571." *English Language Notes* 11 (1974), 250-56.

———. "The Laurence Nowell Manuscripts in the British Library." *British Library Journal* 5, no. 2 (Autumn, 1979), 201-02.

———. *William Lambarde, Elizabethan Antiquary 1536-1601.* London and Chichester: Phillimore & Co. Ltd., 1973.

Wheloc, Abraham, ed. *Archaionomia, sive de priscis Anglorum legibus libri, sermone Anglico, vetustate antiquissimo, aliquot abhinc seculis conscripti, etc. Accessere in hac nostra ultima editione Leges Henrici Primi nunc primum editæ, ex manuscripto in fisco regis habito: Una cum gloßario.* Cambridge: Cambridge University Press, 1644. Rev. edition of Lambarde's *Archaionomia* of 1568.

———, ed. *Historiæ Ecclesiasticæ Gentis Anglorum libri V... paraphrasi Saxonicâ eleganter explicati...... Quibus in calce operis Saxonicam chronologiam ...... contexuimus*. Cambridge: Cambridge University Press, 1643; repr. with additions 1644.

Whitelock, Dorothy, M. Brett and C.N.L. Brooke, eds. *Councils and Synods, with other documents relating to the English Church*. 2 vols., vol. 1. A.D. 871-1204, part 1 871-1066. Oxford: Clarendon Press, 1981.

———, ed. *English Historical Documents c. 500-1042*. 2nd ed., vol. 1. London: Eyre Methuen, 1979 and New York: Oxford University Press, 1979.

———, ed. *From Bede to Alfred: Studies in Early Anglo-Saxon Literature and History*. London: Variorum Reprints, 1980.

———, ed. *History, Law and Literature in 10th-11th Century England*. London: Variorum Reprints, 1981.

———, et al., trans. *The Anglo-Saxon Chronicle. A Revised Translation*. London, 1961.

———. "The Old English Bede." *Proceedings of the British Academy* 48 (1963), 57-90, repr. separately London: Oxford University Press, 1963 and repr. in *From Bede to Alfred*.

Wilkins, David. *Concilia Magnae Britanniae et Hiberniae, a Synodo Verolamiensi A.D. CCCCXLVI. ad Londinensem A.D. MDCCXVII. Accedunt constitutiones et alia ad historiam ecclesiae Anglicanae spectantia: a Davide Wilkins, S.T.P., Archidiacono Suffolciensi, et Canonico Cantuariensi, collecta*. 4 vols. London, 1737 with dedicatory letter to William Wake, Archbishop of Canterbury 1715-37. Vol. 1 *Ab Anno CCCCXLVI. ad Annum MCCLXV*. [Based on Henry Spelman's *Concilia*.]

———. *Leges Anglo-Saxonicae ecclesiasticae et civiles... cum codd. Mss. contulit, notas, versionem et glossarium adjecit D.W.* Londini: typis G. Bowyer, impensis R. Gosling, 1721. [Includes Latin trans.]

Wormald, Patrick. *The Making of English Law: King Alfred to the Norman Conquest* (title provisional). Forthcoming.

———. *"Quadripartitus,"* in G. Garnett, ed., *Law and Government in Medieval England and Normandy: Essays in Honour of Sir James Holt.* Cambridge: Cambridge University Press, 1994.

Wright, C.E. "The Dispersal of the Monastic Libraries and the Beginnings of Anglo-Saxon Studies: Matthew Parker and his Circle—A Preliminary Study." *Transactions of the Cambridge Bibliographical Society* 1 (1949-53), part 3 (1951), 208-37. [Offers samples of the hands of Nowell, Lambarde, & Co.]